C000018189

THE TENTH CHILD

Dear Donald,

Herewith the promised copy of my autobiography, "The Tenth Child". It will be published on February 25th.

I hope you enjoy it. As Bernard Ingham says in the foreward there's a lot of angst there but I hope there's also a little fun!

Regards. See you in mid-year I hope.

Harold.

THE TENTH CHILD

A Life

Harold Bolter

To Donald Avery
In friendship and with best wishes.
Harold Bolter
January 2010

Book Guild Publishing

Sussex England

First published in Great Britain in 2010 by
The Book Guild Ltd
Pavilion View
19 New Road
Brighton, BN1 1UF

Copyright © Harold Bolter 2010

The right of Harold Bolter to be identified as the author of
this work has been asserted by him in accordance with the
Copyright, Designs and Patents Act 1988.

All rights reserved. No part of this publication may be reproduced,
transmitted, or stored in a retrieval system, in any form or by any means,
without permission in writing from the publisher, nor be otherwise circulated
in any form of binding or cover other than that in which it is published
and without a similar condition being imposed
on the subsequent purchaser.

Typeset in Garamond by
Ellipsis Books Limited, Glasgow

Printed in Great Britain by
CPI Antony Rowe

A catalogue record for this book is available from The British Library.

ISBN 978 1 84624 390 5

To Sheila,

My wife, my love, my life

Contents

Foreword
by Sir Bernard Ingham

Like me, Harold Bolter has a lot of angst to get rid of. I am sure he feels better for writing this book. I know I feel refreshed after penning a weekly column for *The Yorkshire Post*. Writing can be a most effective purgative.

What I had not realised was how much we two purgers have in common. Our working class credentials are impeccable. Why, we each even blew a cornet for a time in a brass band. We progressed through grammar school to regional and national journalism. What is more, we both became industrial correspondents, though his accent at the *Financial Times* was on covering nationalised industries whereas I took the labour correspondent's route on *The Guardian* when strikes made labour reporters the most overworked scribes in Fleet Street.

And then, as if some hidden hand were at work, he moved to take charge of the public face of a beleaguered British Nuclear Fuels (BNFL) at the very moment that Tony Benn, my Secretary of State in the Department of Energy, was watering his wicket by dubbing the company's Sellafield plant 'the world's nuclear dustbin'. The fact that the label was pinned on BNFL curiously by the education correspondent of the *Daily Mirror* in no way hid Benn's hand in this affair at the time – as Harold accurately explains. I had responsibility for a Cabinet Minister who, while technically the sponsor of the nuclear industry in a pro-nuclear Government, operated on this and other matters as a rather privileged member of the Maquis behind enemy lines. Life was never tedious with Tony.

So, what have we learned in the course of these closely related voyages of discovery?

Well, I reckon we among many have proved conclusively that there is no such thing as a glass ceiling in modern Britain. If we could make it out of the labourer's ghetto into modest affluence then so could – and can – anybody with hard work and a certain wit. In fact, I think Harold, as the tenth child in a far more poverty-stricken family than mine of two sons makes the point more strongly.

I suspect he shares my contempt for the mass of condescending middle class activists who rail about 'prejudice' and 'exclusion' while wrecking the education system by culling grammar schools and lowering standards. If they cared about the working classes and their still limited horizons they would be hammering those who neglect their parental responsibilities and clamouring for greater discipline and higher standards.

My reading of this book convinces me that the second lesson we have learned is that no matter how well you think you are doing there is always somebody wanting to do you down. I got used to the Margaret Thatcher-haters in the Cabinet and Tory backbenches trying to get shut of me. I survived because I had a Prime Minister who prized loyalty. Harold could not rely on that at BNFL and his account of the audit that brought him down and the associated innuendo beggars belief. Personally, I would not have paid those responsible for its project control in washers. Not surprisingly, the police could not find a case to answer anywhere in the entire mess.

This brings me to the nuclear industry in which I have been fairly closely involved since retirement in 1990 as a consultant to BNFL, eventually translated in 1998 into the secretaryship of Supporters of Nuclear Energy (SONE). This relatively small group of people sought to keep the nuclear flame alive during some very lean times. Harold accurately states that my forthright advocacy of nuclear power (as distinct from any of its institutions) has been seen in the nuclear industry as a bit over-the-top. I take that as an accolade because the industry itself has for too long been distinctly under-the-bottom, to coin a phrase, since Harold gave up the public education role at BNFL.

One of the problems is that the industry grew out of the civil service and had, as Harold instances, a bureaucratic aversion to public exposure, as though it could avoid it with the neanderthal Greens around. At a crucial time it effectively abdicated the field to those who in the words of Professor James Lovelock, the great environmentalist, 'grievously misled the public with a concatenation of lies' about all things nuclear.

Second, it has for too long been under the thumb of a Government that, having bankrupted British Energy, the nuclear generator, and written off nuclear power as 'economically unattractive' in 2003, proceeded to dismantle BNFL and, God save us, sell off Westinghouse just as a global nuclear renaissance was coming. It then changed its mind three years later when it recognised that its energy policy – such as it was and remains – was up the creek.

Harold remains very dubious about whether that nuclear renaissance will be realised. He is right not to put his trust in politicians. Both Labour and Conservatives are now technically in favour of nuclear power but seldom, if ever, speak up in public for it. The Liberal Democrats wish to get rid of both nuclear and coal-fired power stations, thus being the one party that can be guaranteed to put the lights out. At the same time the Nationalists in various parts of the UK won't touch nuclear with a barge-pole, except in Anglesey where they need a replacement of Wylfa to keep their aluminium smelter going.

The prevailing political fashion is to be besotted with every remedy for domestic energy security and global warming that does not work – and grossly expensive with it.

Yet this is where I depart from the author – apart from his membership of the Labour Party since I have steered clear of any party affiliation. There will be a nuclear renaissance because, as the politicians may discover too late for our good, there is no alternative. There will also be reprocessing because without it we shall be throwing away vast amounts of clean energy. That would be madness and the failure to make the THORP plant work properly must not be allowed obscure it.

In all this lies the national tragedy at the substantive heart of this book.

Introduction

Before writing this autobiography I spent some time questioning why people might want to read about my life – or anybody else's life for that matter. Why should people be interested in the impact I may or may not have had on our society? Would those special moments which have given me so much pleasure give pleasure to others? And what about the occasions which have caused me and those close to me so much pain, particularly the time when I was falsely accused of being a fraudster?

I came to the conclusion that there could be no place for modesty in a book like this, whether it was genuine or false. I was not coerced into writing the story of my life, as so many memoir writers claim. That made the answer to the question 'Why do you want to write this book?' simple. The truth is, I have found my life endlessly fascinating, even the worst of my days, and hope that you will too.

As a Fleet Street journalist and later as a director and chief publicist and defender of the company owning Sellafield, Britain's most controversial industrial site, I have had plenty of public exposure over the years and achieved a certain notoriety.

I was even warned by the nuclear industry's security people that my life might be at risk while I was arguing the case for civil nuclear power through the media at a time when scares about a possible link between radiation from Sellafield and childhood leukaemia were at their height. The scares were shown to be just that more than a decade ago but the folk memory lives on and people still have their suspicions.

Although I became well known because of my national and local television appearances as a sort of nuclear industry aunt sally I wouldn't claim to have been a 'celebrity', a description which is bandied around so much today that it's pretty well meaningless anyway.

This memoir is about me, but not only about me. It is placed squarely in the context of someone who met and occasionally irritated prime ministers and royalty, actors and pop stars, industrialists and trade unionists and most of the many other notables who have achieved fame, however transitory it turned out to be. In that way I hope that through my own experiences I can throw new light on issues which seem to be eternal.

Reviewing my life I have been struck by how little has changed in human terms since I entered the world in a Black Country slum more than 70 years ago. I was born into a place of thick smog, with struggling and sometimes broken people trying to eke out a living and enjoying simple, hard-earned pleasures at the football match and the working men's clubs which flourished then.

We are no closer to settling on a fair education system, no nearer deciding what to do about immigration, still unsure about the soundness of our financial structures, still arguing the toss about the need for a written constitution and the future role of the royals and still concerned about the environment and the air we breathe. Childhood poverty is still with us, despite the benefits system we've developed, and there is still very little social mobility, still not enough opportunities through the education system for children of ability living in deprived areas to reach their potential.

As a young journalist in the West Midlands and later in Fleet Street I wrote about the newly created nationalised industries, which were generally considered to be a good thing. Nobody really questioned the need for state ownership of coal, steel, gas, electricity and the railways, despite the greed and disruptiveness of some of the trade unions representing the people who worked in those industries.

We had our very own demons in the industrial relations arena, of course – Jack Jones, Hugh Scanlon and, later, Arthur Scargill among the full-time trade union leaders, and Derek Robinson, aka Red Robbo, at Longbridge trying to bring the motor industry to its knees and in no small measure succeeding. I knew and wrote about them all.

Then there was the UK's eternal bogeyman Tony Benn, now transformed in the eyes of much of the media into a national treasure. It may be difficult for a younger generation to believe but today's avuncular

Tony scared the life out of most people, including many of his Labour Party colleagues, when he was young. Tony Benn has had an impact on both of my careers.

While I was working for the *Financial Times* as the paper's industrial editor I wrote about Benn's plans for workers' control and his support for industrial action by various trade unionists, particularly Scargill. Whereas we are now having to face up to the rigours of recession, with low inflation and low interest rates, the 1970s were a time of raging inflation and high interest rates – and no less frightening for that. There was even talk in some circles of the country's government being taken over by the military, and at the centre of such talk was the spectre of terrifying Tony and the over-reaction of some people to him, including journalists who should have known better.

During my second career, in the nuclear power industry, Benn had responsibility for the industry within a wider brief for the energy industries as a whole. In my time he went from being a staunch supporter of civil nuclear power to one of its bitterest opponents – while supposedly representing and defending it in Parliament. There are plenty of theories about how this came about – and I have expressed mine in this book – but no one is really sure what happened.

In some ways Margaret Thatcher was the Conservative Party's Tony Benn, in that she frightened the pants off lesser men, even in her own party. Suddenly nationalisation was a dirty word and privatisation the thing. But did her policy of selling off the country's industrial crown jewels really change things for the better?

Our energy industries are now largely in the hands of foreign-owned companies, which are milking the situation for all it is worth. The banks, the cornerstone of our capitalist system, have had to be bailed out with billions of pounds of taxpayers' money and some of them effectively nationalised.

The railways are no more efficient today than they were when they were in public ownership, probably less so. Rail fares are the highest in Europe and so complicated that they are a positive deterrent to many contemplating rail travel. What price our supposed need for a better public transport system?

And with the implosion of the housing market and the nightmare of negative equity we have recognised that the Thatcher policy of getting local councils to sell off their housing stock to people who couldn't afford it was probably a bad idea, too.

I have worked in the private sector, the newspaper industry, and in the public sector, nuclear power, and both of them had their pressures. Those journalists who think that working in the public sector is a soft touch should try it. Certainly there are pressures in daily journalism, where you're only as good as your last story, but in my experience they are nothing compared with working for a company like British Nuclear Fuels, which operates in a goldfish bowl atmosphere and is subject to meddling civil servants and opinionated politicians who, with a few notable exceptions, know little of the subject they claim to be experts upon.

Working in the public sector can be vicious and not at all the sinecure it's made out to be by some commentators, some of them of the El Vino variety, looking to cut public sector pay and pensions at a time of economic depression.

I was nearly driven to suicide by the politicians and faceless bureaucrats who control our public sector industries and I'm certain Dr David Kelly, the man who blew the whistle on the phoney prospectus for the Iraq war, did take his own life because of them.

On that note I think it's time to make it clear that my life has not been all angst. There has been lots of fun along the way and my book has plenty of lighter moments. There can't be many – if any – directors of our state-owned industries who have trod the boards in the major musical roles made famous by Maurice Chevalier in *Gigi*, George Sanders in *Call Me Madam*, and Christopher Plummer in *The Sound of Music*!

And no other young journalist can have been sent to see the Beatles record their very first national television programme and to interview them, and found the Fab Four so unimpressive that he didn't bother to write anything!

I have been fortunate in my life to have the love and support, at various levels, of many people. I think primarily of my immediate family, of course – Sheila, my wife, my three children, Helen, Matthew and Sarah and their partners, my grandchildren, James, Laura, Michael and Patrick Doherty and the two young Bolters, Isaac and Solomon. It is a great sorrow that a seventh grandchild, Joseph Doherty, died as a baby and I didn't have the chance of getting to know him.

I have received a great deal of encouragement and support from friends and colleagues during the preparation of this book and I would like to put my thanks to them on record. A few of my friends read early chapters of the book and gave me their thoughts on it, which were usually encouraging and always constructive.

I am particularly grateful to Sir Bernard Ingham, best known perhaps as Margaret Thatcher's chief press secretary, for contributing a beautifully crafted and typically forthright foreword to *The Tenth Child* and to Nicholas Owen, the BBC television news presenter, for his generous comments about the early sections of the book which he read.

Chris and Bill Redman, fellow members of the International Wine and Food Society, almost challenged me to write the book in the first place after listening to me reminisce. It was my idea to write the book but I probably needed a jolt to get going.

Michael Cassell, an old friend and former colleague from my days as industrial editor of the *Birmingham Post* and of the *Financial Times*, was kind enough to read several early chapters and gave me some sound advice as to the need for a more consistent approach in my writing.

David Walker, former features editor, news editor and, most recently, managing editor of the FT checked out the chapter dealing with my time on the paper, which enabled me to correct a few errors and I am grateful to him for that.

I discussed some of my thoughts on the education system in the UK with my good friend Monica Galt, former head teacher of Kings Road Primary School and a member of the Council of the National Association of Head Teachers and, while we didn't always agree, our discussions were always stimulating.

A neighbour of Monica's, Peter King, took me through the intricacies of my computer system and helped me to avoid wiping important passages of manuscript and research notes from my PC. In doing so he had the opportunity to read several chapters of the book and came to like it. We have become good friends.

Finally, I have benefited from the advice and encouragement of Dr David Ingram, who is involved in the drug-testing business and Valerie Ingram, his wife, a former civil servant who was concerned with energy issues for some time. David, like me, left his industry following the mischievous, some would say malicious, activities of some of his peers and understood what I had suffered in my final days in nuclear power.

Michael Cassell is perhaps best known as former chief political correspondent of the FT and editor of the Observer column. He and his wife Linda, are members of what we are pleased to call the FT Gourmets Club, the members of which must have grown tired of me as I tested out a few thoughts on the approach I was taking with *The Tenth Child* at some of our more recent dinners.

I am grateful to the FT Gourmets for allowing Sheila and me to share their company, even though I left the paper over 30 years ago and lost touch with them for some years after I left journalism for the delights of the nuclear power industry. The group is a small and select one and our conversations are invariably sparky and thought provoking.

David Walker and his wife Pat, a freelance journalist of some renown, are also members of the FT Gourmets. So is Tony Moreton, a former industrial correspondent and deputy news editor of the FT and his wife Ena, who is perhaps better known as Ena Kendall, a well-known columnist and feature writer on the *Observer*.

Ray Dafter is probably the most energetic member of the group. He was energy editor and then resources editor of the FT before moving on to various high-powered roles with the Electricity Council, a PR and communications agency and Enterprise Oil, before setting up his communications business and publishing company. His wife Christine has been the driving force and coordinator of the FT Gourmets.

The late Michael Hand was a member of the FT's news desk at the time of his retirement, after an earlier career as labour correspondent, while his wife Anne, still a member of the FT Gourmets group, was a journalist with the *Oxford Mail*.

I miss Mike dearly, as I also miss two more of my friends and colleagues who have died recently, John Hayles, who was Finance Director of British Nuclear Fuels at the time of his retirement, and Jimmy Johnston, another former BNFL man, who gave a great deal to his Cumbrian community as leader of the Labour group on Copeland Borough Council and as mayor of what I still think of as Whitehaven.

There is another group of people from my past who still meet regularly. They are the former main board directors of British Nuclear Fuels from the early days of the industry, when the late Sir John Hill, and his successor Coningsby Allday, were chairmen of the company – the days when things got done and the nuclear industry seemed to have an exciting future.

I think it's fair to say that none of us is impressed by what has been allowed to happen to the company and the industry over the last 20 years or so and rather doubt that our political lords and masters will have the resolve to bring about the renaissance of civil nuclear power which they promise and which is long overdue.

Our group doesn't have a name, but to be a member of it you have to have served on the BNFL Board under the inspirational Con Allday, a man whose service to the nuclear industry should have been better recognised. There are seven of us now – Con himself, Dr Donald Avery, who was his Deputy Chief Executive, and Dr Bill Wilkinson, Alan Johnson, Roy Pilling, George Inglis and, of course, me.

Of the ten children of William James and Harriet Olive Bolter born into the choking slums of the back streets of the aptly named Black Country there are only three left – my sisters Jessie and Brenda and me.

With so many children it might be thought that we would turn out to be a closely knit family group but we didn't. We were all too busy fighting for our own survival I guess and I regret the fact that I didn't do more to maintain contact with my brothers and sisters over the years. I hope that those who follow us will work harder at keeping in touch with each other.

Finally, I would like to thank Carol Biss and all those members of the Book Guild Publishing staff who have played a part in the publication of this book.

I

The Slum Kid

First there was a boy. They named him William Bramwell after the first-born child of General Booth, the founder of the Salvation Army to which they then belonged. Then there was a girl, Jessie, followed by another boy, Thomas, and another girl, Mary.

If economics or forward planning had played any part in their lives they would have stopped there. Two boys and two girls, there was a certain symmetry to it and they certainly couldn't afford more children. But they kept going.

Mary was followed by Eva, Eva by Brenda, Brenda by Gladys, Gladys by Beryl and Beryl by Marina – six girls on the trot, regular as clockwork, every couple of years or so. Then, at long last, another boy, Harold Edward – me – the tenth and final child of William James Bolter and his wife, Harriet Olive Bolter, née Homer, my mother.

That makes me sound wanted, as though my mother and father pressed on with their procreating until they'd produced the Joseph they'd always longed for, the special youngest child. But it wasn't like that, as my mother delighted in pointing out when I got too uppity.

'I caught easily,' she would say, which was her way of describing the act of getting pregnant. 'That's all it was. We never expected you.' The implication was that not only didn't they expect me they didn't want me either. 'I was 42 years old for God's sake and your dad was 46.'

My mother had no problem giving birth either. 'It was as easy as shelling peas,' she would say. So there was no pain or apparent danger in childbirth to dissuade her or my father from producing a few more peas to shell, despite the appalling conditions into which the new child would be born.

My father died when I was 18. Although we became close towards the end of his life I never dared to ask him why he didn't limit the size of his family. It wasn't as though he was a Catholic. I can only assume that after the first half dozen or so children one more mouth to feed seemed an irrelevance. Or perhaps he didn't like the discipline or sensation of wearing one of those new-fangled condoms which, in any case, cost money.

By the time I was born, in 1937, the family should have seen the worst of it. It had somehow survived the Depression, despite my father being unemployed for over a year, and Bram – as William Bramwell was always known – and Jessie had started work. But life always seemed a struggle, I was told. In theory my mother looked after the bills but it was all a bit haphazard, a sort of financial juggling act, with final red notices and warning letters only to be expected.

The date of my birth is as uncertain as my mother's accounting methods. For the first ten years of my life I celebrated my birthday on August 18th, not that there was much in the way of celebration. No money for it, you see. Then, as it neared the time when I had to take the Eleven Plus exam, my birth certificate was checked. It was found that I had been registered as having been born on August 16th.

Although my mother grumbled that 'I ought to know when you were born,' which must be true, officialdom won and I became two days older than I thought I was, which was mildly disconcerting.

My early memories are of 170 Beeches Road, West Bromwich, the mid-terrace slum of a house where I was born. Queen Victoria is said to have drawn the curtains of her railway carriage when it went through West Bromwich, so that she wouldn't have to see the poverty and squalor. No matter that the town was part of the heavily industrialised Black Country, the powerhouse of her empire.

The Black Country was still very black when I was born, still contributing to the nation's wealth, still destroying the health of people working in the factories which belched their fumes and smells out into the tainted environment.

Our house was rented. The landlord was either short of money for repairs or trying to make our lives unpleasant in the hope that we might be persuaded to get out and make way for tenants who paid the rent regularly. The house was on three floors and also had two cellars. One cellar was used to store coal. The coal man delivered it in sacks piled high on a horse-drawn cart. He tipped his bags of coal into the brick-lined hole which led to the cellar and mother watched to make sure that we received the correct number of sacks and that there wasn't too much slack in them. Slack was coal dust and it burned too quickly. You had to make sure that the coalman didn't try to cheat you by adding stones to the coal as well.

The other cellar wasn't as damp or as cold as the coal cellar. It acted as a darkroom for my father's photographic hobby, which he enjoyed inter-mittently and somewhat secretively. This led my brother Tom to speculate (after the old man had died, of course) that he must have been developing pictures of a lady friend.

At ground level we had a front room, which was there for show and rarely used, a living room which was usually over-crowded, and a kitchen-cum-scullery, which had a built-in copper boiler for the washing. The boiler was brought up to the boil every Monday, steaming the place out. A wooden dolly, cut into a cross at the base, was used to beat the dirt out of the clothes. There was a mangle for wringing water from the clothes before they were hung out to dry, when the weather was up to it. The boiler also provided the hot water for my weekly scrub, which took place in a tin bath.

A door led from the kitchen to the backyard, a small patch of bare earth, and an Anderson air raid shelter, half buried in the ground with corru-gated iron sheeting over the top of it. The shelter was generally waterlogged. We didn't use it.

There was also an outside toilet, the only lavatory serving the household. It was greatly over-worked, except in the winter when we looked elsewhere for relief.

On the first floor of the house there was my mother and father's bedroom, complete with wardrobes, a dressing table and stool, an eiderdown, a some-what shabby carpet and other refinements. It also had a 'guzunder', a piss pot, which was placed under the bed when it wasn't being used, hence the name. There were two more bedrooms on that floor, shared by some of my older brothers and sisters – the numbers and mix varied as they left for the war or for marriage.

At the top of the house there were two attic rooms, one of which I shared with the two sisters closest to my age, Marina and Beryl. Marina, two years older than me, shared a bed with me until I was five or six years old, sleeping top to tail. She provided an alternative target for the bed bugs which we squeezed to death, the blood – presumably some of it ours – oozing out of their bodies.

If one of us was taken ill we would be removed to another bedroom, usually the one used by my parents, the one with the refinements, so that the doctor wouldn't see the conditions we slept in. Once the doctor had gone we would be returned whence we came. If we were walking wounded we would be examined in the front room which, as it was rarely used, was clean enough to be used for a medical inspection.

In the middle of the attic room where we normally slept there was a bucket, placed there to catch the rain-water which came through a gap in the roof tiles and through the ceiling. In places the plaster had been washed away from the wooden laths into which it had once been pressed and we could see the sky through the gaps. There were water stains at the edge of the holes, a rusty orange colour, and little bits of paper-covered plaster, hanging by a sliver of wood.

The floor was bare floorboards usually, but from time to time my mother made a rug for us from old clothes, produced by cutting up strips of worn out material a few inches long and pulling them in and out of a sacking base with a tool called a bodger. The three of us shared a guzunder.

There was a fireplace up there but a fire was never lit. We didn't have that sort of money. In the winter my mother spread old coats and the rug, if we had one, across the bed in an attempt to keep us warm. We slept in the pants and knickers and vests which we had worn that day and which we might well be wearing the following day.

The bed itself had an iron frame with coiled springs hooked into it which boinged away like Zebedee if we moved too sharply. The springs regularly slipped out of the holes intended to keep them in place. The mattress was stuffed with flock and collapsed towards the middle of the bed as the springs gave way under the strain.

Beryl, six years older than me, had her own bed. Beryl was backward, simple if you like. She went to a special school with the unfortunate name of Bratt Street. Her bed was underneath the tiny window which provided the only natural light in the room, although there was precious little of it. The window was set in the sloping roof and was never cleaned, inside or out. Inside, the glass was festooned with cobwebs.

Beryl invariably dropped the clothes she took off at night onto the floor. Marina and I obeyed mother's instructions and draped our clothes over both ends of the bed. Some of Beryl's clothes smelled strongly at times, particularly after she'd started her periods. It was only later that I understood what caused the stink. At the time I assumed it was because she'd wet herself.

I can feel Beryl's breath on my cheeks, heavy enough to wake me. As my eyes open her right hand reaches out and with her thumb and forefinger she strokes the eyelashes over my left eyelid, gently, caressingly. I'm too scared to move, in case she pulls my eyelashes out or pokes her finger in my eye.

'What are you doing?' I whisper, afraid to startle her. I keep my head perfectly still, transfixed by what is going on.

'Nothing,' she says. 'I just wanted to feel them.'

'Why? That's silly.'

'Don't call me silly. Everybody calls me silly. I don't like it. I'm not silly. I'll tell mom you called me silly.'

'Okay. You're not silly. Now move your hand.'

'Don't be such a baby.'

Marina wakes. 'What's the matter?' she says sleepily.

Beryl removes her fingers from my eyelashes.

'She's only trying to pull my eyelashes out, that's all.'

'Liar. I didn't do anything. I wasn't going to hurt you. Anyway you shouldn't call me silly.'

'Okay. You're not silly.'

Beryl goes back to her bed, mumbling to herself.

I decide not to tell mom what's happened. There's no point. She won't do anything. Eventually I get back to sleep.

The incident was never repeated. Beryl was harmless enough for the most part although she hit out occasionally when she became frustrated. I tended to ignore her. I even found it useful to have her around at times, blaming her for things I'd done, knowing that her denials would be less persuasive than mine.

If I heard other children teasing her I defended her as best I could, getting into one or two punch-ups as a result. The teasing could be merciless and, backward though she might be, Beryl was sensitive enough to find it deeply upsetting. 'I'm not silly. I'm not silly,' she would cry through her tears. I felt sorry for her, but embarrassed too. As I grew older I tried to avoid being seen with her. It's not something I'm proud of.

Beryl was put into a mental institution when I was about 15. It was years later before I found out why. Apparently she grew up with the normal appetites of a woman and became pregnant. She had an abortion, which may or may not have been legal, and was 'put away for her own safety'. I doubt if she saw it that way.

My mother went to see Beryl regularly when she was in what unkind people called the loony bin. The rest of us pushed her to the back of our minds. When she was past her child-bearing years mental health care had changed and Beryl was allowed to leave the institution and live outside under supervision. She married a man she'd met inside and they were apparently very happy together until she died an early death from cancer. I never met her husband.

My mother had a theory that this simpleton of the family, the one the neighbours' children called barmy Beryl, had ended up that way because she followed Gladys in the seemingly endless procession of daughters. Gladys had died of meningitis when Beryl was just learning to talk and was said to have been the prettiest of the girls. In the end Gladys was simply forgotten under the press of more children. She was dead before I was born.

I was two when the Second World War broke out. West Bromwich didn't see much of the German bombing but there were plenty of air raid warnings. Some nights I was taken to the big air raid shelter at the corner of Legge Street, less than a hundred yards from our house, when the sirens went off.

I didn't mind being woken up in the dead of night to go to the shelter. There were other kids there and we were given cups of hot cocoa. It was exciting. One of my early memories is of standing at my father's side, bleary eyed from being plucked out of bed, ready to be taken to the shelter. He was talking to my mother and we could see a red glow lighting up the horizon. Nearly 50 when war started, my father was too old to be called up but was drafted in for night-time service as an air raid warden. As he talked to my mother he speculated that Birmingham, five miles away as an aircraft flies, was being bombed. He told me later that what we had actually witnessed that night in November 1940, when I was three years old, was the destruction of Coventry, twenty miles away.

I started school in September 1942, at the height of the war. Before that I had accompanied my mother when she did the school walk with Marina and then with Beryl on to the special school in Bratt Street. I couldn't wait to start school, despite Marina's dire warnings that I didn't know what was coming to me.

Beeches Road Primary School was a ten-minute walk away from home, just past the first of the three entrances to Dartmouth Park and next door to St Philip's church. The school had been built around the turn of the century and was much like other schools of the period, but to me it was very special. It was an oasis of cleanliness and order in the middle of the chaos and grime at home.

I liked the headmaster, Mr Griffiths and all of the teachers, particularly Mrs Davis, who taught arithmetic. She was a plump lady with an ample bosom which looked as though it was made from two small batch loaves. I had an auntie Annie, my mother's sister, who had a similar shape. My sister Mary used to impersonate her by putting batch loaves down the front of her blouse. That's how I knew about batch loaf bosoms.

Auntie Annie didn't visit often. None of our relatives did. I think they were a bit ashamed of us and the state of the house. We weren't invited to their houses very often either, except on very special occasions.

Beeches Road itself had a distinct air of 'them and us' about it. On one side of the road there were large detached houses, set back from the road and with long back gardens running down to the park railings and a view over to open fields. Even a small child could recognise that the people who lived in those houses were more fortunate than those of us who lived on the opposite side of the road.

Our run-down terraced houses had very short frontages and at the rear the small dirt yards backed on to a narrow alleyway. Our view was across to the backyards of people living in similar conditions and onto their washing, old bedsteads and rusty bicycles, perhaps the odd chicken run where the Christmas dinner was raised.

One of the wealthier families living over the road, almost opposite us, was the Millichips. They owned a toy shop on the High Street. Bert Millichip, later to become Sir Bert and Chairman of the Football Association, was a member of the family and became a solicitor. But it isn't him I remember. My memory is of the day Marina and I thought we were about to be killed when the air raid sirens sounded in the afternoon, something we'd never experienced before. I remember the grand lady who saw two frightened children standing outside the house opposite hers, uncertain what to do as the siren wailed. For some reason mother wasn't at home when we arrived back from school and we didn't have a key to the house.

Mrs Millichip came across the road and collected us. She took us into her home and gave us a cup of cocoa and a chocolate biscuit each, a rare treat. I remember her with affection for that little kindness but I never spoke to her again. After the war the two sides of the road kept themselves to themselves.

I was eight years old when the war in Europe ended in May 1945. We went to a street party in Legge Street, which ran off Beeches Road. There wasn't a party in Beeches Road. The people who lived on the other side of the road weren't the sort to have a knees up, I was told by my mother.

My own little world changed with the arrival of the Mears family. They had moved to West Bromwich from a little village called Abertridwr, near Caerphilly, in south Wales and had found a house in Beeches Road. Ted, the father of the family, had worked in the coal mines during the war and had moved away from the area to make sure his two sons, Dennis and Colin, never went down them.

Colin, the younger son, was sent to my school and was put in the same class as me. He was a sturdy little boy with an impenetrable Welsh accent – impenetrable that is to someone used to speaking in a Black Country dialect and listening to others who spoke in the same way. Somehow, though, we made ourselves understood and we quickly became friends. That friendship has survived for over 60 years.

It was from the Mears family that I discovered that there was a social stratum somewhere between the Bolters and the Millichips. Colin's mother and father both found jobs when they moved to the Black Country. With two wages coming in the Mears family could afford the occasional treat, little pleasures that I could only dream of, and their house, empty all day during the working week, always seemed clean and tidy.

Colin and I found school work easy and were usually near the top of the class. After school we played out in the street with three or four other boys, much to the annoyance of some of the neighbours and the occasional car driver. We didn't care. Our families didn't have cars and those who did were snobs.

Beeches Road Primary School was not just a place for study. It was also an adventure centre. It had a large concrete air raid shelter with several dark rooms, a place to sneak into when the teachers weren't watching or to clamber over, daring each other to hang from the roof edge by the finger-tips and drop to the ground.

I had my first real fight in the school playground near the shelter. It was over a girl. I can't remember what she looked like or what her name was but I do know that I had decided that she was my girlfriend. Unfortunately, another small boy thought she was *his* girlfriend. I suspect that neither of us would have known what to do with her if she'd agreed to take on the role.

The fight wasn't any ordinary rough and tumble. This one took place with coats marking the corners of what we thought of as a boxing ring. We had a referee, too, my friend and protector, Timothy Austin, a tough-looking lad nobody wanted to fight. We intended to go three rounds, each of three minutes, because someone had heard that was what amateur boxers did.

I'm not sure whether there was a teacher on playground duty that day but no one prevented the fight going ahead. Tim, the referee, even contemplated charging the eager young spectators for the privilege of watching it. He was ignored. The boy I fought was a better fighter than me. I must have hit him a few times but he was quicker and probably braver. He soon had me in tears. My friend Tim eventually brought the bout to a premature end, declaring the fight a draw and making us shake hands. I thought he'd saved my life. Neither of us pursued our interest in the girl.

The school's air raid shelter was still there years after the war ended and by then we also had Dartmouth Park to play in. During the war we weren't allowed into it because of the barrage balloons and anti-aircraft guns. I was somewhat wary of the park. Just inside the main entrance there was a huge statue of an angel, with wings for arms, placed there as a monument to local men killed during the First World War.

The statue worried me. I'd been told by somebody that if you walked under the angel's left wing you would die. The problem was that I was never sure whether that meant the angel's own left wing, as I looked up at it, or the one to my left, the angel's right wing. And which was the angel's left wing on the way out of the park? I used one of the other entrances when I decently could.

Mr Griffiths, our headmaster, believed in teaching the three Rs and in rewarding high achievers, singling them out for special praise and the occasional treat in front of the whole school. He would be regarded today as politically incorrect, I suppose, but I thrived on his approach and loved him for it. I've always revelled in competition.

One of the headmaster's treats in our final year at junior school was to take the five top performers in the class to a lunchtime concert given by the City of Birmingham Symphony Orchestra in the city's monolithic Town Hall. Colin and I went. I was thrilled by the experience of watching and listening to the musicians, who were being kept up to the mark by an extremely animated conductor. Colin seemed less impressed.

I already knew a little about conducting, because I'd seen my extrovert father at work. Although the rent might go unpaid we usually had several musical instruments around the house – an old piano on permanent display but rarely played in the holy of holies, the front room, a trombone, a euphonium and even a violin, when they weren't earning their keep at the pawn shop.

Bram played the euphonium and Tom the trombone when they were home on leave, Bram from the navy and Tom from the army. I expressed an interest in learning to play the trumpet and my father pointed me in the direction of the Salvation Army, where he knew I'd be provided with an instrument and given free music lessons.

I had lessons on the B flat cornet for three years at the Army's wooden citadel at the top of Spon Lane. Eventually I reached the stage where I was allowed to play with the band in the streets, resplendent in my red Salvation Army vest. I ducked the trickier musical phrases.

It was while he was a member of the Salvation Army that my father had learned to read music. He was also given the chance to conduct the band. He went on to conduct brass bands, male voice choirs and even the music coming out of the radio. Music, together with his involvement in the Labour Party and the trade union movement, gave him the fulfilment which working in the stores at the Kenrick and Jefferson printing factory on West Bromwich High Street never could.

During the 1945 general election campaign my father made our front room available as a committee room for the Labour Party. There was a big poster with red lettering on it signalling our support for John Dugdale stuck in the window, an obvious provocation for our blue-postered neighbours across the road. I doubt if our candidate set foot outside the front room during his brief visits to our house. If he had, even to go to the lavatory in the backyard, he would have seen living conditions which gave real meaning to the socialist causes he espoused.

According to my sister Eva, my father had the chance to fight the safe

Labour seat at West Bromwich, or was it Smethwick? The family had lived in Smethwick before I was born. Eva said he had turned down the opportunity to become an MP because he couldn't see how my mother would cope with him away in London. I believed the story at the time. I believed everything Eva told me and I had every faith in my father's ability to do anything he turned his mind to, apart, perhaps, from earning a decent wage.

Latterly, I've had my doubts. Both Patrick Gordon Walker at Smethwick and John Dugdale at West Bromwich were public school and very much Labour Party Establishment figures. Maybe my working-class dad made the candidates' shortlist.

In addition to politics and music, my father was a writer and an avid reader, especially of the works of William Shakespeare. The showman in him which led him to front prize bands and male voice choirs also led him to learn the more popular speeches written by Shakespeare, as well as all of Stanley Holloway's monologues.

I particularly remember the Hamlet soliloquy, which he would declaim from time to time when the mood took him or he'd had a beer or two down at the Wrexham pub. His favourite Stanley Holloway story was the one about Sam and his musket. He was probably a bit of a ham, my dad, but I loved him for it.

Dad's writing was largely confined to a competition called Bullets, published in *John Bull* magazine. The competition involved the magazine publishing a list of two or three words and the competitor providing no more than three other words to produce a pithy, witty, poignant or humorous phrase. The finished list was then entered in that week's competition, for a small fee. My father won a few prizes for himself but, because he couldn't afford the multiple entry fees, he earned more by selling his efforts to others, who took a chance on his wit and wisdom and paid the fee and pocketed any prize.

Dad was largely self-taught. As the eldest member of his family he'd been sent out to work in the stables at the home of some rich family at the first opportunity. There he was kicked by a fractious horse, breaking his arm. I don't know whether it was set by a vet rather than a doctor but someone made a mess of the job. The accident left him with a right arm which was permanently bent into a boomerang shape. This infirmity never seemed to worry him though and somehow it gave his conducting even greater panache. With his arm across his chest he looked positively Napoleonic.

It was at the big house or some other like it that my father met his future bride, Harriet Olive Homer, who had also been put out to service when she was young. Apparently she was a very attractive girl, recently returned from America with her widowed father and siblings, failed emigrants. My father probably found this slightly exotic and attractive.

The fact that my mother and father met at all was surprising and wouldn't have happened but for the industrial revolution. Born in Chipping Norton in 1890 into a family of farm labourers who'd lived in Oxfordshire for generations, my father was taken to Llangollen as a small boy. His father, Thomas, was a railway plate layer and presumably followed the tracks as the railway system expanded into Wales. The family finally ended up in the Black Country, where most of my extended family still live.

My mother had an even more adventurous early life. She was the daughter of an American, Martha Timmins, who for some unknown reason had been sent to Rowley Regis in Staffordshire, which is also part of the Black Country, when she was 12 years old. There she joined a family called the Westwoods, who may have been relatives. Martha also met Walter Homer, my maternal grandfather, and married him.

They began their married life at the home of Harriet Westwood, by then a widow, but it can't have been much of a life. The whole family had to work at home as chain makers to make ends meet. No surprise then that they decided to try to make a new life for themselves in Martha's home country.

My mother, the first-born child of Walter and Martha, was born in 1894. She was known to all and sundry as Hattie. She was just six years old when the family set sail from Liverpool on a ship called *Germanic*, bound for New York. It's as Hattie that she's shown in the ship's manifest. The *Germanic* was built by Harland and Wolff and owned by the White Star shipping line, like the *Titanic*.

It must have been a hell of a journey for them – Walter, Martha, Hattie and three of her even younger siblings, Lucy, Annie and baby George – and it can't have been easy for them to settle in Syracuse, New York, with relatives, where another child, Sheldon, was born. But worse was to follow. Only four years after reaching the promised land, Martha died. My mother was not quite ten years old. It didn't take long for her widowed father to up sticks again and return to England with his five children.

My mother rarely talked about her father or how the family survived, but it seems he was a drunken brute. According to my mother he once threw her down the stairs. She blamed him for the fact that in later years her back was bent almost double. Mind you, she still lived until she was well into her nineties.

I believe that my mother and father loved each other and despite the appalling conditions in which we lived I felt secure enough. I received plenty of love and encouragement from my sister Eva, who delighted in my progress at school. I sensed very early on that my mother didn't know what to make of this strange child, the son who actually liked to go to school and who had the irritating habit of challenging everything she said.

Apart from my delight in proving how clever I was and having boys of my own age to play with or fight, the other appeal of Beeches Road School was that it was kept lovely and warm, unlike my attic bedroom. This was never more important than during the winter of 1946, when I was nine years old.

During that bitterly cold winter the railway tracks and points were frozen solid and little coal or oil could be moved around the country. Most of what there was had to be used to keep the electricity power stations and gasworks going to supply the needs of manufacturing industry in that heavily industrialised part of the Black Country.

Very little coal or coke reached domestic users – at least not poor payers such as us – but there was coke on sale at the local gasworks on Saturday mornings for those prepared to queue for it. Anyone, child or adult, was entitled to a bag of coke if they could haul it home through the snow. Marina and I were sent to fetch the coke on several occasions, no matter what the weather was like.

It's the early hours of the morning, a Saturday morning, and Marina and I are roused from our sleep by our mother. Her touch is gentle and I realise that she regrets having to wake us up. Beryl is left to lie on in bed. Lucky Beryl. Our older brothers and sisters are married and living elsewhere or they've left for work.

There's ice on the cobwebs at the window and the dirt on the window itself has formed into a pretty pattern. I want to touch it, but I can't reach. Our breath is like steam.

It's bitterly cold and Marina and I dress as quickly as we can in the several layers of clothes provided for us by mother. We each put on two vests and two pairs of pants or knickers, our shirts and blouses and two pairs of socks. With the extra socks my shoes are tight, pinching my toes.

Mother gives us some more socks to wear on our hands and on top of all this we pile on some old jumpers and our coats and we're ready to go. It's seven o'clock.

Dad is leaving for work after spending a couple of hours working on his entries for the Bullets competition. There's a huge brown pot of tea on a trivet by the fire. It's been there since Dad made it when he first got up. He's added hot water and tea leaves to the pot from time to time, turning the contents into a thick brown stew. Marina and I are given cups of the mixture, with milk and plenty of sugar. I feel a lot warmer.

'Off you go,' Mother says. 'Take care.'

Marina and I go out through the back door, shivering as the cold hits us. There's a trolley waiting for us outside, leaning against the wall. The trolley's made from pieces of wood bolted onto the axles of an old pram, which was probably once mine and possibly Marina's as well. A piece of rope is tied to the front axle, which is what we pull it with. The trolley will be used to bring back our precious cargo.

We have a long walk ahead of us and the roads are covered in snow, the footpaths slushy under foot. Our destination, Swan Village gasworks, is two or three miles away and mainly downhill. The sky is getting lighter.

A queue has already formed. It will be some time before we reach the head of it and we can only hope that there will be some coke left. Sometimes there isn't.

We jump up and down, trying to bring some warmth to our feet, blowing on our hands through the layers of old socks. Marina is crying quietly, but trying to hide her tears. I'm braver than her, but I feel like crying. There's an acrid smell in the air and dark grey dust everywhere. I can taste it. Spilt coke crunches under my feet.

I hold out my sack, the neck wide open. The man shovels coke into an over-sized coal scuttle, dangling from what looks like a big clock face. It's the weighing machine for the coke. Satisfied, he tips the coke into my sack.

I have to drag the sack off the weighing machine myself, tugging at it until I have it on the ground. I've been told that it's a rule that you handle your own sack. I don't know whether it's true but I take no chances. Then it's Marina's turn.

A man helps us to load our sacks onto the trolley, which bends under the weight, and we set off for home. Our way home is uphill as far as the Tower, a cinema which is halfway along our route, and then it levels out, with only a slight incline from then on.

The trolley seems to get heavier as we go along and we take it in turns to pull it, while the other one pushes from behind.

My back is killing me.

2

The Grammar Grub

As that awful winter gave way to spring I began to think more and more about what would face me when I left junior school in the summer. At times I felt worried, at times excited by the prospect. I didn't know it then, but I was to be one of the early beneficiaries of the Butler Education Act of 1944. This brought in the Eleven Plus, paving the way for boys and girls like me to obtain a grammar school education and the chance of a better future.

For all the opportunities it provided, 'Rab' Butler's legislation also caused considerable upheaval, leading to tensions and divisions within the families and communities from which the chosen ones came. Under the Butler system the least academic went off to one of the secondary modern schools, branded as failures far too early in life. It was anticipated that they would become factory workers, bus conductors and shop assistants or take up some other menial form of employment. They were to be the wage earners of society.

Children of middling ability were transferred to a secondary technical school, where they were taught the more demanding skills which would one day equip them for jobs as mechanics or shorthand typists. At least that was the intention. In practice very few secondary techs came into being.

Then there were the grammar schools. There had been grammar schools for centuries, of course, but entry to them was largely reserved for those whose parents could afford to pay for their children's places. They were for the top few percent of the child population destined to become academics, lawyers, accountants, and captains of industry, or so it was thought.

There was never any doubt in my mind that I would become a grammar grub, as the secondary modern kids called us. I sat examinations for two grammar schools, the co-educational West Bromwich Grammar School, within walking distance of home, and Holly Lodge County Grammar School in Smethwick, a boys-only school which was a bus ride and a couple of good walks away.

I passed both of the examinations I took during the summer of 1948, creating a dilemma for my father. He took time off work to visit the two schools and picked up leaflets explaining what items of uniform and sports gear would have to be bought for me, what meal and travel subsidies were available and how I was expected to behave. I was feeling pretty pleased with myself and couldn't wait to hear which school my parents had chosen for me. My own fancy was for West Bromwich Grammar, where I knew Colin would be going.

My parents' bedroom was immediately below the attic room I shared with Marina and Beryl, and one night I could hear raised voices coming from their room and caught the odd reference to me. I crept out of bed and sat on the stairs to listen to what was going on. My mother and father were having a ferocious argument about my future. My mother took the lead.

'What's so special about him? None of the others went to grammar school.'

'They didn't have the chance. Now it's free. He's going I tell you.'

'What about the uniform? They wear uniforms.'

'We'll manage.'

'It's easy to say, Will. Anyway, the others have done all right. Bram's in the police force now and Tom's got himself a job as a nurse at that mental hospital.' She didn't mention the girls.

'So what? Harold's going to have a chance they couldn't have. He's the lucky one if you like.'

'Lucky? I don't know about lucky. He's a cheeky little devil, I know that. Gives me nothing but lip all the time. Thinks he knows everything. Full of himself.'

'What's that got to do with anything? Anyway, give it a rest. He's going to grammar school. You stopped Eva going to art school, you're not going to stop Harold getting on. We fought to get kids like him into the grammar schools.'

'Oh you and your politics. We'll have to get him football boots and things as well as the uniform. Shorts and God knows what else. He'll be with a bunch of snobs.'

'He's going and that's that.'

The argument continues to rage back and forth as I creep back to the attic, convinced that I'm going to be packed off to one of the secondary modern schools.

Next day I get up early and join my father by the fireside, where he's doing his writing. He pours me a cup of thick black tea and lightens it with milk before adding the sugar.

'You're going to Holly Lodge,' he says.

It's not the school I want. I want to be with Colin. But it will do. It's a grammar school. I nod my agreement.

'Thanks dad.' I feel like giving him a hug but we don't do that sort of thing.

My father never did explain his decision to plump for Holly Lodge. I suspect it was because the buildings were modern and the boys and girls were in separate schools, kept apart by a wide drive and sports fields. The school was set well back from the road in a quiet area. It looked fresh and roomy by comparison with the collection of old buildings which formed West Bromwich Grammar School, squashed together on the main road opposite the Kenrick and Jefferson printing works where dad worked, close to the town hall, the gala swimming baths and a hospital. He may also have felt that having girls in the same classroom would be too much of a distraction for me as I got older. He could have been right.

As I prepared to change schools during the summer holidays my mother put together the cheapest version of the Holly Lodge school uniform she thought we could get away with. I was bought a new pair of short grey trousers, several sizes too big, and a new blazer, which was navy blue. The Holly Lodge badge, bought separately, was stitched onto the top pocket of the blazer, not very professionally. It was slightly lop-sided, a dead give-away.

The school had also provided a list of the sporting kit I would need – shorts, swimming costume, football boots and socks, cricket flannels and a white shirt, plimsolls – a seemingly endless list which challenged my mother's ingenuity. She made the shorts herself from an old bed sheet and the swimming costume came from a woollen jumper. Mom cut the arms and parts of the shoulders off it and tacked round the edges of the holes she'd made to stop it unravelling. The first time I used the costume it clung to my private parts as soon as it got wet. I felt stupid.

Shoes were always a problem. My mother complained that I kept growing out of them and that I ruined them playing football in the street and the playground. She was right on both counts. When the shoes became worn they would be patched up with cardboard, which was useless when it rained, or stick-on soles were applied to them. They didn't stick on for very long. I suppose that was the football. On one occasion Tom cut the heels off a pair of Marina's shoes and I was told I would have to make do with them. I was painfully aware of them, even though none of the other boys seemed to notice. I was glad when they were replaced.

I wasn't the only one wearing makeshift and hand-me-down clothes. Others had their own versions of the school uniform and we soon learned to take the teasing of the better-off children or shut them up by threatening to give them a thump round the ear.

Life at 170 Beeches Road was a noisy, crowded affair, with a great deal of coming and going. I think Jessie got married first and Bram and Tom, recently demobbed, weren't far behind. This seemed to inspire the rest of the girls, who vied with each other to be next in the helterskelter scramble to get to the altar or the register office. If things went wrong for them they simply came back home for a while, sometimes with a husband in tow, sometimes not. This led to a great deal of turmoil.

It seemed to me that beds and bedrooms were constantly being shuffled, although this didn't really affect me. Nobody wanted the attic room which Marina, Beryl and I slept in. All of this movement didn't totally pass me by, though. Brenda was allowed to start married life with her husband Tommy Mann in a sort of bed-sitter arrangement in the front room. I'd been doing my homework there till then. It was the only reasonably quiet downstairs room in the house.

Emotionally there seemed to be a fair amount of sexual action or discussion as the girls fell in and out of love. I suppose my sisters thought I was too young to understand what was going on when they talked and giggled about their own or somebody else's romantic adventures, but I wasn't.

Mom tried to exercise some sort of control over them, not always successfully. I knew exactly what she meant when she told one of my sisters that a friend of hers was 'no better than she should be'. I thought the girl was pretty. My mother thought she was a tart.

My mother talked in clichés as she tried to keep the girls 'on the straight and narrow', using expressions like 'You made your bed now lie in it' and 'Marry in haste, repent at leisure.'

Abortions were illegal, even I knew that. But I understood the whispered gossip about girls who had 'got themselves in the family way' and were trying to get rid of an unwanted child by drinking 'the best part of a bottle of gin' and taking hot baths. There were other friends of my sisters who'd been to see the old woman living round the corner who knew how to sort out 'the mess they've got themselves into', apparently using a knitting needle for the purpose.

In some ways life at Holly Lodge was as turbulent and disturbing as it was at home. Instead of the 10-minute walk to school I'd been used to I had a journey which could take anything from 40 minutes to an hour. It meant getting up much earlier than before, leaving Marina behind in bed. By then she had a bed of her own, but we still slept in the same room. So did Beryl.

The journey to school now involved walking to the town centre and catching a Number 16 bus to Smethwick. It left from the top of Spon Lane, just off Dartmouth Square. At the terminus outside the Spon Croft pub I disembarked and walked or ran the rest of the way up the hill to Holly Lodge. I didn't have to pay on the bus. I had a bus pass, courtesy of the local education authority.

It was a rule that we had to wear our caps to and from school. I'd never worn a cap before and thought I looked stupid in it. I quickly learned that very few of the boys wore their caps until they were within sight of the prefects stationed at the end of the school drives. The prefects were there to ensure that we had the caps on our heads and they entered our names in a book if we didn't. That meant detentions or lines.

At the end of my first year at Holly Lodge the new entrants sat an examination which decided the course their education should take for the rest of their time there. There was an annual intake of 90 boys, divided into three classes of 30 pupils. The top 10 boys in each class of 30 were put into the most academic arts stream, specializing in English, history, French and Latin. The middle group were siphoned off into a class which put more emphasis on the sciences – biology, chemistry and physics – plus English,

French and German, which had taken the place of Latin. The bottom stream concentrated on what were seen as less demanding subjects, such as mechanical drawing. They also studied English and French, but there was no Latin or German for them.

We all did mathematics up to GCE 'O' level standard and there was an element of choice between other subjects such as geography, music and art. There were probably ten subjects available to us in all – not the dozens now on offer.

I was in the top stream, the boys seen as potential academics and high flyers. I began my grammar school career at the top, a carryover from junior school, but it was pretty much downhill from then on. Everything had come so easily at Beeches Road Junior School. It was different at Holly Lodge. I was among equally bright, perhaps brighter, boys and was expected to work.

I should have worked harder than I did but chose to put such effort as I was prepared to deploy only into the subjects, particularly English and history, which interested me. There was no tradition of study at home to help me either and no pressure from my father – and certainly not my mother – to do my homework. I worked at home from time to time but it was never easy to find peace and quiet. Increasingly I fitted my homework in during the lunch break at school or cribbed it from others first thing in the morning. I was careful to crib from boys who I knew were of only average ability. I didn't want to attract attention by appearing to be too clever.

For the most part the teaching staff at Holly Lodge treated all of the pupils the same, rich or poor, apart from Mr Watson Taylor, who taught history and was an out-and-out snob. He gave special attention to the dwindling number of pupils whose places in the school had been paid for. Watson Taylor had little time for me, nor I for him.

Apart from teaching me history, Watson Taylor was my form master. He singled me out for special attention, remarking on the holes in the heels of my socks, my dirty neck, the state of my fingernails, that sort of thing. He turned humiliation into a fine art. He was also into physical violence, hitting me across the knuckles with a ruler when I'd done something which he found particularly annoying.

By contrast, my English teacher saw qualities in me which he was determined to nurture and protect. I was fortunate to have 'Sniffer' Jones, so-called because of his sinus problems, as my main English teacher throughout my time at Holly Lodge. I owed much of any later success I had in life to his early encouragement.

Holly Lodge was designed with the classrooms built in a square, with a lawn in the middle of what was called the quadrangle – a new word to me. As far as possible we were taught in our form rooms and the teachers came to us. We only moved for such subjects as science, where we were transferred to the labs, and physical training in the gym.

There were strict rules about how we could move round the school. Teachers were allowed to walk across the central lawn area. Prefects could show their seniority by walking on the path surrounding the lawn. The rest of us made our way along the covered arcades which fronted the classrooms. It was all very regimented.

One day it was raining and Sniffer decided to keep dry by taking the arcade route, which was covered, to his next lesson. All of the classrooms had full-length plate glass windows, which meant he could see what was going on inside them.

As luck would have it Sniffer glanced into the classroom just as Watson Taylor whacked me across the knuckles with his ruler. He stormed into the room and snatched the ruler out of his fellow teacher's hand.

'Don't let me see you doing that ever again,' he shouted. 'You have no right to do that. If there's any caning to be done, send the boy to the headmaster. And you'd better have a good reason for that, too.'

Sniffer then turned on his heel and marched out of our form room, which had gone very quiet, taking Watson Taylor's ruler with him. We sat in stunned silence, looking on as a visibly shaken Watson Taylor tried to recover his composure. Watson Taylor never hit me again but the taunting continued. I got used to it in the end.

I was caned on three occasions, twice by my first headmaster, Mr Boden, a mild-looking, white-haired old man who had a surprisingly strong arm, and once by his successor, the Reverend Thorp. Both knew how to inflict pain. I don't think I deserved any of the canings.

My first came after I tried to protect a weaker boy, a lad called Badham, from bullying. Badham was being flicked across the face with a milk straw and was in tears. It wasn't serious bullying, I suppose, but Badham was unable to put a stop to it. I told the bully to pack it in but he wouldn't. A fight broke out as I pulled him away from Badham and snatched the straw out of the bully's hand.

In the melee which followed a classroom window was broken – one of the full-length ones. Watson Taylor sent me and the bully to the headmaster for a caning. I thought this was grossly unfair and told the headmaster so. I was still caned. I regarded the stripes across my bum as a badge of honour.

I can't remember the reasons for the other two canings. If they were meant to teach me a lesson about my future behaviour there couldn't have been much point to them.

The inside windows of some of the classrooms, including my form room, looked out on to the school playing field. I found this a distraction when there was a game being played. I was sports mad and had no trouble getting into the house teams for cricket, football and athletics as I progressed up the school.

Then there was boxing. I like to think that I was a sensitive soul but I'd learned very early to stand my ground if anyone tried to pick on me at school or if one of the secondary modern kids tried it on as I made my way home. The usual trick was for one of them to snatch that damned school cap and kick it down the road. At Holly Lodge the art teacher, Mr Barker, was responsible for teaching boxing. He was an unlikely tutor, long, thin and aesthetic, but he seemed to know his stuff. To find out which of us young boys had the makings he paired off a couple of boys at random, tied boxing gloves on them and let them loose in a marked square of boxing ring size in the gym. No account was taken of relative heights or weights.

My first bout was against a boy called Baker. He was short and stocky. I was thin, with long arms, which gave me an enormous reach advantage. The contest was like an old-fashioned bare knuckle fight. Neither of us knew how to box, so we stood toe to toe and slugged it out, as the other boys cheered us on.

Our tutor loved it, so much so that at the school's annual boxing tournament he pitched us against each other again and we were the first contestants, being the youngest. We were in a proper ring this time but the action was much the same as before. We tried to knock the living daylights out of each other. There was no skill about it. I was deemed to be the winner by Mr Barker. My opponent, Baker, failed to progress after that but I continued with boxing lessons from the scraggy art teacher and eventually became school boxing captain.

My father only saw me box once, towards the end of my school days. It was my last bout and my father, suffering from failing health, had struggled to get there. A lad from another school, a secondary modern pupil far tougher than me, effectively beat me up and Dad decided it was time to call it a day. I didn't mind too much.

My motives for taking up another sport, ice skating, when I was about 15 years old had nothing to do with any perceived need for more exercise. I'd started to take an interest in girls again and someone must have told me that the girls at the ice rink, many of them girls from the school next door, wore extremely short skirts.

I was never a very good ice skater but I rarely missed one of the Saturday afternoon skating sessions at the Birmingham Ice Rink, unless I was broke. I was occasionally given some pocket money by my mother or by Eva but it soon went. I decided to go out to work

I found a job helping to deliver bread on Saturday mornings for a relative of my brother-in-law, Harry Powney, who was married to my eldest sister Jessie. Saturday was his busiest day. It was the day customers paid their bills. Anyone who said they'd pay later or had no change got stale bread. I'd sometimes wondered why the bread we got at home was stale so often.

I earned enough from the bread round to persuade my mother that I could pay for a bicycle on what we knew as 'the never never', hire purchase. Because I was so young the bike was bought in my mother's name and she was notionally responsible for the monthly payments which I, of course, provided from my earnings.

I was very proud of my bike, particularly as Colin's father had just bought him one and we could go for rides together. My bike was bought from Bert Shinton's shop near the town centre. Bert's daughter had been a pupil at my primary school and my father knew Bert slightly. Unfortunately, it wasn't long before the hire purchase agreement began to unravel.

One day my father came across a letter from Bert Shinton, informing my mother that as the HP payments had not been made he intended to repossess the bike. My father was furious.

'What's all this about?' he asks my mother. 'You told me Harold could pay for the bloody bike. Now we get this. Why haven't the payments been made?'

I look across at my mother, waiting for her to speak, willing her to tell

him the truth. My mother looks distinctly uneasy but keeps quiet as my father rants on.

Eva is just home from work and enters the room, attracted by the row. 'What's going on?' she asks.

'Harold's not been paying the HP on his bike. Bert Shinton's taking it back. Makes me look a damned fool. God knows we have enough money problems already without this.'

'But he gives mom the money every Saturday, as soon as he gets home from the bread round,' Eva says.

'Why the hell didn't you tell me that?' my father demands, first of me, then of my mother. 'Why, for God's sake?'

Neither of us speak. We just look at each other.

I know what I feel though. It's a mixture of disgust and pity. How can my mother stand by and allow me to take the blame?

The money was found from somewhere to pay off the debt and I kept my bike. I suspect Eva paid at least part of it. The incident not only affected my relationship with my mother but how I came to regard my father as well.

I had long recognised that my mother had been ground down by the drudgery of keeping the family fed, the clothes washed and the shopping done. My father rarely took her out and she had no outside interests of her own to break the monotony of it all. I began to see my father in a new light, questioning why he'd ignored so much of what was going on around him over the years, why he'd never sorted out that attic bedroom in which my two sisters and I had slept.

For the most part he'd been content to dress up in the smartly pressed suit, the shirt with the starched white collar and cuffs and the gold cuff links, and to take himself off to choir or band practice or one of his Labour Party meetings.

I began to love my mother a little bit more and my father a little bit less. At the same time I felt guilty about thinking of them in such a judgemental way. I guess it was all a part of growing up.

As I reached my early teens it became obvious that my father's health was deteriorating rapidly. The doctor said he had acute bronchitis and he used an inhaler when his breathing was at its worst. He was in his early 60s but looked older and didn't get out as much. As a result he had less to occupy his mind.

For me this had its advantages. I began to talk more and more to my father, learning from him. There was no set pattern to it. We would debate anything and everything – the nature of society, politics, religion, anything. Without making a point of it we took to role playing, justifying attitudes which we despised. One day I'd be the Tory, another day I'd be a Communist. The more extreme the cause the better. Taken together with the conversations I had with Sniffer Jones I was developing debating skills which were to prove invaluable, without knowing it.

When I was 15 and despite the lack of effort which I'd put into my school work, the head teacher, the Revd Thorp, came to the conclusion that I would benefit from a sixth form education, and asked my father to see him. The head's perception of my ability was obviously coloured by the views of Sniffer Jones. I had talked to him about my ambition to become a lawyer, or perhaps a journalist.

My father must have wondered what I'd done wrong when he was summoned into the head's presence. Like me, he'd assumed that I was only a year away from leaving school and earning my living. My sisters had left school at 15.

There were perhaps a dozen boys who the school thought would benefit from taking 'A' (for Advanced) level examinations in the sixth form but realised that their parents were unlikely to allow them to stay on at school for the extra two years. This would have taken them to 18 years old, when the chances were that they'd be off doing National Service. There was never any talk of university for me. 'That's not for the likes of us, our Harold.'

The school came up with a compromise. The plan was for the important 'O' and 'A' courses and examinations to be pulled together. I would study for a further two years (taking me to 16 when I took the exams and just 17 when I left school). This proposition was put to my father, who didn't hesitate, although he knew my mother wouldn't be pleased. He told the head that I could stay on for the extra year.

Because I hadn't worked hard enough in earlier years I left my grammar school with an excellent English 'A' level and not much else in the way of academic distinction. The idea of telescoping 'O' and 'A' levels together didn't work as well as expected and it was soon dropped by the school.

My school leaving certificate probably owed a lot to the influence of Sniffer. I suspect it was the inspirational Mr Jones who wrote that I had 'a keen critical sense and a fluent English style' and 'a good brain, which he uses to form his own personal judgements'.

My leaving certificate also informed potential employers that I had played for the school first elevens at cricket and football and been a member of the athletic and boxing teams. I couldn't see that having much influence when it came to getting a job. Words like able, conscientious and diligent also appeared, written by someone with a supportive nature or a sense of humour, and I hoped that might help.

I knew that I hadn't made the most of the opportunities presented to me at Holly Lodge but I did have an ally, Sniffer Jones, the man who saw something in me that others had missed. And Sniffer was a friend of W. Vaughan Reynolds, the editor of *The Birmingham Post*.

3

The Copy Boy

I was a few minutes early as I walked through the impressive front entrance of the *Birmingham Post and Mail* building. I'd spent nearly an hour walking the city centre streets, killing time. I was still at school and was wearing my school uniform – the blazer with its prefect's braid edging the lapels, the trousers well pressed for once and my shoes polished. I would have liked to have worn a suit but I didn't have one. I was about to have my first job interview.

The entrance to the *Post and Mail* building on the corner of New Street and Colmore Row was opposite the Midland Hotel. I later discovered that at the back of the hotel there was a bar which was one of the favoured watering holes of the senior reporters, mainly those working for the morning paper, the *Post*. Their working hours were from 2 pm to 10 pm, which provided plenty of time for them to have a pint or two of beer before starting work, a few more around 6 pm if things were quiet and a chaser at the end of the day.

There was a strong smell of furniture polish as I entered the building, similar to that in our unused front room in Beeches Road, the one with the rarely used piano. An array of half a dozen or so young men and women faced me. They sat at a long counter with a low grille in front of them and there were people waiting patiently to speak to them. They were writing furiously and seemed very important. The scene was positively Dickensian.

'Excuse me.' It was my turn to speak to one of those in authority, a smartly dressed young man. He was in his early 20s. I was 17. That probably justified his air of superiority. I was aware of my school uniform. He wore a suit.

'Yes?'

'I have an appointment with Mr Reynolds.'

'Mr Vaughan Reynolds?' he said questioningly, emphasising the Vaughan. 'He likes to be known as Vaughan Reynolds. He's the editor of the *Post*. Is it him you want?'

'Yes,' I said, already intimidated.

Off the young man sauntered into an inner office, leaving me to fester a little longer. 'Somebody will come and get you,' he said on his return, in an offhand sort of way.

'What are you doing?' I asked politely.

'Small ads,' he said. 'Taking advertisements,' he amplified, sensing my bemusement. 'Next.' I moved to one side as an old lady pushed past me to place her small ad.

I was eventually collected by the formidable Patricia Latham, who at that time was secretary to W. Vaughan Reynolds. I could sense immediately that she was someone to be reckoned with. Pat Latham, a striking woman with lots of make up and a loud voice, controlled the editor's outer office – and the editor – with a rod of iron, I later discovered. There was no getting into the editor's presence without Miss Latham's say-so.

As far as I'm aware she had no journalistic training but she went on to become woman's editor of the *Post*, either because she instructed Vaughan Reynolds to give her the job or because he felt in need of a less ordered, controlled working environment.

Miss Latham marched me up an impressive wide staircase to the first floor. The editor's office was practically opposite the top of the stairs and I was ushered straight into it. I can't remember what Vaughan Reynolds looked like, which suggests he was not particularly imposing. I had few conversations with him of any real length or depth, although I worked for him for about six years and can still picture most of the other people I worked for. He seemed to keep well away from the reporters' room.

As Miss Latham left the room Vaughan Reynolds came straight to the point.

'Gwyn Jones is a friend of mine. He tells me you have the makings of a journalist.' Good old Sniffer.

'I hope so sir.'

'What have you been studying?'

'English, French and History at "A" level. Maths and Economics at "O" level.'

'When will you get your results?'

'Some time during the school holidays I think.'

'Never mind. Gwyn says you'll do well. Can you start here at the beginning of August?'

'As soon as you like, sir.' Sniffer obviously has more confidence in my GCE exam results than me.

Vaughan Reynolds seems to be unsure of what else he should ask me.

'Unusual spelling, Bolter,' he says. 'No "u" in the middle.'

My name's no stranger than yours, I think. I'd noticed the W. Vaughan Reynolds sign on his door.

'I think there was a "u" in Bolter once. Ages ago.'

'Is W. J. Bolter a relative of yours?'

'Yes. I think so. My father's name is William James Bolter.'

'Does he do the Bullets?'

'Yes,' I say, wondering where this is taking us.

'I do the Bullets,' Vaughan Reynolds says. 'Your father's better at it than me. Clever man. Anyway tell Miss Latham I've given you the job – trainee journalist. She knew I was going to anyway. Good morning.'

After thanking him I practically skip out of Vaughan Reynolds's office. Apparently he's concluded that I must be able to write because my father is better than him at a somewhat obscure word competition and his friend Gwyn Jones, a Welshman, has taught me English.

My father was tickled pink when I told him that his entries in the *John Bull* competition had helped me get my first job as a trainee journalist with the *Birmingham Post*, one of the biggest regional daily morning newspapers in the country, second only to what was then the *Manchester Guardian*.

Neither of us read the *Post* as it happened but that didn't matter. I was going to get the start in journalism which I had dreamed about. Dad's morning paper of choice was the *Daily Herald*, which was tied to supporting official Labour Party policy and was part owned by the Trades Union Congress. If he couldn't get the *Herald* for some reason he would pick up a copy of the *News Chronicle*, which backed the Liberals. That was as far as he would drift to the right in his search for information and opinion.

Never in his wildest dreams would he have imagined that the *Herald* would one day become the *Sun*, owned by the Australian Rupert Murdoch and supporting whichever political party its owner fancied at the time. He wouldn't have expected the *News Chronicle* to be absorbed into the right-wing *Daily Mail* either.

It was 1955 and the *Daily Herald*, like the other national newspapers and even the *Post*, had started to write about the flood of immigrants arriving in Britain from the West Indies and India and Pakistan. My father didn't know what to make of it all.

'The Millichips have sold up you know,' the old man says. We are sitting by the fire one evening, having one of our increasingly frequent conversations.

My father's chronic bronchitis seems to be getting worse and he wheezes and coughs a lot as we talk, spitting phlegm into a handkerchief or on to the fire, where it sizzles. I wish he wouldn't. He's now having to use a nebuliser to help him breathe.

He's usually off work and doesn't get out much at all now. I can sense that he looks forward to talking to me. I suppose I make a change from the radio, which is turned on most of the day.

'Half the houses over the road have been sold to Pakistanis,' he says. 'They pack them in like sardines – a dozen or more of them in one house, all of them men. They sleep in shifts you know. It's not natural.'

As usual I adopt an opposing stance.

'The government says we need them. According to them we need the West Indians over in Handsworth as well for that matter. There's a labour shortage.

'The blacks are needed on the buses and the railways and the Pakistanis and Indians are working in the heavier industries – the foundries and rolling mills and so on. They're doing jobs our own people don't want.'

'Who says so?' the old man challenges me. 'Where's the evidence? According to the Herald some of the unions are opposed to them coming over here. They tried to block the blacks getting jobs on the buses in Birmingham.

'The unions are worried that we'll end up with these people working long hours and being paid low wages. Before you know it the employers will use it to try to force our wages down. Not mine, of course. Too late for that.

'We went through a war to stop Hitler invading us and now we're told that we have to spend a fortune on defence to stop the Russians swarming all over us. So what do we do? We let a bunch of blacks and Indians come into our country without a fight. Invite them here. It's crazy. They're not like us. Never will be.

'It's all right for the politicians. They don't have to live next door to them. We were never consulted – not even by the Labour Party. The Party takes the working class for granted nowadays. Oppose immigration and you're called a racist.

'Your mother says the Pakistanis and the Indians stink when she sits near them on the buses. Something to do with the stuff they slick their hair down with.

'And some of them chew some sort of nut – betel nuts I think you call them – and spit the stuff out on to the pavement when they've finished chewing it.

'I'm not against them because of their colour, mind. But one day this immigration policy will come home to roost. Mark my words.

'I'm only glad we're moving in with Eva and Bob and the family. Get away from here.'

It was another 13 years before Enoch Powell delivered his famous 'Rivers of Blood' speech warning of the dangers of uncontrolled immigration. I suspect my socialist father would have agreed with what he had to say, if he'd been alive.

My sister Eva, her husband Bob and the children lived in a three-bedroom council house at Hill Top, on the fringes of West Bromwich, just off the main road to Wednesbury. The house was barely big enough for the two of them and their three, later four, children but they had invited my mother and father and me to go and live with them.

I don't think that the offer was made because of the Asian takeover of Beeches Road – although that might have been a factor – but because of my father's failing health and the rotten conditions in which we were still living. His heavy smoking – a couple of packets of Players or Capstan full strength each day – can't have helped. There had been no improvements in the fabric of 170 Beeches Road since my first memories of living there and Eva, who loved our father as much as I did, was worried that the damp conditions in the house were making his bronchitis worse.

I guess our landlord wasn't sorry to see us go. He found new tenants straight away – more Pakistani immigrants.

Despite being overcrowded Eva and Bob's new council house seemed like a palace after the slum property we'd been living in. There was a bathroom and an indoor toilet and every room was heated by radiators. I slept downstairs on a camp bed in what was intended to be the lounge.

Patricia Latham greeted me when I arrived at the *Post and Mail* building for my first day's work. I was wearing my first suit, bought off the peg. She steered me through the instructions on what was expected of me and I signed some papers, not bothering to read them too closely. I would have joined the *Post* for nothing.

'You will be paid three pounds and ten shillings a week,' Miss Latham said, making it sound like a fortune. 'Now come and meet Leslie Duckworth and Ron Lerry.'

Leslie Duckworth was a tall, stern-looking Yorkshireman and he was introduced to me as the news editor of the *Birmingham Post*. I didn't know what a news editor was but it sounded important. Mr Duckworth was my real boss, I later discovered, and a very fine journalist.

Ron Lerry was smaller and less boisterous and I never did understand his role on the paper. He was called Chief Reporter but never went out on reporting assignments. I suppose he acted as Leslie Duckworth's assistant, but nobody bothered to explain his role to me.

My principal contact with Mr Lerry came when, as the office junior or copy boy, I was sent off to change his wife's library books at Birmingham's large and imposing Central Library at the top of Colmore Row. I had to think *old lady* when I made my choices, but there were no complaints from Mrs Lerry.

Apart from that, my main regular task during the year or so I spent with the *Post* before leaving for National Service was to file copies of each successive edition of the paper when I arrived in the office. The newspapers were penetrated by a couple of sharp spikes and then laid flat on the previous day's papers. The spike was then turned over. The pile of papers sat on top of what looked like a lectern and were rarely consulted by the reporters for whom they were intended.

After a few days I discovered that reporters – even trainee reporters – didn't enter the office through the front entrance of the building. They went in at the tradesmen's entrance at the back, through a narrow doorway in Cannon Street. The doorway was next to the bays where newspaper delivery vans were loaded and over the road from it was a pub, which the reporters knew as Annie's Bar. The stairs up to the reporters' room took a route which enabled the reporters to by-pass Vaughan Reynolds's office and the newsroom – useful if journalists were late back from Annie's or the back bar of the Midland.

In addition to filing newspapers and changing Mrs Lerry's library books I was made responsible for telephoning one of the City Council departments each day to check the state of the Elan Valley reservoir in Wales which supplied Birmingham with its water. I used a proforma prepared for the purpose: 'Elan Valley Rainfall – Streams are yielding less/more than the city's demand' it read and I had to strike out the incorrect statement. The first time I did it I read the next day's paper with great pride. My piece was there. I was in print for the first time, albeit anonymously. I'm not sure why the rainfall situation in Wales mattered but I guess it was important to someone.

I also had to check with contacts at the two Birmingham cathedrals and the main churches each Friday, preparing copy for the Saturday paper which informed the faithful what and who they could look forward to – or avoid – on the following day.

On some days there was an old man in the office when I arrived, reading from a cuttings file and scribbling away in a notebook. Eventually I plucked up courage and introduced myself. I asked him who he was and what he was doing. The venerable gentleman told me that he was Dicky Ross and that he'd once been a reporter. After he'd retired the *Post* had found him a job updating the obituaries, on a part-time basis. He seemed to choose his own working hours. Dicky looked as though he wasn't too far away from the time when his own obituary would appear in the paper, but I didn't say so. I wondered if he kept his own obit up to date.

I found my occasional chats with Dicky Ross about journalism illuminating. He'd obviously had a full and satisfying career and I suspect he'd been quite a character in his day. 'You'll love being a reporter, my boy,' he assured me. 'Nothing like it – but mind the booze. Mind you, you'd earn more money as a printer. The comps earn more than the reporters and all they have to do is retype what the reporters write. It's crazy. I'd be a rich man now if I'd been a comp. The printers run this place.'

'What's a comp?'

'Sorry. A comp is a compositor.'

'Right.' I wasn't much wiser.

Occasionally a reporter allowed me to accompany him on an assignment to a City Council meeting, an exhibition, or an auction. The only woman reporter on the staff wrote about clothes and shopping and compiled the weekly women's page. Sometimes I was sent out to the market to check out the prices for the different fruit and vegetables which made up the standard shopping bag she'd invented.

On one memorable occasion Cyril Chapman, the football correspondent, let me join him in the press box at the Hawthorns, the home of West Bromwich Albion, the team I supported. I still do, in theory. The football writers took their trade seriously. I simply cheered the Baggies on like any other supporter, to the annoyance of the gentlemen of the press scribbling away by my side. Cyril didn't ask me to go to the match again.

It was the mid-1950s and it didn't take long for me to sense that the *Post* was more suited to the mid-1930s. It wasn't only that the offices had an old-world charm about them, some of the reporters had a distinctly casual attitude towards time keeping and news gathering and much of the writing seemed old-fashioned as well. The *Birmingham Gazette*, the opposition paper, was much livelier and had more of the tabloid about it. I wasn't sure I was on the right paper.

The *Post*, but not the *Gazette*, still covered such events as important funerals and agricultural and pigeon shows and caged bird competitions – all of which called for the names of mourners or winning owners to be recorded by me, the copy boy, for posterity. I found the funerals pretty unpleasant. I had to stand outside some church or cathedral, whatever the weather, asking people who they were as they passed me by, even those who were genuinely upset. I knew that if I got the spelling of their names wrong in the list of mourners I prepared there would be a complaint.

There were a few people who seemed to turn up at every important funeral, making a hobby of paying their respects to the dead. I suspected that some of them didn't bother going into church once they'd planted their calling cards in my hand.

Leslie Duckworth argued that it was good training for me, that it would teach me the importance of accuracy. Not for him the lazy reporter's maxim 'If in doubt leave it out'. Leslie was an 'If in doubt find out' man.

The agricultural shows could be fun. I attended them with Bill Jones, a portly, shambling old reporter of Welsh extraction, who talked ninety to the dozen and chain smoked, like my dad. He lit one cigarette off another, keeping one lit and permanently in his mouth as he talked, blowing the ash off the end onto the front of his jacket. When Bill was busy he would send me off to talk to some of the prize winners.

'Just ask them about themselves. People like to talk about themselves. Then ask them about their animals. I usually find the animals more interesting. You'll get the hang of it.'

The *Post* carried reams and reams of show results, in a regimented style which had probably been established by old Bill. The style had an unconscious humour to it, which the show winners didn't seem to notice and Bill Jones certainly didn't. An example might be: 'Best cow in calf: Mrs Margaret Smith (Buttercup Lady the First)'.

I spent some of my lunchtimes playing snooker with Colin, my best friend, who was studying to be an architect in Birmingham. There was a snooker hall next door to the *Post and Mail* building. We had corned beef sandwiches topped with HP sauce for lunch. The cues were looked after by a scruffy old man known as Tiny, who didn't wear socks. His feet were so black some people thought he did have socks on.

One of the reporters I came to know was Alexander Walker, who learned his craft as a film critic on the *Birmingham Post*. Alex went on to become the best-known film critic in the UK, working for the *Evening Standard* for 43 years and writing dozens of books about the cinema and its stars.

'Harold. I'm thinking of going swimming this weekend. Would you care to join me?' Alexander Walker asks. He's the newly appointed film critic of the Post and about seven years older than me. His hair is piled high in a bouffant style.

'I'm not sure. I'm not that good a swimmer,' I reply.

'That doesn't matter. We'll take a picnic and swim in the river at a little spot I know near Worcester. It's quite shallow. You'll enjoy it.'

'I'll think about it, Alex.'

'Right. Let me know. I'll make the arrangements.'

Alexander Walker leaves the reporters' room, a smile on his face.

John Solon, one of the senior reporters, comes over to speak to me. He's been sitting at his desk at the far end of the room, apparently taking no notice of Alex and me, staring out of the window which faces out towards the Midland.

'Harold. Do you have a girlfriend?' John asks.

'Yes Mr Solon,' I reply, surprised at the question.

'Alex doesn't. He prefers young boys. I wouldn't go swimming with him if I was you. Not if you like girls.'

'Oh. I see what you mean. I wasn't going anyway. I went swimming with my new girlfriend and a few friends last weekend. A group of us cycled across to Sutton Park and went swimming in the open air pool.

'I decided to show off and did a racing dive into the water without testing how cold it was first. I ended up getting palpitations. Sheila had to help the others drag me out. Sheila's the name of my new girlfriend by the way.

'I don't really fancy the idea of swimming in a river. And I don't fancy Alex Walker either.'

4

The Airman

I'd been a copy boy with the *Post* for about a year when I received my call-up papers for National Service. There was some suggestion that the *Post and Mail* group might try to get me a deferment by making me an apprentice journalist but nothing came of it and I didn't pursue the idea. I wanted to get away from the overcrowded house where I was living as soon as I could, for Eva and Bob's sake. I also thought that a change of scene would help me get over my grief.

My father died while I was a copy boy, when I was just 18. Even though he'd been ill with chronic bronchitis for several years his death still came as a shock.

My father's death was not caused by bronchitis but by a burst ulcer which led to peritonitis. The ulcer had never been diagnosed or treated. His constant complaints about stomach pains and excess acid had been ignored by his doctor for years and I had told him to stop his moaning. He died very quickly in the end. The whole process took only three days. I was left feeling extremely angry about the doctor's incompetence, as I saw it, and guilty about my own insensitivity towards someone who had been dying in front of my eyes, someone I loved.

I felt guilty about the way I'd spoken to him towards the end of his life. During some of our conversations I'd tried to jolly him out of his depression, his conviction that he was dying, reminding him that the doctor had said that there was nothing wrong with him apart from his bronchitis.

William James Bolter, storeman, political activist, musician, writer, raconteur and my beloved father was just 65 when he died. I still miss him.

I didn't want to share my grief or offer my support to anyone else either. I wanted it all to myself. I was also convinced that my mother wasn't mourning my father's death as deeply as she should have done. I realise now that I was being unfair, that death affects people differently, that outward display can be fraudulent, that people deal with pain in all manner of ways. My mother, as was her way, simply got on with things.

My instinct was to run for cover. It seemed best all round for me to join one of the services and get my National Service over with. But which service?

Surprisingly, perhaps, given the awful conditions in which I'd been brought up, I passed my services medical as Grade A – with one exception. I was deemed to be Grade 7 as far as the vision in my right eye was concerned, a condition of which I was totally unaware. I remembered the eye feeling sore and blinking it a lot a few years earlier, but this was put down to a silly childhood habit. It must have been another missed diagnosis by that damned doctor.

It turned out that the eye had been infected by bacteria carried in the faeces of a mongrel dog, Spot, which we had when I was younger, a dog I loved to stroke and play rough and tumble with. The disease had left a scar on the pupil of my right eye. But Grade A7 Vision didn't stop Her Majesty's Government accepting me as a conscript.

Asked which of Her Majesty's armed forces I wanted to serve in I opted for the Royal Air Force, explaining that I had one brother who'd been in the Royal Navy and another in the Royal Army Medical Corps during the recent war. It would square the circle, I suggested, if I joined the RAF.

To my delight it was agreed that I should be recruited into the RAF for my two years of National Service and I was sent off to RAF Cardington in Bedfordshire to be kitted out. Nothing happened there to worry me about what lay ahead, but it was a false dawn.

When I joined up it was already known that conscription couldn't go on for much longer. I sensed that the regular servicemen who had to decide what to do with me were less than pleased to have me on board. They were already looking forward to dealing with men who wanted to be part of a professional fighting force

I was told that if I signed on for another three years there was a chance that I would get a commission and become an officer, but I declined. Five years was too long to wait before I became the journalist I knew I was destined to become and I didn't see myself as an officer anyway. For one thing I didn't speak like one.

I was then told by the officer interviewing me that I would be trained as a cook, an appalling prospect. I told him I was sure I would make a lousy cook and might even poison somebody. If, on the other hand, I was trained in the skills which would help me in my career as a journalist I would work exceptionally hard on behalf of the RAF. The argument worked. It was agreed that after my basic training I would take a six-month course in shorthand and typing and become a secretary.

I didn't much fancy telling Colin and my other mates that I was going to become a secretary, which they would certainly regard as a girl's job, but I knew that typing and shorthand were essential tools for a reporter at that time. There were no pocket-sized tape recorders in those days and no computers with spellcheck software either.

But first I had to survive basic training, eight weeks of the physical endeavour and emotional battering known as square bashing.

I arrived at RAF Padgate, near Warrington, after a long and tiring train journey from Cardington, via a train change at Crewe. It was a particularly hot day at the height of summer and I was wearing a greatcoat and carrying a heavy kit bag. The journey took about eight hours because of a delay at Crewe. On arrival at Padgate I was presented with an empty mattress and told to fill it with straw from bales which looked as though they had been left out in the open for some time.

The drill instructors, or DIs as they were always known, then marched the new arrivals over to the billets to which they'd been assigned. There were 20 of us to each of the wooden huts, built on stilts, which had highly polished floors, two stoves down the centre of the room and ten beds and bedside lockers each side of it.

After dumping our gear on our beds the group of young men I was to share the next eight weeks with were told to stand to attention. The DI responsible for our hut, a Corporal Benson, then ordered us to march up and down the billet and to grind our boots into the polished boards. When he was satisfied that we'd done enough damage we were given cleaning and polishing materials and ordered to get down on our knees and restore the floor to its previous pristine condition.

As far as I could see our drill instructors had one objective, to teach their charges to obey any order they were given immediately and without question. I found myself doing stupid things like cutting grass with scissors and crawling under the billet to smooth down dirt I had disturbed by getting under the billet in the first place.

Instead of being lectured on the effects of gas, we had to be marched into a concrete bunker, where we were locked in. Various gases were then fed into the bunker, so that we could experience their effects. There was a song going the rounds at that time about some idiot who loved to go a-wandering with a knapsack on his back, laughing his head off. The chorus went something like 'val de ree ha ha ha ha; val de rah ha ha ha ha . . .' We were made to sing this inane drivel as laughing gas was fed into the bunker, bringing tears to our eyes. The DIs found it funny anyway.

One poor devil, a qualified solicitor older than the rest of us, couldn't take the pressure and opted to sign on for an extra three years so that he could go on an officer's training and assessment course, thinking the square bashing there would be easier and he would one day be called 'Sir'. Unfortunately, he failed the course and was sent back to us, still committed to serving for five years and still struggling with the square bashing.

The men in the billet I shared were a mixed bunch – frightened mother's boys, would-be roughnecks, petty thieves and keen young men who took to the services life like ducks to water. I simply did my best and tried not to attract the attention of the bullies called DIs. By and large I succeeded and passed out on time. Some failed and had to endure another couple of weeks. There were two suicides while I was at Padgate.

I sat on a bare bed in the hut, waiting for a bus to arrive to take me to the station, where I was to get a train to Hereford and my new camp, RAF Credenhill, where I was to undergo trade training. Corporal Benson was sitting on another bed, writing.

'What are you doing Corporal?'
'Writing a few notes for the next lot to find when they arrive.'
'I don't get it. What are you writing?'
'Benson is a bastard. Watch out for Benson – he's the worst of the lot. That sort of thing.'
'I don't get it. You are Benson.'
'And I am a bastard, aren't I?'
'Yes corporal.' (I had learned to agree with everything Benson said.)
'Did you lot find any notes about me in your locker when you arrived?'
'Yes. We thought they'd been written by earlier recruits. Warning us what to expect.'

42

'They were written by me. All of the DIs do it. Conditions you before you even get started. Now bugger off. Your bus is outside. Good luck.'

By the end of the eight weeks square bashing I was a new man – confident that I could take anything the Royal Air Force could throw at me. The RAF had certainly smartened me up – trousers pressed, boots shining, cap badge sparkling. This had an interesting, possibly life-changing, side effect. For a few months before I was called up I'd been seeing a new girlfriend at the youth club attached to Guns Lane Methodist Church in West Bromwich which I attended – as much as anything because it attracted girls who attracted me. My new girlfriend had become rather special. My racing dive into the cold water of the pool at Sutton Park, which I'd told John Solon about, had been performed specially for her. We'd cycled to the park with our friends, Colin Mears and his girlfriend Joyce, who later became his wife.

We started off with me on the bike which Bert Shinton nearly reclaimed and Sheila on her father's bicycle. We swapped on the way back, because her dad's old bike didn't have any gears and was very heavy. She rode my lighter bike, which did have gears. Maybe that act of chivalry impressed her more than my racing dive.

I was only 18, a bit early to make my mind up about such things, but I thought of her as someone I would like to be with forever. I thought she felt the same about me, although I must have been difficult to be with, a volatile mixture of despair over the death of my father and excitement at the prospect of leaving home for the RAF.

Sheila Powis was a few months older than me, but looked much younger. She was petite and had a simplicity and sweetness about her which contrasted well with some of the other girls I knew, who could be quite knowing, hinting at sexual experience which I certainly didn't have and which frankly scared me.

Sheila had a superb dramatic soprano voice. When she sang such pieces as 'One Fine Day' from *Madam Butterfly* and 'Velia' from *The Merry Widow* at local clubs and theatres, the back of my neck tingled.

My father met Sheila only once, shortly before his death. Like me, she was one of a small group of young people from the chapel which went round people's homes carol singing at Christmas. We called at my house and the group sang a few carols around the piano in the front room. Sheila sang 'Silent Night' as a solo, to my father's considerable delight.

That night, when I returned home from our carol singing round he said to me: 'The little girl. The one who sang "Silent Night". That's the girl you will marry.'

I liked Sheila very much but regarded her as just a friend and had a girl-friend at the time. I laughed the old man's remark off and told him not to be so stupid. My father turned out to be right. Sheila Powis and I did marry and we are still married today. I know that I couldn't have chosen a more loving and loyal partner. Or did my father choose her for me?

All that was ahead when I first started to date Sheila, shortly before I started my National Service. I thought we were getting on well but when I received my call-up papers Sheila informed me, as gently as she could, that she didn't want to continue our totally platonic relationship. She was 19 years old and didn't want to stick around for two years waiting for me, she said. I was devastated.

Subsequently I discovered that it wasn't so much that she'd lost interest in me as the fact that she wasn't happy about being seen with me because of the scruffy way I dressed and the poor state of my laundry. She felt sorry for me, but knew that I would have been deeply hurt if she'd told me that she was too embarrassed to be seen with me or that her mother had offered to do my laundry for me.

It's amazing what a uniform and laundered shirts can do. After I'd completed my basic training at Padgate I was allowed a few days' leave. By coincidence – and it was coincidence – Sheila and one of her friends, Enid Dyke, saw me walking down the High Street in West Bromwich. I was on the opposite side of the road from them. We stopped and waved at each other, unsure what to do. Eventually I crossed the road, trying to look nonchalant. I was wearing my smart grey uniform.

Our conversation was a bit stilted, but as we moved apart to go our separate ways Enid said she would like to write to me and asked for my address. I gave it to her, disappointed that it wasn't Sheila who'd asked for it. In fact Enid was asking for the address on behalf of Sheila, who was too shy to tell me that she wanted to renew our friendship. Sheila wrote to me as soon as I arrived at Credenhill for my trade training.

The RAF approach to training was typically intense, rigorous and regimented. For three months I did little else than learn to type. For hour on hour, day after day, I sat at a heavy, old-fashioned typewriter which had a metal plate covering my hands as they rested on the keyboard, so that I couldn't see the keys. The idea was that this would force me to use all of my fingers and touch-type – and it worked. When I reached a certain proficiency, which I think was 60 words per minute, I was considered to be ready for stage two, shorthand training.

The approach was much the same. For hour on hour, day after day, I did little else than learn Pitman's shorthand outlines, mixed in with short forms which were peculiar to the Royal Air Force such as 'I have the Honour to Be, Sir, Your Obedient Servant' with which most RAF letters were signed off. They probably still are.

I attained a shorthand speed of over 120 words a minute, which is practically verbatim speed. When I hitch-hiked home for the odd weekend and took Sheila to the cinema (for which she invariably paid) I found myself writing shorthand on the palm of her hand, taking a note of the film dialogue. It drove her mad at times.

Having completed my trade training as a secretary I was promoted to Leading Aircraftman (LAC) which meant I had a two propeller blades badge attached to the arm of my uniform and a few shillings extra pay. I was told that I would be stationed in Cyprus, at the time of the Cypriot terrorism campaign. The idea of being a possible target for a terrorist's bullets or bombs didn't exactly thrill me.

I was given two weeks' embarkation leave so that I could break the news to what remained of my family and to Sheila. She was extremely concerned, because we really were in love by then and I think we both sensed that we would marry one day.

Ours was a tearful farewell as I left to go back to Credenhill for instructions on how I was to be transported to Cyprus. I assumed that I would be flown there – my first experience of flying – but was told that LAC Bolter would not be going to Cyprus after all. The RAF didn't have a ship going there. Obviously I wasn't worth the cost of a seat in an aircraft. Instead, I was told, one of the airmen on the secretarial training course which followed mine would be going to Cyprus in my place. I was to go to RAF Buntingsdale Hall, near Market Drayton in Shropshire, which is only 40 miles or so away from West Bromwich.

RAF Buntingsdale Hall was the home of Headquarters 22 Group, part of Technical Training Command, and it really was centred around an old hall. I doubt if there was ever a cushier post. There were only about 80 people there as far as I recall. About half of them were officers, most of them living in married quarters, and the other half of them were 'men'.

I was one of the 'men', the other ranks, a mix of regulars and national service conscripts, the lowest of the low. Even so we lived in extremely good conditions, better in many ways than those I had enjoyed at home, certainly at my first home. Because it was such a small camp, the domestic services at Buntingsdale Hall were provided by civilians. They not only did the cooking and cleaning, they even waited table in the other ranks mess which we used.

My job was to act as secretary to a Squadron Leader Anslow, who was responsible for setting up courts martial for offences committed within Technical Training Command, of which HQ 22 Group was a part, and dealing with the paperwork when decisions were reached and offenders sentenced.

The importance of accuracy in my work was emphasised at the outset. Charge a miscreant under the wrong section of the Manual of Air Force Law (MAFL) and he might get off and we can't have that can we airman? Of course not, sir.

There were plenty of sporting opportunities at Buntingsdale Hall, which had its own tennis courts and cricket and football pitches. With so few people on site it was almost impossible not to get into the camp teams. We were never very good, of course, with so little in the way of talent to choose from, but we had a lot of fun playing against the fourth or fifth teams from larger stations such as RAF Ternhill, just up the road, or RAF Cosford near Wolverhampton.

Squadron Leader Anslow was the self-appointed captain of the cricket team. He turned out in impeccable whites and had a cravat tucked into the neck of his shirt. During matches he addressed any fellow officers who were playing as Jimmy or Tony or whatever – the rest of us were simply 'Airman'.

'You'll be opening the batting today Bolter.'
'Yes, sir.'
'They've a particularly good fast bowler. Don't go trying to hit him out of the ground. Just stick in there. Wear him out.'
'Yes sir. Did you win the toss?'
'Yes I did.' Anslow says it as though it's a major achievement.
'Are we batting or bowling?'

'We're bowling first.'
'Any chance of a bowl this week, sir?'
'We'll see.' That's a no then.
'Who's opening the bowling sir?'
'I am. With Flight Lieutenant Brown.'
'Fine.' No surprise there.
I'm sent to field on the boundary, where I'm always placed. After an hour of doing not very much I light up a cigarette.
'Airman. Put that cigarette out,' Anslow calls out. 'What the hell do you think you're doing?'
Not a lot.

My interest in sport had an unexpected advantage. In fact, it almost certainly saved me from having an even worse conduct rating than the one ascribed to me when I was demobbed.

No one volunteers for anything in the forces lightly, but after a great deal of thought I agreed to a request from Squadron Leader Anslow to run the sports store in my spare time. Tennis rackets, cricket bats and footballs were kept in the store and the most frequent users of the equipment were the RAF special policemen (SPs) who guarded the perimeter fence. They seemed to have plenty of time on their hands.

Buntingsdale Hall had a small armoury and because of a perceived threat from the IRA it had to be guarded day and night. It might be thought that this was a job for the SPs, too, but that was far too obvious. At night erks like me would be detailed off to sleep on a camp bed in the armoury and were given a cricket stump to protect ourselves with if the armoury was invaded. If only the IRA had known.

The main duty of the SPs, it seemed to me, was to cause problems for me by reporting me to my superiors if I was late back to camp after a weekend at home with my girlfriend and family, even if I was only a few minutes late. I used to hitch-hike both ways, occasionally taking eight or nine hours to travel the 40 miles. I tried very hard to get back to camp on time. On one occasion I collapsed with pneumonia on the snow-covered field which led from my sister's home to the main road because I was scared of being late. Sometimes I failed miserably to get a lift. That meant some form of punishment and another black mark on my record.

Looking after the sports store gave me the chance to begin a campaign of mild irritation against the SPs – nothing serious enough to get me charged with an offence, just enough to make a point to them on the lines of 'I'll scratch your back if you scratch mine.'

'You want a tennis racquet, corporal? Certainly. Here you are. Sign here.'

'The strings look a bit loose to me.'

'I know. All the good racquets are out at the moment or getting re-strung. I've been trying to persuade the camp commandant to get some new ones.'

'Corporal Jones always seems to get a decent racquet.'

'Luck of the draw, that's all. Good man Corporal Jones. I was a few minutes late back to camp last Monday and he told my boss, old Anslow, that I'd reported in sick and gone for treatment. I suppose it's a matter of give and take. I don't do this job for fun you know.'

Apply the same process to the provision of footballs with slow leaks and cricket bats with weakened splices and you get the picture. The message soon got through and I was never charged with being absent without leave again.

When my two years service in the RAF was drawing to a close I was promoted to the rank of Senior Aircraftman, almost certainly in an attempt to get me to sign on as a regular airman. No chance.

A few weeks before I left the RAF I was summoned into the presence of a man called Flight Lieutenant Howrilowicz for a career interview – the first I'd been given. He was a Pole left over from the war – no doubt a brave man in his time – who was now holding down some sort of personnel job. Most of the administration officers seemed to be former pilots who obviously missed the excitement and fun of flying.

The flight lieutenant told me that I had done pretty well during my service and asked if I'd thought of staying on in the Royal Air Force. If I signed on for five years or more he could pretty well guarantee I would get a commission, he said. I thought of the solicitor who had been made a similar promise but didn't say anything.

'What would I be doing, sir? If I did become an officer, I mean.'

'You would be working in the Administration Branch, much as you are now.'

'Like Squadron Leader Anslow?

'Well, not at first. You'd be a Pilot Officer.'

A couple of ranks below you, I thought.

'Sorry, the air force is not for me, sir. Nor being stuck in an office all day or living in married quarters here on the camp. I really don't know how you put up with it, sir. It might be different if there was a real war on I suppose but I don't see much point to it all in peacetime.'

5

The Apprentice Boy

I went to see Vaughan Reynolds, the editor of the *Birmingham Post*, as soon as I was demobbed. I was anxious to resume my training as a journalist and didn't think there would be a problem. As I understood it anyone who'd worked for a company for more than six months before being called up had to be taken back when they were released from the services. As I entered the editor's office Vaughan Reynolds was reading some papers. They were my release papers from the RAF.

'They've given you a conduct rating of Fair, Harold. That's only one level above 'Dismissed the Service'. What on earth happened? What did you get up to?'

'I don't know. It doesn't make sense. They promoted me to Senior Aircraftman just before I was demobbed and asked me to sign on for three more years.'

'I see. Right. It says here that you were often late back to camp after going home for weekends.'

'That's a bit unfair. I was only late twice – well, only charged twice. I wasn't very good at hitch-hiking at first, but it was okay once I got the hang of it and the SPs understood that I wasn't going AWOL or anything. Nobody seemed that bothered. The punishment on both occasions was doing an extra night in the armoury, protecting it with a cricket stump.'

Vaughan Reynolds looks bemused. I tell him the story of how RAF Buntingsdale Hall protects its armaments against the threat of an IRA attack.

'Good Lord. Do they really do that? Anyway, what about this comment

that at times you have an insolent manner? That does surprise me. It doesn't sound at all like you. Did you upset somebody?'

'I'm not sure. I suppose I could have annoyed one of the officers by smoking while I was fielding on the boundary in one of the cricket matches – but cricket wasn't compulsory anyway. Who signed the report you're reading, sir?'

'Two people. Squadron Leader Anslow and a Flight Lieutenant Howrilowicz.'

'Ah. Howrilowicz. I think I understand now, sir. I only spoke to Flight Lieutenant Howrilowicz once. It was him who tried to get me to stay on in the RAF. I told him that the idea of spending my life behind a desk in an RAF camp appalled me and that I didn't know how he put up with it.'

A look of comprehension comes over the editor's face.

'I see. At least I think I do. Very interesting. I'm sure you will make an excellent journalist. You certainly tell a good story.

'You'll be glad to know that I'd already decided to give you an apprenticeship before I received this report from the RAF. Just as well perhaps. Anyway, forget about it. You'll start here and then we'll find you a place on one of the weeklies.

'Oh. By the way. Gwyn Jones sends his regards.'

'Thank you, sir.'

'You can forget the "sir" business now,' Vaughan Reynolds says. 'This isn't the Air Force.'

Thank the Lord for that.

Because of my two years in the RAF I was rather old, at nearly 21, to be starting a three-year apprenticeship, it seemed to me, particularly working on a weekly newspaper out in the sticks, such as the *Walsall Observer* or one of the other group papers. National Service was coming to an end and young men and women were being apprenticed as journalists when they were 17 or 18 years old. I felt that I had much more affinity with the older journalists than with a bunch of kids.

Nevertheless, I felt sufficiently secure in my own ability to propose to Sheila and she was sufficiently secure in her ability to make something of me that she accepted. We became engaged. We shared the cost of the ring.

Ours was a strange courtship, complicated by the fact that I worked from

2 pm to 10 pm while she worked from 9 am to 5 pm as a clerk-cum-telephonist at a factory in West Bromwich. The only way we could meet during the week was for me to take a chance on getting to the council house where Sheila lived with her mother and father and brother Stan before 11 pm, the time at which her mother placed a curfew round her.

To do that I had to get away from the office promptly (or even early if it was a thin news day), and run across Birmingham from New Street to Colmore Row, from which the bus to West Bromwich left. Then I had to get another bus from West Bromwich town centre to the bottom of Wilford Road, where Sheila lived, and see if the downstairs lights were still on in her house. Lights on and I could enter.

Occasionally I didn't make it, rushing up the road only to see the lights go off. When I did make it I was only allowed to kiss my fiancée goodnight in the doorway and murmur endearments for 20 minutes or so, then her mother would call out, 'Come on Sheila. Time that lad went home. They're playing the Queen.'

That meant that the national anthem was being played at the end of the night's TV programmes, a signal that it was time for me to go home to my sister's house in Heronville Road, a couple of miles away. I had to walk there, the bus service having finished, or beg a lift from a passing milk float or lorry. I was rarely in before midnight.

The weekends were our time for getting to know each other during our walks together, hand in hand around Dartmouth Park, singing in the choir at Guns Lane Methodist Church alongside Colin and Joyce, or cuddling in one of the double seats on the back row of the Tower or one of the other local cinemas.

While I was courting Sheila I was also learning my craft as a reporter. The newspaper industry had set up an organisation called the National Council for the Training of Journalists while I was in the RAF. The older generation of newspaper reporters regarded it with complete disdain. I was one of the earliest trainees subjected to the courses patched together by the NCTJ – at least, that was the idea.

Part of the syllabus involved the trainee obtaining a shorthand and typing qualification, which I already had, and learning English to a reasonable level, which I'd already bettered through my GCE English 'A' level. There was little else left, apart from a course on the elements of English law, particularly libel as it then related to the media.

Leslie Duckworth, my first news editor, was still there and he didn't see any need for the NCTJ proficiency certificate which I was supposed to be working towards through day release and evening classes at the Birmingham College of Commerce. As a result I attended very few classes. Leslie simply absorbed me into the reporters' room fold, gradually extending the size and complexity of the stories he sent me out to cover on my own or in partnership with one of the senior reporters.

In terms of strictly technical ability I was a cut above most of the old stagers, who generally typed with two fingers not the full set and whose shorthand-cum-longhand notes were decidedly idiosyncratic.

Success in any job, it seems to me, is the product of three things – ability, opportunity and extreme good fortune. It was for others to decide whether I had the first quality, ability, and for them to ensure that there was a chance for me to benefit from the second, opportunity. The third quality, a lucky streak, was something I had in abundance for most of my career in journalism.

It was not unknown for the established reporters to wander in to the office closer to 3 pm than 2 pm, some of them having had a liquid lunch before starting work. I, on the other hand, was determined to please Leslie Duckworth and Ron Lerry, whose wife's library books were now changed by a new copy boy.

I was back living with Eva and Bob and still travelled in to work by bus. I was usually in early and as the new boy I wasn't expected to join the older reporters in Annie's Bar or in the back bar of the Midland. That was a pleasure still to come.

I had only been out of the RAF for a few months when the news desk received a tip-off, confirmed by the police, that there had been a multiple shooting in the city centre. It was thought that three people had been killed.

I'd just arrived, early as usual, and was the only person around with any sort of claim to be a reporter. Leslie Duckworth knew that the first senior reporter was probably at least an hour or so away. He sent me out on the assignment, reasoning I suppose that the first available senior reporter could take over from me later. It must have seemed a safe bet to him because the *Evening Mail* would be covering the event for its final edition. Anything I obtained in the way of information could be checked against what the *Mail* printed and news agency reports.

In the event I had a free run, covering the story for about two hours. By the time a senior reporter caught up with me I had so much information in my notebook from eye witnesses and police briefings that Leslie Duckworth had little choice but to let me have my head.

Through this stroke of extreme good fortune – and with the help of experienced journalists covering Birmingham and the West Midlands for the national newspapers – I had my first front page lead, the 'splash' as it was called, within months of coming out of the forces and while notionally an apprentice.

From then on there was no more talk of me going out to one of the weekly papers to train. I worked as a fully fledged reporter on the *Birmingham Post*, but was paid as an apprentice, gaining more and more confidence as Leslie Duckworth tested me on new assignments.

I learned some important lessons from Leslie. He taught me not to jump to conclusions about how people would react to stressful situations. He encouraged me to plough my own furrow and not share information with other reporters in an informal pool arrangement. 'They're just covering their backsides,' Leslie would say.

My first brush with other people's emotions came when I was still formally an apprentice. I was doing the duty calls one night – phoning round the police, fire and ambulance services every hour to see if anything of note had occurred – and was told that all three services had been called out earlier in the evening to an incident on the railways which had led to the deaths of three men.

The incident itself was over, I was told. The three men were gangers who'd been using one of those hand-operated trucks to pump their way along the railway track to the place where they were working. In a tragic accident a train came along the same line, hitting the truck and the men. All three were killed outright.

The police said that the men lived at the same address and that relatives had been informed. They gave me the address and I reported to Leslie Duckworth. 'Write up what you've got from the calls and get out there with a photographer,' he said. The photographer and I sped off to the address we'd been given. I was wary of being accused of intrusion and determined that if no one came to the door immediately when I knocked it I would get away from the scene as quickly as I could.

I knock the door and a woman aged about 30 answers it straight away.

There is no escape. The woman's eyes are red from crying and I can see several children and perhaps half a dozen adults, some of them muscular young men. She tells me her name and asks who I am.

'Sorry to trouble you,' I say. 'I'm from the Birmingham Post. *I wonder if you'd mind speaking to me about what's happened. The police have told us about the dreadful accident.'*

I expect to be told to go away. Instead I'm invited into the house and taken into the kitchen, which is quieter.

'They were lovely men,' she says. 'All three of them.' She speaks with a soft Irish accent.

The woman explains that one of the men who was killed was her husband and the other two were his brothers.

'We came over from Ireland three years ago,' she says. 'The boys found work as gangers on the railways. I don't know how we'll manage now.'

It's obvious that the woman wants to talk. Maybe it's easier talking to a stranger than to the friends and relatives in the room next door.

I notice a photograph of three men in a frame on the mantelpiece. They're holding glasses of what looks like beer and smiling.

'Is that them?'

'Yes.'

'Do you mind if I borrow it? I'll make sure it gets back to you. Tomorrow.'

'Yes. I'd like a picture of them in the paper.'

'What about you? Do you mind if the photographer takes a picture of you?'

'I don't want a picture of me. It wouldn't be right.'

'I understand. We'd better get off now. Thanks for talking to me.'

I felt drained and didn't say much as we drove back to the office.

'Where on earth have you been?' Leslie Duckworth demanded when I reported to the news room. 'It's nine o'clock. Get a move on or you'll miss the early editions. I'll get somebody to collect your copy as it comes off the typewriter. It's the splash.'

I tried to explain to Leslie why I had taken so long, how I'd found the experience of talking to someone who'd lost three members of her family in such terrible circumstances emotionally disturbing. I handed the photograph of the three men over, expecting a pat on the back. All I got was:

'Well knock out a caption for the picture before anything else. We don't want the three of them being mixed up do we? Now get a move on.' I thought he was an insensitive old so and so.

I went upstairs to the reporters' room and wrote the piece. I then went down to the news room and handed it in. Leslie read it and nodded as he came to the end. 'Fine,' he said. 'Now pop across to the pub and get yourself a pint. You look as though you need it.'

It was nearly closing time but there were still about half a dozen other reporters in the bar when I arrived and I told them about the story I'd been working on. Leslie Duckworth joined us, which was unusual for him. He commuted from Birmingham to Wolverhampton and rarely hung around after he'd finished his day's work.

'Are you okay Harold?' he asked, as one of the reporters got him a drink. I nodded. 'I'm sorry if I seemed a bit rough on you but it was necessary. You won't meet too many situations like that but if you do there's no sense in getting involved. Just get the facts and then push what's happened to the back of your mind. Worry about it if you have to – but after the job's done.'

Leslie Duckworth's injunction to think outside the box and make up my own mind about what constituted a story was perhaps best exemplified when a 20-year-old Teddy Boy arrived at the office and asked to see a reporter. I was sent down to find out what he wanted. I think that Leslie thought there might be trouble and I looked as though I could take care of myself.

Teddy Boys had a bad name. They were the hoodies of the 1950s and 60s. There were instances of serious gang warfare with razors and knives and some Teddy Boys had fascist tendencies, aligning themselves with groups that attacked the West Indians who had emigrated to Britain in the mid-1950s. The Teds had played some part in the notorious Notting Hill race riots of 1958.

The Teddy Boy phenomenon had its roots in the gangs of East End toughs who plagued parts of London. The name was coined by the *Daily Express* and grew out of the Edwardian-style drape jacket worn by these teenagers. 'Teddy' made for a shorter headline than 'Edwardian'. The drape jacket wasn't entirely innocent. It was made of wool and had lots of pockets. It kept the owner warm as he hung around the streets and was also good for concealing weapons and alcohol.

Augmenting the jacket in what became an easily identified uniform the Teddy Boy wore suede shoes with thick crepe soles, so-called 'brothel creepers', narrow 'drainpipe' trousers, a smart shirt and a loud tie, usually of the 'slim Jim' or boot-lace variety. Most of the boys had their hair cut long and kept it greasy, quiffed at the front and with the sides swept back so that they met in what became as known as a DA, which stood for duck's arse.

A young man looking like the archetypal Teddy Boy waited for me at the back entrance of the *Post and Mail* building in Cannon Street. His name was Tom Gauntlet, he was 20 years old – just a year younger than me – and he surprised me by what he had to say.

Tom told me that he was fed up with what the newspapers were writing about Teddy Boys. 'Most of us just like the look,' he said. 'We're not all out to cause trouble like you lot say. Most of us just want to be left alone to get on with our lives and enjoy our sort of music and so on.'

'Fine,' I said. 'So what are you going to do about it?'

'I'm going to set up a National Association of Teddy Boys to speak up for the Teds, but I don't know how to get going.'

'Well, for a start, tell me exactly what you have in mind and we'll see what a bit of publicity does for you.'

So that's what we did. Instead of writing yet another story about the Teddy Boy threat to society, I wrote about a young man who felt he had every right to dress as he liked and have his hair cut with a DA without being branded as a thug because of it. I sympathised with him. I had a crew-cut at the time.

The *Post* ran the story and it was picked up by the nationals. The National Association of Teddy Boys came into being and held its inaugural meeting in October 1958. Tom Gauntlet was there with a Birmingham youth leader and an elderly Quaker who must have been dragged along to give the event some respectability. From my interview with him I suspect Tom was articulate enough not to need them.

The Times reported, somewhat sniffily I thought, that only 22 Teddy Boys turned up for this meeting and that they were outnumbered by the reporters and photographers who were present. The aim of this new Association was 'to lend respectability to this lawful and, as they claim, innocuous manifestation of youthful high spirits,' *The Times* said. It didn't sound a bit like Tom Gauntlet. I thought a turn-out of 22 Teddy Boys prepared to be counted among the teenagers who weren't looking for trouble was pretty impressive.

I lost track of what happened to the National Association of Teddy Boys. I doubt if it lasted very long. But there is still a Federation of Teddy Boys, a world-wide organisation, so perhaps my piece in the *Birmingham Post* led to something.

Leslie Duckworth wasn't the only man who helped my early career in journalism. There were several others, men like John Solon, the clever and sensitive writer who'd advised me not to go swimming with Alex Walker, David Talbot, the tennis correspondent, and Jack Hay, whose daughter Sally was to marry Richard Burton. Jack was motoring correspondent and at that time a very good one. Towards the end of his career he ended up working for me. Tragically, Jack became an alcoholic. When Sally married Burton one of the tabloids ran a picture of Jack sleeping rough under the arches below a railway line in London and another of Burton looking tired and emotional elsewhere. The obvious inference was that Sally was going from one drunk to another.

Basically I was a jack of all trades, expected to turn my hand to anything thought to be of interest to the *Post*'s readers – sport, crime, the proceedings of the City Council, the arts, natural and man-made disasters, industry and commerce, politics, anything at all. Being the youngest reporter I was given most of the stories calling for a bit of action.

Although I'd served in the RAF I'd never been in an aircraft. My maiden flight was in a small four-seater while I was an apprentice with the *Post*. There had been heavy flooding in the West Midlands and I was sent to fly over the area with a photographer. His constant movement in the plane threatened to destabilise it and the pilot had to keep reminding him not to throw himself about so much. Photographers, armed with their large black cameras, were like that.

I wrote a piece which was given the headline 'I Fly Over The Floods' – dramatic stuff. One of the places that was flooded was the Worcestershire County Cricket Ground, I remember. Not much has changed. It still gets flooded fairly regularly.

As the paper's action man I was sent up to the Lake District when a Birmingham schoolboy went missing while on a school camping holiday. I joined the search for him near Coniston and was up there for three days, filing stories every day. The weather was glorious. Eventually the boy's body was found, his face buried in the grass where he'd fallen. It was established that he'd had a fit. I did the follow-up pieces, too – reporting on the inquest and carrying out interviews with the boy's parents and his school's head-master.

Leslie Duckworth also tested me out as a potential showbiz writer, sending me off to jazz concerts and shows at the Town Hall starring young singers such as Shirley Bassey, Tom Jones and Tommy Steele. I particularly remember the piece I wrote about Tommy Steele when I reviewed his first perform-ance in Birmingham.

His manager, Larry Parnes, told me before he went on stage that Tommy had endured an extremely tiring day, with lots of press, radio and televi-sion interviews. I was about to see someone who combined the universal appeal of a Gracie Fields, the humour of a George Formby, the footwork of a Fred Astaire and the sterling qualities of goodness knows who else.

I faithfully reported what Parnes had said about Tommy's many qual-ities and went on to describe what I actually saw. Tommy, playing the cheeky Cockney chappie role for all it was worth, had appeared on stage and proceeded to lie on his back, clutching the microphone. He'd then burped into it, which didn't strike me as particularly edifying.

I quoted what Larry Parnes had told me about all of the things Tommy had done that day and concluded, 'And thus ended a tiring day for Tommy Steele – and for at least one member of his audience.' For a young man I could be very pompous.

Writing about the theatre and concerts carried with it an important perk. I was always provided with two tickets, so I could take Sheila with me for free. My regular venues were the two variety theatres, the Birmingham Hippodrome and the Aston Hippodrome, a few miles outside the city centre. Sheila was happy enough to accompany me to see the top variety acts at the Birmingham Hippodrome. She was less keen on the Aston Hippodrome, which was out in the sticks and pretty dilapidated, with gas lamps still lighting lavatories that smelled strongly of disinfectant.

The Aston Hippodrome put on shows with such exotic names as *Nudes Neat and Naughty*, *My Bare Lady*, and *The Original Jane of the Mirror*, clearly intended for the dirty mac brigade. These shows had nude tableaux, with near-naked young women posing as 'Venus Unadorned' or 'Britannia'. They were not allowed to move and there was nothing to be said about them in my critical notes for the *Birmingham Post*. I had to wait for the second half of the programme, which usually contained a few second-rate comedy acts, acrobats, illusionists and wannabe musical turns. Then I had to dash to a phone box and pour out my artistic soul to a copy taker who typed up my words of wisdom and fed them into the publishing process.

My pieces of peerless prose were attributed to me, vaguely, by carrying my initials, H.E.B., at the end of each review. After a few months of this W. Vaughan Reynolds asked Leslie Duckworth who H.E.B. was and was told it was the apprentice.

'We can't have this,' Reynolds said. 'What would his mother say if she knew we were sending him to look at nude women?' I doubt if my mother would have said very much or been very interested. My trips to Aston didn't stop, of course, but my initials no longer appeared.

Accuracy was paramount, even when writing about something as dire as the nude revue-cum-variety shows at the Aston Hippodrome. One of my predecessors as apprentice reporter once covered a touring production of *The Archers*, the radio series. He first wrote about it when it played the Birmingham Hippodrome. A few months later, in one of the Aston Hippodrome's rare ventures into straight theatre, the piece moved there. Or so the reporter thought.

He decided that there was a better way of spending his Monday evening than watching *The Archers* for a second time. He simply re-worked his original 'crit' of the performance at the Birmingham Hippodrome and phoned it in as though it was an original criticism of the performance down in deepest Aston. Unfortunately, the cast from Birmingham had been replaced by lesser lights. He panned and praised actors and actresses who would not be found dead in a dump like the Aston Hippodrome and ignored the poor devils doing their best to make it from there to the bright lights of a city centre theatre.

The young reporter's career was brought to an abrupt end by the *Post*. He stayed in the profession, though, and made a living working for one of the more inventive tabloids.

After hearing this cautionary tale I was extremely careful, although I did once call the creature used in a performing animal act at the Aston Hippodrome a monkey instead of a chimpanzee, which is apparently important in the primate scheme of things. This might not seem too important an error, and it wouldn't have been if the compositor who set the type for the piece hadn't replaced the 'm' in monkey with a 'd', translating the poor

61

animal into a donkey. The chimp's owner wrote in complaining, calling me an ass, and the *Post* published his letter.

Despite this I moved on to greater things in the arts world after I'd completed my apprenticeship. I was sent to cover the legitimate theatre at the Alexandra Theatre or the Birmingham Repertory Theatre occasionally standing in for the renowned theatre critic J.C. Trewin.

I was even given the job of writing about a touring ballet production featuring Nureyev and Fonteyn. It was the first ballet I'd ever seen and I took the editor's secretary with me when Sheila, by now my wife, couldn't make it. The secretary, who had succeeded the indomitable Patricia Latham, was a balletomane and with her prompting I had the good sense to describe the performances of Nureyev and Fonteyn in glowing terms.

For a time I was the *Post*'s television critic. Commercial television, as it was known, was just starting up and Lew Grade's Associated Television (ATV) had the weekday Midlands franchise. As the man famously said, he'd been given a licence to print money. He didn't waste too much of it on production costs.

One of his money-making vehicles was *Crossroads*, one of the first soaps. To my mind it compared very badly with *Coronation Street*, produced by Granada in Manchester, which began at much the same time. ATV didn't much like me making the comparison. The only thing remotely professional about *Crossroads*, in my view, was Noele Gordon, which says a lot.

ABC had the franchise for the weekend television schedule in the Midlands. One of its offerings was *Thank Your Lucky Stars*, a popular music programme which featured a young girl called Janice Nichols, who was born in Wednesbury just down the road from where I was born. Janice became famous for little more than being able to say 'Oi'll Give It Foive' in the sort of Black Country accent which I was beginning to lose. It didn't strike me as a major accomplishment but she built a career out of it.

I went to see *Thank Your Lucky Stars* produced at ABC's Aston studios in mid-January 1963 at the invitation of Jimmy Bake, ABC's persuasive press officer. As luck would have it the headline act that week was a new group called the Beatles.

The occasion left me cold. It seemed to me that the performance began before the Beatles even made it past the heaving mass of screaming young girls circling the stage door. We now know, of course, that Brian Epstein, the Beatles' manager, had organised this apparently spontaneous demonstration of devotion.

Inside the studios the Beatles mimed to one of their early records, 'Please, Please Me'. The pretence was made that the performance was live but it was obvious to those watching the programme being made that the screaming girls allowed into the studio would have drowned out any sound coming from the mop-headed four.

At the end of the show I was taken by Jimmy Bake to meet John, Paul, George and Ringo in what passed for a green room at the ABC studios. I remember the boys, who were two or three years younger than me, being hyper-active, constantly jossing each other and clearly affected by the adoration of their fans or some other stimulant.

I can't remember a word of what passed between us and have an awful feeling that I was so unimpressed that I didn't bother to write anything. So much for my part in the history of the Beatles.

6

The Bridegroom

Two weeks before Sheila and I were to be married, Sheila's mother knelt at her daughter's bedside and prayed that she wouldn't go ahead with the wedding. Fortunately, Emmie Powis's prayers weren't answered. Her daughter ignored her and took me as her lawful wedded husband despite her mother's weeping and wailing.

Sheila and I had become engaged soon after I left the RAF, when I was 20 and just starting my apprenticeship. We'd bought a Yorkshire terrier, Lady Jane of the Vale, better known as Tottie, to mark the occasion. We'd decided to get married as soon as I became a qualified journalist and now the time had arrived. I'd finished my apprenticeship and even had the National Council for the Training of Journalists proficiency certificate to prove it, despite attending so few lectures.

Two weeks before the wedding Tony Cheesewright, one of the young reporters from our rival paper, the *Birmingham Gazette*, reached his maturity. A general invitation went out to journalists of a similar age to join him at his parents' home in one of the posher areas of the city for a drink after work. Tony's father was Maurice Cheesewright, the *Gazette*'s editor, a man of influence. I accepted the invitation.

I was running a small car by this time, a black Ford Popular, and was the designated chauffeur for the four reporters from the *Post* who joined me when we set out after work for Tony's bash. The party was a reasonably sober one and at the end of it I began to ferry my four passengers back to their various homes.

My last passenger was Margaret Cooper, a young reporter on the *Post* who subsequently married a good friend and colleague, Alan Hughes. Margaret had moved up to Birmingham from the southwest and lived in a flat in Handsworth, which was on my route back from the far side of Birmingham where the party was held.

Weather-wise it was a reasonable night, although there was a bit of mist around. Margaret was sitting in the back of the car, where she'd been for the whole of the return journey. Her flat was at the bottom of a steep hill and as I rounded a sharp bend we ran into a wall of fog. More precisely, we ran into the back of a lorry which been parked with no lights on.

There were no seat belts in the rear of the car and Margaret was thrown forward and over the front passenger seat, which wasn't anchored. She flew head first over the top of it and into the front window, breaking her nose. I was uninjured.

Someone driving in the opposite direction saw what had happened and took charge, waking a nearby resident to call the police and ambulance services. Margaret and I were rushed off to hospital, leaving my car firmly wedged under the rear of the lorry. The car wasn't badly damaged, but the accident repair crew who went out to tow it away made its condition worse. They dragged it away without letting the front tyres down first, leaving the bonnet and part of the front of the car behind and still wedged under the lorry.

By the time Margaret's broken nose was fixed it was early morning and I rang Sheila at her office to tell her what had happened. I explained that Margaret was obviously traumatised by what had happened and asked her whether she thought I should take the poor girl home to her empty flat or back with me to my sister's house. 'Take her to Eva's,' was the instruction.

One of the things you learn very early on in journalism is that dogs really do bite dogs – that reporters like nothing more than embarrassing other reporters. On the routine calls to the police, fire and ambulance services the *Evening Mail*, the *Post*'s sister paper, learned of my car crash. It ran a story on the front page of its first edition, which hit the streets around 11 am, giving brief details of my accident with the headline 'Journalists Hurt in 1 am smash' – or maybe it was 2 am.

My future mother-in-law rarely read any newspaper and certainly not the first edition of the *Evening Mail*. But she read that issue, or had its contents drawn to her attention, and was very suspicious indeed. So for that matter was my sister Eva and quite a few of my friends and Sheila's.

Sheila seemed to be the only person who believed my version of what had happened. It didn't help that Margaret was a tall, willowy blonde who had done some part-time modelling. Sheila's mother certainly didn't believe that I hadn't been up to some sort of mischief and did her bedside prayer act.

Neither of our families had any money to pay for the wedding or to help us to get started in married life. We'd saved what we could out of our salaries to pay for wedding clothes. Sheila's wedding dress cost her £8. It was meant to be white but had faded to a uniform shade of ivory in the shop window. 'It's okay. Ivory's the "in" colour,' Sheila told me. The bridesmaids dresses were made by my sister Marina.

I had a new suit for the occasion, which looked very smart. The effect was somewhat spoiled by the shirt I'd bought to go with it. The collar of the shirt was too big, revealing my young man's Adam's apple.

Sheila and I paid most of the costs of the wedding reception and some of our relatives rallied round making sandwiches and jellies for the many family children brought in for the occasion. I spent the morning ferrying food round to the community hall where the reception was held, in between making a few urgent phone calls, trying to sort out a serious transport problem.

One of the consequences of the accident in which Maggie Cooper broke her nose was that I didn't have a car to take Sheila and me on honeymoon to south Devon. There was no chance of us affording the repair costs immediately, with the cost of the wedding itself lying so heavily on us.

Sheila's friend Enid and her husband Roy had kindly offered to lend us their van and we thought our problems were over. Unfortunately Enid and Roy had an accident in the van the day before the wedding and sent me a telegram at my sister's house to say that it was no longer available.

Eva thought it was a greetings telegram and left it to be opened by my best man, my brother Tom. Fortunately, he opened it a few hours before the marriage ceremony and the wedding reception. When he did open it he gave me the bad news. I spent several hours before the ceremony trying to sort the problem out, chasing friends and relatives, some of them already getting ready for the wedding, to see if they could help.

Eventually, in desperation, I rang the office to see if I could get a phone number for Jack Hay, who was still motoring correspondent then, to find out if he knew a reasonably priced car hire firm. The operator put me through to John Lewis, the *Post*'s municipal correspondent, who happened to be in the office.

John was extremely helpful and generous. He told me that his wife, Jennifer, had driven into the city in their second car that morning and was out shopping at Rackham's. If he could track her down he would arrange for her to leave the car, a 1934 Bullnose Morris, in Cannon Street, at the back of the *Post and Mail* building, for me to pick up. I could borrow it for the full two weeks of the honeymoon. It was a wonderful gesture.

Our wedding took place at All Saints, West Bromwich, commonly known as Old Church. I'm not sure why we didn't have it at Guns Lane Methodist Chapel, where we had met, but I assume we wanted a somewhat grander setting.

I went through the wedding service in a daze. The various upsets over the weeks preceding our marriage and that morning had taken their toll and I was no longer certain that I was doing the right thing, whether I was ready for the responsibility of marriage. My new wife, on the other hand, looked remarkably calm and told me later that she had no doubts about the commitment she was making.

I have only three strong memories of the wedding ceremony itself. My new wife looked beautiful in her ivory wedding dress. The vicar was annoyingly insensitive, reminding people before the ceremony began that there was a collection box at the back of the church and that they were not to throw confetti in the churchyard or on the pavement outside.

And finally, the atmosphere was lightened by Peter Robinson, a *Birmingham Post* photographer. The paper's photographers had decided to produce a wedding album for us as a wedding present and Peter was given the job of taking the pictures. It was typical of him that he wanted to take more than the routine photographs which any wedding specialist might be expected to take. Peter wanted new angles on a very old subject.

To get everybody into the family group picture, Peter balanced precariously on the narrow edge of a gravestone. He prepared for the shot and then pretended to fall off, succeeding in getting a smile from everyone, even me. Peter didn't have any truck with the vicar's injunction about confetti throwing either. He encouraged the vandalism.

Sheila and I didn't stay long at the wedding reception. We left as Sheila's brother Don broke open a barrel of beer, drenching those closest to him. We had Tottie the Yorkshire terrier with us, reasoning that no one would think we were newlyweds with a dog for company. We said our goodbyes and departed with an instruction from Sheila's brother Stan to me to 'watch what you're doing with our wench', an oblique reference to the car crash incident, I assume.

My new mother-in-law was still not talking to me.

One of my brothers-in-law, Marina's husband Billy Pincher, gave us a lift into the centre of Birmingham where, to our great relief, the Bullnose Morris awaited us. The *Post and Mail* printers on duty that Saturday afternoon, producing the *Mail* and its sporting sister, had obviously been tipped off about what was going on. They'd tied pieces of printer's lead and other bits and pieces in a long string from the rear bumper of the car.

The workers cheered and cat-called us on our way as we left for the first stage of our honeymoon, an overnight stay in a hotel in a suburb of Bristol. As soon as we turned the corner into New Street I was instructed by new wife to stop the car and remove the debris. I did as I was told, of course.

Just outside Bristol, at Sheila's insistence, I stopped the car again and walked around it, checking to make sure that there was no longer any evidence that we were just married. I couldn't see anything obvious and we went on our way to the hotel.

'Just married then,' the girl at the reception desk said.

'How did you know?' Sheila asked.

'Look at your dog. It's covered in confetti.'

Before going to bed with my new wife, for the very first time I may add, I had to help her get the bits of confetti out of our Yorkshire terrier's mane. Then I had to get down on my hands and knees to clear up the bits of confetti I'd removed, along with more of the stuff which came out of our suitcases.

We managed to consummate our marriage that night – sort of. We were both exhausted.

The next day we set off on part two of our journey, heading for south Devon, where we were to stay at a farm owned by a family called the Perratons for a couple of weeks. The choice had been made at random and we had no set plans – well, maybe I did.

We got as far as Somerset when the Bullnose Morris spluttered to a halt. John Lewis had warned that this was a possibility and had told me over the phone that all that was required was to give the electric petrol pump a tap with a spanner if it happened. I had no idea where the petrol pump was or what constituted a tap.

I decided that it would be safer to push the car to the nearest garage, wherever that might be. Sheila didn't have a driving licence but I thought she was capable of steering the car and, if necessary, braking. I was aware that strictly speaking someone without a driving licence should not be behind the wheel but decided to take a chance.

Fortunately, the road was fairly flat and we must have gone about a mile when a policeman on a motorcycle pulled up in front of us. Sheila braked, thank goodness.

'On your honeymoon then,' the policeman says, in a delightful West Country way.

'How did you guess?' I ask, wondering when he will want to see Sheila's non-existent driving licence. I was sure there was no more confetti lying around.

'The suit,' he says. 'Your wife's. She's wearing a going away outfit.'

'I see. Well, you're right. We're on our way to Devon. If we can get there. It's not our car. We borrowed it from a friend.'

'What's wrong with it?'

'No idea. I think it's something to do with the petrol pump. It's electrical.'

'There's a garage down the road. Not too far. They should be able to fix it.'

'Thanks very much.'

'Get in the car lad.'

'What?'

'Get in the car. You're on honeymoon. Got to keep your strength up.'

Delightful blush from my new bride.

Sheila moves over and I get behind the steering wheel. The policeman then proceeds to push the car to the garage, a further mile or so away.

He explains our problem to the garage owner and they have a little chuckle together. I am shown how to tap the petrol pump with a spanner in just the right place.

'Temperamental old buggers,' the garage owner says. 'But they go all right.'

'How much?' I ask, as we prepare to leave. 'What's the cost?'

'Nothing. Go on. Enjoy yourselves. Have a nice honeymoon.'

Another blush from the new Mrs Bolter and we are on the way to the farm owned by the Perratons, where we will be staying.

I can't imagine a country bobby or a garage attendant behaving in the way those two did nearly 50 years ago, not with all the pressure there is today on the police force to meet arrest targets and on small businesses to maximise profits.

The Perratons turned out to be a delightful couple who couldn't do enough to make us feel welcome. Our room was comfortable, we had the use of their lounge and our meals were generous. Mrs Perraton even brought cups of cocoa up to the bedroom at night to help us to sleep. She clearly had no idea we were on honeymoon and I wasn't allowed to go to bed with my new wife until the cocoa ritual had been completed.

Liz, the Perratons' daughter, and husband Norman were not to be fooled, however. After a few days they asked us if we were newlyweds and we confessed that we were. The whole family seemed genuinely delighted and Mrs Perraton went out and bought us a wedding present. But the evening cocoa routine didn't stop.

We were married in 1960 and we are still friends with Liz and her second husband John, and with Norman, her first, for that matter. They are lovely people living in a lovely part of the world. The South Hams are still our favourite part of Britain, followed closely by Cheshire, where we have lived for the last 32 years.

Ours has been a good marriage, with much to be thankful for. It's not been without its problems, of course, usually of my making. I know that I've given Sheila cause for concern from time to time and that sometimes I've taken her for granted, accepting her unfailing loyalty as a matter of course. I am sorry for that.

Most of the problems we have had to face can be put down to my self-obsession, my preoccupation with what seemed right for me in terms of my career and my determination to live my life to the full, almost at any cost – just like my father, I suppose. Despite that our marriage has grown stronger with the years. I am thankful for it. I owe so much to my wife.

By today's standards our marriage has been unconventional. For 26 of the first 30 years of our married life there was a third person in it – but not in the Diana and Camilla sense. We had one or other of our mothers living with us, another throw-back to earlier days when familial responsibility was the norm amongst the working class in the Black Country.

We'd been married for just two years when my mother came to live with us. She'd stayed on with Eva and her husband Bob Vince and their family after my father died and I'd finally left them. Despite the reduction in numbers the small council house was still overcrowded. The situation wasn't helped by the fact that my mother tended to meddle in the affairs of Eva and Bob, usually taking the side of her daughter in any argument, a recipe for disaster. Eventually it all became too much for Bob and I could sense that the Vince marriage, Eva's second, was coming under threat. Sheila agreed that we should offer to take my mother into our new home.

When we first got married we'd lived as lodgers with two friends, Iris and Philip Bradley, for a year while we put together enough money to take out our first mortgage. We'd been living on our own, with our first child Helen Elizabeth, in a semi-detached house at Hasbury, near Halesowen, for less than a year.

So two years into our marriage I made the offer to take my mother into the bosom of my new family. I did so partly out of a feeling of guilt over my attitude to my mother over the years and partly as a gesture of thanks to Eva and Bob, particularly Eva, who'd done so much for me.

I'd largely ignored my mother as I drew closer to my father, particularly towards the end of his life. I felt that I should have done more to get to know her, that I might have found more things to admire in her if I'd taken the trouble to look for them. I also felt sorry for the situation my mother found herself in, dependent on one of her children or facing the prospect of being put into an old people's home. In a way offering her a home was my way of saying thanks to my father for all that he'd been to me. He would have wanted my mother looked after.

My mother lived with us for six years. I can't say they were particularly easy years, certainly not for Sheila who spent most time with her. It wasn't that my mother deliberately stirred things up, at least I hope not, but she had a way of making remarks which a more sensitive person would know were likely to cause friction.

It therefore came as a relief that when I left the *Birmingham Post* to join the *Financial Times* and moved to the London area my mother didn't come with us. By coincidence she'd had been invited by Bram, the eldest of her ten children, to join him in Australia for a couple of years. In the event this didn't happen but by then Sheila and I had moved and my mother went to live with my sister Mary.

Within 12 months duty called again. Sheila's father died, rather suddenly, shortly after we'd left for a two-week package holiday in Spain. The family took the decision not to tell us and so Sheila wasn't even at his funeral.

Sheila's mother was left on her own and I could hardly argue when asked whether she, then in her early 70s, could come and live with us. We knew that we could rely on Ray, Sheila's brother, who was a widower, to help us with respite care if it became necessary.

Ann, Sheila's sister-in-law, was similarly understanding. Ann's husband Gordon, Sheila's eldest brother, died in an industrial accident at far too young an age but she has done a wonderful job keeping her close-knit family together. Ann has become the sister Sheila never had.

Emmie Powis stayed with us for 20 years and as time went by she forgot that she had once prayed that her daughter wouldn't marry me. For the most part it was good to have my mother-in-law around.

Grandma, as everyone called her, even me, was a tough character. She'd had to be. Her first husband had died leaving her with four sons, and her second husband, Albert, Sheila's father, had a nervous breakdown. It had been brought on by pressures of work during the war and disappointment that his career had taken a down-turn when it was all over and younger men returned to the factory where he was employed.

The voluntary treatment Albert received included electric shock therapy and this had clearly affected Pop, as he was known. He could become very angry at times for no apparent reason, but for the most part Emmie knew how to cope with him. In his lucid moments he had a dry sense of humour and showed signs of being the educated, civilised man he had once been. I liked him. He never lost his temper with me.

Our three children grew up assuming that it was natural to have an old lady in the house. I don't know what effect it had on them, but I'm pretty sure they saw enough of the problems which having an elderly relative as a permanent house guest can cause to hesitate a long time before offering me somewhere to live if I become incapable of looking after myself. Sheila might be a different matter.

Sheila and I have three very different children. We love all three of them dearly and are inordinately proud of the people they have become. As of now, we also have six grandchildren who are a constant delight to us, even though we tend to worry about what faces them in our increasingly complex and difficult world.

In recent years I've been told by her husband, Philip, that Helen, our eldest child, would have liked more stability in her early life than her restless father was prepared to give her and the rest of the family, although she didn't tell me that at the time. If she did find my various career moves and associated housing transfers unsettling, I'm sorry. I still believe that they were essential if we were to stay together as a family.

The search for emotional security led Helen to explore various forms of the Christian faith in her early teens and this led her to Roman Catholicism. Her faith is very strong and very necessary to her. She prays that my wife and I will one day share it.

Helen has an inner strength which is palpable. That strength was needed when our grandson Joseph, less than a month old, died from an infection caught in the hospital where he was born. To my deep regret I never held him in my arms and I still feel a great sadness and sense of loss at the memory of Philip carrying Joseph's tiny white coffin to the altar at his funeral and Helen reading the beautiful eulogy she had written for him at his grave side.

I do not cry easily but at Joseph's funeral mass I couldn't stop the tears flowing as I held three-year-old Michael in my arms. Michael slept throughout the service and I clung on to him for my comfort as prayers were said over the body of the boy who would have been his baby brother.

Helen had asked the priest conducting the service if she could read the eulogy she had written about her dead child and had expected to be called to the lectern to do so. For whatever reason that didn't happen. It's probable that the priest thought she might find the task too emotionally draining. He didn't know my daughter.

As that tiny white coffin was lowered into the grave Helen stepped forward and began to read from her notes:

'If Joseph had lived to old age, hopefully someone would be standing up to say what a great guy he was at his funeral. I couldn't bear to let it pass without saying what he meant to us. This will probably be hard for me to say and hard for you to hear but I felt it to be one last thing I could do for Joseph.

'For us nothing will ever be the same again. Our family, our home, our livelihood have been ripped apart and thrown upside down. There is a big hole in our family, which we cannot fill.

'His whole short life was a contradiction. He wasn't expected but was so very much wanted. His death has put our family back to the place we were before we knew he was coming but those plans are no longer of any importance to us. Everything that seemed so important is now shown to have been worthless.

'His gift was to give us an understanding of love. Though we didn't plan to have him our love gradually took shape and grew for him during my pregnancy. As I touched his unborn head between my ribs I marvelled that this child was already well known and loved by God, when I could only guess his sex and what he looked like.

'I thought how God knew and had planned the layout of every hair on his head. After he was born and I couldn't hold him because of the Caesarian operation, I studied the pattern of his hair and touched his beautiful head. It was all that I could reach.

'As he grew he so loved to have his head touched. And as he became ill I was left with just his head to touch, as the medical attention in his last two days of illness covered his whole body. As he died his head remained the most recognisable part of him and his hair remained beautiful.

'He taught us that we have a capacity to love just one more child and therefore have the capacity to love as many children and other people as God brings our way.

'His birth and death let us see the depth of our family and friends' love and concern for us, which we might never have known the full extent of.

'His short life taught us and our other children to love him so deeply and fully that we cannot believe we only had him for 25 days and not a lifetime.

'Even though we can be sure that he is one amongst Jesus's most precious saints, we grieve for his loss and that of his future and ours. Joseph Jonathon Doherty we love and miss you and will always remember you.'

Typically, Helen turned that tragedy into something she could draw upon to help others and became a voluntary counsellor helping parents who have lost young children. She still is, ten years after Joseph's death. She wrote to Gordon Brown when he and his wife Sarah lost their first child and Sarah wrote back to her thanking her for the consoling words of someone who knew how they must be suffering.

Joseph is still very much part of the Doherty family and recognised as such by Helen and Philip's four remaining children – James, Laura, Michael and Patrick. Patrick followed Joseph and Barnabas, his second name, means child of consolation.

Matthew, our second child, has always been something of an enigma to me, a strange mixture of the insecure and the quietly confident. When I moved from Birmingham to London it took us nine months to sell our house and I saw the family only at weekends. Matt was only a toddler but he seemed to be particularly upset when I left on Sunday nights to get back to London in time for work on the following day. It was a stressful time all round and during it my son developed a stutter, which he has had to battle hard to overcome. Perhaps that was my fault.

Matthew seemed to be happy enough at his primary school, despite that stutter, but hated the secondary school we sent him to. He said nothing at the time, though, preferring to grin and bear it, assuming that the slipper beatings dished out by various teachers at the fee-paying North Cestrian Grammar School in Altrincham were the norm. I do wish he'd said something at the time, but that's Matt.

He's now a musician, house husband and part-time department store worker. He married Karen relatively late, more than ten years later than his mother and father had married, and I guess that the insecure side of him led him to agonise over the responsibilities of marriage and fatherhood before he took the plunge. The confident side, which he has in equal measure, has led him to work hard at his several roles, juggling them successfully, and he has become a brilliant, caring father to Isaac and Solomon.

During his miserable time at his secondary school Matt asked us to buy him a guitar. It was probably the most useful thing we've ever done for him. He has found solace in his music and gained and given a great deal of pleasure from it. Like many other people with a stutter he also has a fine singing voice, with not a trace of hesitation in it.

To our astonishment, remembering his introverted nature, he appears to have no worries about performing in public, sometimes to very large audiences indeed. He has become the lead singer, lead guitarist and principal song-writer with several pop groups and one of those groups almost made it in a big way.

There have been times when Sheila and I have found it hard to believe that it was really our son up there fronting a group on live television and playing in front of hundreds of fans at concerts up and down the country.

Matt and his mates have now settled for a part-time role on the music scene, performing their own music through a group called Statedancer. Music is still an essential part of Matt's life, a place to retreat to and to expand his horizons from.

Unlike the other two, who live nearby, Sarah effectively left home 17 years ago when she went to university and never came back. We miss her very much, although we keep in constant touch and visit her as often as we can. When Sarah was at Altrincham Girls Grammar School, which Helen also attended, she'd acted in a play at the boys grammar school – the only girl in it – and put on a very convincing performance. Sheila and I thought she might become an actress and suggested she try for RADA. Instead she studied drama and English at university.

After leaving university Sarah went into teaching, which seemed a safe profession for a young girl, if stressful at times. Very soon, however, she took the even more courageous step of moving to France with her partner Helen to manage a ski chalet in the French alps, with the objective of building up capital to build a chalet of their own.

Having always worked for an employer I admire people who sink or swim by their own efforts. I was never brave enough to branch out on my own as a writer or freelance journalist or set up my own public relations business, ideas which I've toyed with at various times.

Sarah is a very determined young woman. She makes it very clear, in the nicest possible way, that her life is her own – that while her mother and father may be informed and even consulted about the bigger decisions she has to make, we are not there to give permission any more.

In the same way that Matt surprised us when he started to front a pop group, so Sarah amazed us when she first went into the chalet business. One of the duties she took on was that of cooking meals for as many as a dozen people. That may not seem much but she was cooking meat and fish dishes and for a life-long vegetarian that must have been a challenge. She hates the smell of dead flesh.

Sarah and her partner's energy and confidence and their willingness to learn the multi-faceted business of chalet construction and management give me every confidence that they will make a success of a very challenging undertaking. But it doesn't stop me worrying about them. I probably worry more about my children now than when they were at home and dependent upon us. I have more time to do so than I ever had when I was working.

I have always been ferociously ambitious and very self-centred in my determination to get ahead. They are not always attractive characteristics.

7

The Industrial Journalist

I became an industrial journalist by accident. It wasn't a career path I'd planned to take, although I knew that I couldn't remain a general reporter on the *Birmingham Post* forever. My brief contact with the Beatles phenomenon had taught me that I wasn't destined to be a showbusiness columnist and I didn't really fancy crime reporting or writing about sport. At that stage in my life my ultimate ambition was to edit one of the national newspapers.

By my mid-twenties I'd become reasonably well known as a news reporter and had started to attract the attention of the talent spotters on the nationals, who noticed that their West Midland correspondents were being forced to follow up stories I had written more often than they liked.

I was approached by the *Guardian*, which had just gone national and was trying to shake off its regional newspaper image as the *Manchester Guardian*, and asked if I was interested in joining its Midlands correspondent, Roger Silver, as his deputy. Roger had just been promoted to the number one position in succession to Keith Gascoigne, who had rejoined the *Birmingham Post*. I decided it was time for a move, although I wasn't sure this was the right one.

After meeting the *Guardian*'s news editor, Harry Whewell, I was taken in to be interviewed by the editor, Alastair Hetherington. Both interviews seemed to go well enough and I knew that I was the choice of Roger Silver himself. Nevertheless, I didn't get the job. It went to a reporter named Dennis Barker, who was then on the *Wolverhampton Express and Star*. But before Dennis's appointment was promulgated the Birmingham newspaper grapevine, centred on the Press Club, had convinced itself that the job was to be mine. The rumour reached the ears of Vaughan Reynolds and Leslie Duckworth, who decided that they wanted to keep me if at all possible.

At that time the national broadsheet newspapers, led by *The Times* and *Sunday Times*, were starting to establish business sections and the *Birmingham Post*, in a more modest way, decided that it must also take commerce and industry more seriously. That was why Keith Gascoigne had rejoined the paper. He was to be its first business editor.

Until then the *Post*, despite being at the centre of the West Midlands with its huge commercial and industrial base, had limited its business coverage to the occasional news item about the Birmingham Chamber of Commerce and Industry and the frequent strikes then occurring at the British Motor Corporation's Longbridge Works.

I was offered a pay rise to stay on the *Birmingham Post* as Keith's number two and as I knew I wasn't going to get the *Guardian* post anyway, I accepted with alacrity, expressing my enthusiasm for the challenge of being involved in this important new venture.

The new section was warmly welcomed by the business community and, equally important, the advertising industry. Very soon we reached the stage where we were expected to provide enough stories to fill up to a page of space in the paper every day, even on days where our better stories were lifted for the front page.

As a rule of thumb Keith Gascoigne looked after the business-oriented stories and I covered the industrial relations scene when we first started up the new venture. When I wrote about the trade unions in the Birmingham area I was fortunate enough to get to know three of the country's most impressive and influential trade unionists, two of whom became general secretaries of the UK's biggest union, the Transport and General Workers Union. The third, arguably the most capable of the three, chose not to take the top job at the TGWU.

Jack Jones was already famous when I met him. He had served with the British Battalion of the XV International Brigade in the Spanish Civil War and had been seriously wounded in the Battle of Ebro in 1938. During the Second World War he'd helped to keep Coventry's munitions industry working through the blitz.

After the war Jones played a key role in organising the workforce of the West Midlands motor industry as regional secretary of the TGWU. During this time he was a strong supporter of the shop steward movement aimed at promoting trade union and industrial democracy, a cause shared with equal enthusiasm by Tony Benn.

In his time Jack Jones was voted the most powerful man in Britain – ahead of the then prime minister, James Callaghan. When I knew him he was regarded as a left-wing firebrand, vying with Hugh Scanlon, of the Amalgamated Engineering Union, as the main scourge of the engineering employers in the West Midlands.

When Jones moved out of the Midlands to become general secretary of the TGWU he was succeeded as regional secretary of the union by the intelligent and urbane Harry Urwin, who was more middle of the road than the left-wing Jones, but widely respected as a thinker within the trade union and Labour Party movements.

I knew Harry Urwin better than I knew Jack Jones and I think it's fair to say that we had a strong personal rapport, based on mutual respect. Harry knew that although the leader writers of the *Birmingham Post* might attack the trade unions, somewhat indiscriminately at times, they would get a reasonable crack of the whip from me. I believed that there were two sides to any story and that they should both be displayed in any news stories I wrote.

This worked to my advantage when I covered the story of a car worker at the British Motor Corporation (BMC) factory at Cowley, Oxford, who claimed that during an industrial dispute which he hadn't wanted to join a group of his fellow workers had put him on trial, found him guilty, put a noose round his neck and threatened to hang him. It was either a terrifying experience, which is what he claimed or, if it was a joke, it was in pretty bad taste.

The threatened hanging story hit the front pages of every national newspaper and the news bulletins on radio and television. The incident was written up in 'kangaroo court' terms and the worker involved was extensively interviewed by the tabloids, and possibly bought up by one of them to stop other reporters talking to him, a not unusual situation in those days. I couldn't get near him.

I turned the story on its head and went to see Harry Urwin. He told me that he would be carrying out a thorough investigation into what had gone on at Cowley and that was what I based my story on, using quotes from the apparent victim supplied by the Press Association to ensure balance.

My willingness to listen to the official trade union viewpoint, which no one else had sought, pleased Harry Urwin. A month or so later, when interest in the story had died, Harry rang me and asked if I was free to pop round for a chat, an offer I never refused. When I arrived at his office in Broad Street, Birmingham, Harry dropped his bombshell.

'On my desk I have the official report of our investigation into that business in Cowley,' he said. 'I have to see someone and I'll be out of the office for about an hour or so. I wouldn't be surprised if you read the report while I'm away, but I didn't show it you. Right?'

That is how I obtained my exclusive on what had really happened at Cowley. What had happened was precisely nothing. The worker who claimed that he had been threatened with being strung up had admitted to the union investigators that he had invented the story. He was a fantasist.

The pack of reporters who had believed his yarn were forced to follow up my story, which led the front page of the *Post*. Initially, one or two of them tried to make out that the TGWU's report was a whitewash, but they were quickly forced to accept that they had been conned by an attention seeker – and beaten to an exclusive by me.

Later on Harry Urwin joined Jack Jones in London as Deputy General Secretary. When Jones retired in 1978 he wanted Harry to succeed him but Urwin decided that with only a few years to go to retirement a younger man would be a better bet. That man was Moss Evans, the third of the powerful TGWU men I came to know in Birmingham. Urwin stayed on as deputy to Moss, having been his boss in the Midlands.

Despite my closeness to Harry Urwin and Moss Evans there were times when I felt that the lower echelons of the TGWU, the shop stewards, were out of control when they were in charge of the Midlands region. I suppose that's what made the Cowley 'hanging' tale credible as far as Fleet Street was concerned.

Maybe Urwin and Evans inherited a situation which they could do very little about. Jack Jones had long been a supporter of the shop steward movement as a means of promoting trade union and industrial democracy and was an early supporter of the Institute for Workers Control, alongside Tony Benn.

There are lots of theories why the shop stewards in the car industry, especially those at Longbridge, gained so much influence and enjoyed so much autonomy. My view is that the die was cast during the Second World War when the country was so desperate for the output from

Longbridge and other factories in the West Midlands, including Coventry where Jones was a full-time official during the war. Power and influence were handed over to the stewards through the 'joint production committees' set up to boost war production by involving workers in the decision-making process. A generation later this power was taken away from them, but they continued to have ambitions in that direction, encouraged by Tony Benn.

Another war-time emergency measure that led to problems later was the so-called 1941 Coventry Tool Room Agreement, which laid down pay differentials for the next 30 years, inspiring many disputes when skills were in short supply. For some years I attended the Confederation of Shipbuilding and Engineering Union talks in York where the subject of pay differentials dominated consideration of individual pay claims, causing a great deal of inter-union conflict.

Finally, the Longbridge shop stewards were allowed to control recruitment during the 1960s. Anyone applying for a job on the factory floor had to be cleared by the stewards, and trade union membership was obligatory. To all intents and purposes the stewards had the right of hire and fire, not the management – true power without responsibility. Inept management and government interference could be blamed when things went wrong – sometimes, it has to be said, correctly.

One in four of the shop stewards at Longbridge during this period were members of the Communist Party. They were able to find jobs for political activists who wanted to create trouble, with the longer-term aim of bringing down capitalism.

This was well known to the security services. One day I was approached by a softly spoken man who told me that he could provide me with information about what was going on in exchange for me providing him with any useful information I picked up. He was obviously working for Special Branch and I declined the offer. It seemed to me that spying on their contacts was not something that objective journalists should involve themselves in.

Not only that, I believed then and still believe that not all of the Communists employed at Longbridge were subversives. Nor were they regarded as such by the company's top management. Some were respected for their integrity and single-minded pursuit of better conditions for their members.

Dick Etheridge, who was convenor of shop stewards at Longbridge for thirty years from 1945 until 1975, was one such man. Dick was an active and influential member of both the AEU and the Communist Party. He was a tough negotiator – but also someone who believed that a bargain once made should be kept. He also regarded the strike as a weapon of last resort and kept the worst of the hot-heads under control.

Derek Robinson, dubbed 'Red Robbo' by the tabloids, was different. He was also a member of the Communist Party and became union convenor at Longbridge. With a network of supporters in the 42 different BMC plants around the UK he led a campaign of strikes which were ostensibly in protest at the mismanagement of the company. Maybe, but some of the men I talked to undoubtedly went on strike without knowing what they were striking about. Blacklegs could lose their jobs.

In one year 'Red Robbo' was credited with causing 523 walk-outs at Longbridge, costing an estimated £200m in lost production.

It may seem strange that the car industry employers allowed this state of affairs to go on. But in 1965 the British Motor Corporation, centred on Longbridge, was selling all the cars it could make. In a sellers' market production costs were not given the attention they deserved and the wages bill spiralled, making the car workers the envy of employees throughout the rest of UK industry.

I lived next door to a car worker at the time. His relative affluence was readily apparent in the top of the range car and the upmarket caravan parked outside his house. His car was changed annually, under a scheme which provided vehicles at heavily discounted prices for the Longbridge workers.

The contrast with the lifestyle of another neighbour of mine, a qualified engineer managing a plant at a Stewarts and Lloyds steel factory not that far from Longbridge, was marked. He serviced his own somewhat venerable car and there was no caravan. I was in a similar position, except that I was no use as a mechanic.

The car worker also seemed to spend more time at home than the rest of us living in the street. Part of the explanation for this may be that he worked shifts – but then my working hours were from 2 pm to 10 pm while I was on the *Post*. Arguably those hours are even more anti-social than shift work.

Apart from being on shifts, the other reason that my neighbour could spend so much time working on his garden or decorating his house was that he was regularly called out on 'downers', as unofficial strikes were called. 'Downer' was short for 'down tools'.

With so much happening on the industrial relations scene and with advertising building up in response to the establishment of the new business section, leaving more and more space to be filled with editorial material round it, it soon became apparent that we needed more industrial reporters.

We were being driven to fill some of the space by running press releases provided by the public relations agencies intact, without challenging their accuracy. We knew that if this went on for too long we would discredit what we were trying to achieve. Instead of a section with a reputation for authority and objectivity, we were in danger of being regarded as a receptacle for PR 'puffs' and not to be taken seriously.

We set out to recruit more staff. We decided that what we needed was younger people with careers to build and a bit of fire in their bellies. There were two reasons for this. Younger reporters might be expected to want to make a name for themselves and be self-motivated. And secondly, younger reporters would not be as expensive as more experienced journalists.

In the space of less than a year we picked up some of the finest journalists ever to work on the *Post* or in Fleet Street for that matter. They all made their way on to national newspapers, where they had highly successful careers.

Among our new members of staff were Andrew Goodrick-Clarke, who was to become the city editor of *The Times* and a noted financial pundit, and Roger Vielvoye, who became oil industry correspondent of the same paper at a particularly interesting time in the North Sea oil exploration programme.

Anthony Rowley made it to the new business section of *The Times* and Alan Hughes joined the *Daily Telegraph*. Michael Cassell went to the *Daily Express* for a time before joining the *Financial Times* where he had several roles over the years, perhaps the most notable being his time as the FT's parliamentary sketch writer, during which he won many admirers.

For a time after the new boys arrived in the mid 1960s I continued to concentrate on the industrial relations scene, covering the annual conferences of the largest unions, such as the National Union of Mineworkers, and the smallest, such as the National Society of Metal Mechanics.

The mining industry was employing close on 400,000 workers at that time – 600,000 fewer than at the coal industry's peak – and the NUM still had some influence within the trade union movement and the Labour Party. But it was obvious even then that the pit closure programme was far from over. Concerns over pit closures and pay rates were well to the fore on the agenda of the NUM Conference in Margate which I attended.

Will Paynter, the NUM's General Secretary, provided me with a different take on the issue in a long and fascinating conversation which I had with him during a day trip on board a ferry taking hundreds of delegates from Margate across to France on a mid-week day trip.

'Never forget that mining is a dirty, dangerous, degrading activity which no human being should have to undertake,' Will says.

'If there were alternative jobs I would like to see all of the pits shut down. There will be people who won't like me saying that, in the current climate, but it's how I feel.

'But as there's no other work in the mining communities – and unlikely to be – I see it as my duty to get the best possible pay rates for my members.

'Somehow we have to convince the politicians that it is economic madness to depend on oil and gas imported from the Middle East and that security of supply is worth paying for. And that means that the miners have to get decent wages and decent working conditions as well.'

'The trouble is Will,' I say, 'some of your members make such militant noises that even reasonable politicians are beginning to worry what the NUM is up to. At times you make it sound as though you want the workers – well the miners really – to run the country. That isn't democracy.'

'That's nonsense. I want the workers to have more influence in the industries in which they work but although I'm a Communist I still believe in an elected parliament.'

The NUM failed to convince successive governments that the UK shouldn't depend on imported coal, oil and gas, in much the same way as the nuclear power industry – once seen as the biggest enemy of the coal industry – has also failed to make the case for an indigenous energy resource. Twice as much imported coal is now used in the UK than home-produced coal and the number of miners working in Britain's coal industry is less than one percent of what it was at the industry's peak.

The annual conference of the Birmingham-based National Society of Metal Mechanics was very different from that of the NUM. There were probably fewer than a hundred delegates at their conference but they were well aware of the muscle they could bring to bear in the car and machine tool industries. Their approach towards conference debate was interesting. Like other unions they had a list of resolutions from which to choose, but unlike any other that I know of they asked me, a journalist, which were of most interest to me. They then debated these resolutions during their afternoon session. This was important. It meant that the debate was too late for the evening papers to cover.

Not surprisingly, perhaps, the NSMM became part of a larger union shortly after I stopped attending its annual conferences and is now buried somewhere within Unison, the engineering union, along with several more of the smaller unions.

In time I wrote less and less about labour relations and more about the more positive side of industry and commerce. Trade union affairs were left to the up-and-coming Alan Hughes, who found a novel way to discover what was going on in the largest union, the TGWU. Alan started to date a young lady who worked on the switchboard at the TGWU's office in Broad Street, Birmingham. She monitored all the calls coming in from the union's many shop stewards and tipped Alan off when she overheard a particularly interesting conversation between the steward at one of the factories – usually Longbridge – and one of the full-time officials. To protect his source Alan then allowed a couple of hours to pass by before contacting the official with the bare bones of the story leaked to him, much to the poor man's surprise.

This must have gone on for a year or more, but eventually Alan and the TGWU switchboard operator fell out and the source dried up, much to my horror. I implored him to settle his differences with the girl but he remained obdurate and our flow of stories from the TGWU became a trickle.

In the mid 1960s those journalists who had grown used to having a quiet life on the *Birmingham Post* suffered a severe shock to their systems. Vaughan Reynolds retired, to be succeeded by a campaigning journalist whose tough guy reputation preceded him. Being only 26 I found the prospect of a shake-up invigorating.

David Hopkinson joined the *Post* from the *Sheffield Daily Telegraph*, where he had won a Hannnen Swaffer award as provincial journalist of the year for his paper's campaign to expose the use of a rhino whip by detectives to intimidate suspects.

In 1963 the CID in Sheffield had set up a sort of hit squad, with orders to do what was necessary to deal with persistent burglars who were proving difficult to catch by conventional methods. The squad got off to a disastrous start when the first pair of suspects appeared in court looking much the worse for wear. The Sheffield morning newspaper had a reporter in court as the solicitor acting for these two men alleged that they had been beaten up by two detectives in the interview room and that the officers had used a rhino whip to extract admissions from them. The magistrates ordered the Chief Constable to investigate the matter.

Senior CID officers told the two detective constables that they would have to be charged with using violence to prisoners, but that if they pleaded guilty and kept their mouths shut they would only be reprimanded. They duly pleaded guilty at the disciplinary hearing and were shocked when the Chief Constable fired them. Realising they had been duped they immediately told the whole story to the *Sheffield Daily Telegraph* and David Hopkinson, after some hesitation, ran it, causing a national furore.

The detectives appealed against their dismissal and in an unprecedented move the Home Secretary appointed a QC to hear their appeal and instructed that the hearing must take place in public. The result was a public relations disaster for the Sheffield police force – and a tremendous success for the local newspaper's campaign.

The QC, Graham Swanwick, found that senior officers had indeed formed a squad with orders to ignore the Judges Rules governing the conduct of police officers and to get results by whatever means they thought necessary. The unfortunate detective constables lost their appeal, but the Chief Constable felt obliged to resign, as did several senior detectives. David Hopkinson's reputation was made.

When the news got out that Hopkinson was to take over from Vaughan Reynolds as editor of the *Birmingham Post* it was as though the editorial staff expected the new man to turn up with a rhino whip in his hand, kindly provided by the Sheffield police as a memento of his journalistic triumph. They weren't totally wrong, either.

David Hopkinson set about shaking the place up immediately, by putting up a notice 'inviting' members of the reporting staff to arrange an appointment with his secretary to meet him in order to 'make their number' with him. It wasn't an expression I would have expected Vaughan Reynolds to use. The invitation was, of course, an instruction, and recognised as such by the reporters.

'Okay, so what do you do?' my new boss asks. I'm surprised he doesn't know.

'I'm industrial editor. I write about industry, working with Keith Gascoigne.'

'You might be doing that at the moment, but not necessarily in future. I will be assessing everyone's performance over the next few weeks and making my mind up about them. Till then just carry on with what you're doing.'

'I'm not sure I understand what you're saying. Are you saying that my job is on the line or that you may decide to move me to another job here?'

'Both. We'll have to see how things go. Don't worry I won't take long to make my mind up.'

'I think you should know that I'll be making my mind up about you, too. I'm young enough and have enough confidence in my own ability to believe that I'll have no difficulty finding another job if I have to.'

'Fair enough. I like people who know their own value. Let's see what happens.'

'Talking of value. Vaughan Reynolds promised me a pay rise just before he left and I haven't had it yet. I've been waiting three months already. I guess it must have been held back until your arrival. I'll give it a couple of months so that you can make up your mind up about me and I can make my mind up about you. But if I don't get the rise I was promised I'll be leaving anyway.'

'We'll have to see.'

We ended our conversation on that unsatisfactory note and I went home that night in a foul mood. I didn't like that 'I'll be making my mind up about you' tone one little bit. I told Sheila that I hadn't made a very good start with the new editor and that I didn't think I could work with him. I warned her that I might have to look for a new job and that there was unlikely to be anything suitable in the Midlands.

Loyal as ever, she agreed with me that if the promised pay rise wasn't forthcoming I had no alternative but to start sending off copies of my CV to the national newspapers in London.

In the event I was totally wrong about David Hopkinson. I got my pay rise within weeks and despite our confrontational first meeting I found working for him an invigorating and generally enjoyable experience. Some of his methods upset other reporters, however, particularly the daily bulletins he introduced at the start of his reign. In his bulletins he dissected that day's paper, praising some pieces and criticising others. Copies of this bulletin were put on the noticeboards in an open plan office which was shared with members of the editorial staff of the *Evening Mail*. They became a source of much amusement to them and considerable annoyance to those chosen as targets for criticism by Hopkinson.

John Solon, to my mind the *Post's* most talented writer – although not its best news reporter – was normally the most gentle of men, with a wry sense of humour. He took exception to something David had said about a piece he had written in one of the bulletins and stormed in to see the editor, threatening to sue him for libel if he ever wrote a disparaging note about him again and stuck it on a noticeboard for all to see, including potential future employers.

The daily bulletin system was quickly brought to an end, with Hopkinson explaining that they had served their purpose. I think John Solon's unexpected outburst helped to make his mind up for him.

My career flourished under David Hopkinson. He was someone who loved to take brave decisions and gave me several opportunities to explore new avenues in journalism.

Although I had no experience of sub-editing, which involves cutting stories down to size and writing headlines for them, or of page layout, where decisions are taken about where particular stories are placed, he put me in over-all charge of the *Post's* front page at the time of a general election.

On a provincial morning newspaper the front page changes continually between editions on election night as results come in, with the updated information on the anticipated result beginning to take over more and more space. The trick is to start off with enough small, filler pieces which can easily be dropped to make way for the election news. I remember one such filler very well. It concerned a ship which was thought to be in danger of being blown up somewhere in the Channel because an old wartime mine had attached itself to it.

The sub-editor handling this particular story put up the immortal head-line 'Mine Dangles Over Ship's Bows'. It is a given that all sub-editors – indeed all journalists – must have dirty minds and I could not believe what I was reading when the first page proofs came up.

'Get that headline changed,' I shouted across the room.

He changed it all right. That edition of the paper went out with the headline: 'Mine Dangles Over Cruiser's Bows'. The idiot thought I was complaining that the headline hadn't been specific about the type of ship involved. At least, so I assumed.

Early on in David Hopkinson's editorship of the *Post* the Royal Radar Establishment at Malvern decided to open its doors to the press for the very first time, probably in a bid to secure or increase its funding from the government of the day. The RRE was particularly keen on the public understanding the importance of its research into infra-red technology, then in its infancy, but there was some nervousness too, because of the research going on there into possible military applications of thermal imaging.

Those running the Establishment decided that the *Birmingham Post*, their local morning newspaper, could be relied upon to treat the subject seriously, accurately and sympathetically. It was agreed that I should cover the event. At that night's editorial conference David Hopkinson asked me what I had for the following day's paper.

'I'm not sure,' I said. 'I'm writing it all up now. The trouble is I've either got one very big news story or enough material for several features. I don't know how to play it. I've also brought back some amazing pictures which show what infra-red technology can do.

'After what I've seen I'm convinced that infra-red is going to revolu-tionise several industries and whole sections of medicine and the military.'

'The best thing you can do is sit down and finish writing up what you've started – all of it. I'll decide what to do with it when you've finished,' Hopkinson said.

When I'd finished I took what I'd written into the editor's office and left him to read it. I described how infra-red technology could be used to identify heat sources at night, helping to fight crime, how it could direct weapons onto their targets, how it could show that smoking cigarettes stopped the blood flowing to the ends of people's fingers, and how it had a variety of other fascinating applications.

After 15 minutes or so he joined me in the office I shared with Keith Gascoigne. 'Okay Harold, we're going to run the lot tonight as a series of separate news stories. I'm clearing most of the front page for it,' Hopkinson said.

And that's what he did, surprising me, the RRE and much of the newspaper industry, which had its Midland correspondents and science writers scrambling around to catch up with this multiple scoop by the industrial editor of the *Post*.

This was more than 40 years ago and it was the first time anyone had written about infra-red technology and its applications in a way that lay readers could understand. There were follow-ups in all of the national newspapers and on radio and television. A single story or a series of features over several days would not have had the same impact.

My enthusiasm for thermal imaging was well placed, although some of the applications to which it is now put were only just being thought about then. Because it can be used to detect the smallest of temperature variations it is used to predict emerging problems with power transmission lines and machines, to monitor processes and to assist with energy audits carried out in people's homes and factories. In the environmental area it can identify the source and course of oil spills and chemical spills and identify buried wastes and noxious stack emissions.

There have been enormous benefits in terms of surveillance techniques, too, including uses for border patrol work, loss prevention, perimeter and security fencing, forest fire fighting, navigational aid and search and rescue.

Finally, infra-red technology is used in our hospitals as a diagnostic tool for many conditions, from breast cancer to vascular disease. My amazement at the pictures I saw 40 years ago of the effect which smoking could have on blood circulation was simply a start.

Computing was at a similarly early stage. Its potential uses in industry, medicine, crime prevention and the military were also starting to be identified and IBM was competing against ICL, the UK's own government-owned manufacturer, at that time on the new uses of the computer. It held a conference on the subject in Stockholm and I was there for the *Birmingham Post* and once more I wrote several stories, without the impact the Malvern infra-red pieces had. No doubt IBM was happy enough – it received many column inches of free publicity.

Equally important for me, I met Dennis Topping, who was then the industrial correspondent of the *Financial Times* but about to leave that newspaper for the newly established *Times* business news section. During one of our conversations he asked me whether I intended to remain a provincial journalist or to go to Fleet Street. We agreed that at the age of 30 I had to make my mind up soon.

'If you're interested I'll put a word in for you at the FT,' Dennis said. 'You won't get my job but there'll be a vacancy down the line and I think you would do well in London.'

'I'm interested Dennis. Let's give it a go.'

8

The Gate Crasher

Lionel Bart's mansion house in Fulham had at least two lavatories. One of them had mirrors covering the walls, floor and ceiling, which was somewhat disconcerting, and the other had a toilet shaped like a throne. The throne had a wooden crown at the top and on investigation I discovered that this was the flushing mechanism. Twist the crown to the right and whoosh, a royal flush.

I know about Lionel's loos because a couple of months into my new job as an industrial reporter on the *Financial Times* I became one of the freeloaders who took advantage of Lionel's generous hospitality. In my small way – the cost of three glasses of wine – I must have helped him towards his eventual bankruptcy. At that time, though, in 1967, I was more worried about my own financial situation.

I found myself at Lionel Bart's house as a result of meeting a total stranger one evening after work when I went for a drink in the bar at the Mermaid theatre, near the old *Times* and *Observer* building, just down the road from Bracken House, opposite St Paul's Cathedral, which was then the home of the *Financial Times*. There I struck up a conversation with a reporter from the *New Musical Express*.

I told him how miserable I was living in a bed-sitter in Earls Court, how I hated spending the week in London and weekends in Birmingham, how I was convinced that I'd made the wrong decision leaving the *Birmingham Post*, where I meant something, for the FT which didn't seem to know what to do with me. I must have been a real bore.

'There's a party on at Lionel Bart's place,' the NME reporter said, probably because he'd had enough of listening to my troubles. 'Why don't you come? Lionel won't mind.'

I didn't take much persuading. When we arrived at Lionel Bart's house in Chelsea the composer of the hit musical *Oliver!* greeted us at the door.

'Hello Lionel. This is Harold Bolter. He's with the *Financial Times*,' the *New Musical Express* journalist said, introducing me.

'Hello Harold. Good to see you again,' Lionel responded, although we'd never met before. 'Come in and have a drink. Make yourself at home.'

That was the last I saw of my host and the last I saw of the man from the NME, who probably found more congenial company, someone who kept his troubles to himself. I started to chat to an attractive young woman whom I'd noticed looking at me quizzically over her glass of something bubbly.

'You remind me of someone,' she said, thoughtfully.

I waited to see how long it would take her to recognise my Cary Grant profile.

'I've got it. Max Bygraves.'

Not even his son, Anthony, who was just getting started in show business.

I needed as much distraction as I could get from my worries about the move to the *Financial Times*. These concerns were so severe that they began to have an unfortunate effect on my bowel movements, diagnosed by my GP as symptomatic of a serious case of the blue funks.

The problem was that I'd jumped at the chance to move to London far too quickly, before I'd found out what the FT was all about. I had no idea what plans it had for the future and how I might fit into those plans. Christopher Johnson, the managing editor, conducted my job interview, which was brief. I was offered a job on the spot, probably because I came cheap.

I didn't get to see the editor, Sir Gordon Newton, at my interview – I guess I wasn't regarded as important enough – but I suspect that I wouldn't have learned much from him anyway. As I was to discover, the taciturn Sir Gordon, held in awe by his staff, found it difficult to explain what he wanted and usually didn't bother to try.

To secure my position on the FT I had seriously under-sold myself, a mistake I never made again. I'd been earning £2000 a year with the *Birmingham Post* (this was 40 years ago remember) and accepted the first offer the *Financial Times* made me – £2200 a year. To make matters worse it took nearly 12 months to sell our house in Birmingham and I was forced to rent a cheap but less than cheerful bed-sit in Earls Court.

To pay the rent on that and the mortgage on the house in the West Midlands as well as pay the rail fares to and from Birmingham every weekend I had to eat into the cash lump sum I'd accepted from the *Birmingham Post and Mail* Limited in lieu of my pension contributions, rather than switch the money over to the FT pension scheme.

I didn't know it when I joined the *Financial Times* but the paper was in the throes of a major upheaval and my appointment was very much a product of it. The FT was getting over the excitement of a merger with *The Times* that didn't quite happen, and was agonising over the direction it should take in its wake.

Prompted by the FT's managing director, Lord Drogheda, who was later to become chairman, and supported by the editor, Sir Gordon Newton, the Pearson group had made a bid for *The Times*, owned by Lord Astor. The intention was to take the best of both papers, financially and editorially, and with the FT taking the lead, produce a new paper capable of taking on the *Daily Telegraph*.

But the *Financial Times* didn't follow up its first tentative bid with much sense of purpose and nothing came of the idea. Instead *The Times* went to the Canadian Roy Thomson, later Lord Thomson, to the horror of the other Fleet Street proprietors.

Having lost out, the FT decided to try to broaden its appeal by recruiting more news reporters. It brought in eight more reporters with a provincial newspaper background in a very short time, including my old friend Michael Cassell and three people who became good friends of mine, Michael Hand, Ray Dafter and David Walker.

As the FT moved uncertainly towards becoming a more general newspaper, *The Times* decided to go in the opposite direction and develop a business news section, entering *Financial Times* territory. There was a lot of rivalry and some animosity between the owners of the two papers and some of their journalists as well. Some members of the FT's editorial staff spoke of the new *Times* business news section as 'Comic Cuts'.

Most of the established journalists on the FT had been recruited straight from university and were mainly Oxbridge graduates. As I understand it they'd been given some pretty rudimentary training on the job and left to get on with it. They regarded themselves as writers rather than newspaper reporters – as though that was by definition a superior occupation.

The Lord Snooties looked down their noses at journalists engaged in the mundane task of news gathering. There was a gentlemen versus players atmosphere about the place. It was simply not a newspaper in the sense that I understood the term, more a glorified trade journal which happened to be produced every day.

The news desk set-up was unusual, too. Doug York, the news editor when I joined the paper, was a quiet, cautious man, not at all like Leslie Duckworth, the news editor of the *Birmingham Post*, or any other news editor I've met before or since.

The story goes that under York the FT acquired the reputation of being the paper that got everything right – the day after everyone else got it wrong. Doug would have taken that as a compliment. The *Financial Times* wasn't in the business of looking for exclusives, scoops if you will – but I was. In the end Doug and I achieved a sound working relationship and I came to respect him for his unflappability. But it took time.

At first I found Doug York's caution thoroughly depressing. For some weeks after I joined the paper he only used me to rewrite hand-outs provided by public relations people or to regurgitate statistics provided by over-zealous trade associations – monthly machine tool production figures, that sort of thing. I began to think of myself as the widget-counting corres-pondent.

One advantage of living in London on my own – there weren't many – was that I had plenty of time to make contacts and to get to know some of the reporters from other papers, notably Maurice Corina, who had left the FT for *The Times*, and Roland Gribben, business editor of the *Daily Telegraph*. Both of them became friends as well as rivals.

Despite Doug York's reluctance to allow me any headroom I began to build up some useful new contacts and to develop stories for myself, rather than wait to be given hand-outs to rewrite. With acres of space to fill in the paper and very few news reporters to fill it York was grateful, if still a little wary.

My breakthrough with Doug York came when he started getting phone calls one afternoon from some of the early supermarket chains to say that they were lowering their prices for cigarettes and other goods. He passed the calls over to me to deal with. Kelsey Van Musschenbroek, the recog-nised expert on the retail trade, was away from the office.

This was the first indication we had that resale price maintenance had finally been brought to an end, and the FT splashed on the story. To Doug's great relief there were no complaints about the accuracy of the piece I wrote and from then on he trusted my judgement and placed more confidence in me.

Nevertheless I was still uncertain what sort of future I had on the FT. Maurice Corina was aware of this and suggested I might like to leave the paper and join him and Dennis Topping on the newly formed business news section of *The Times*.

I was interviewed for an industrial reporter post, similar to the one I had with the FT, by William Rees Mogg, editor of *The Times*, and Anthony Vice, editor of the business news section. Both of them were former journalists with the FT, having been taken on as potential high flyers direct from university by Sir Gordon Newton. I say I was interviewed but in truth all I had to do was listen to the two men telling me how good their new business section was going to be.

I was offered a job on the spot, with a salary of £2600 a year. I went straight back to the office and wrote out my resignation letter, which I handed to Christopher Johnson. Within a couple of hours I was summoned to appear before Sir Gordon Newton, the great man himself. It was like appearing before the beak.

'What's all this?' he asks, waving my letter in the air. 'Surely you don't intend to leave us for The Times? *Their business section is going nowhere. It won't last.'*

'I've no alternative. They've offered me £400 a year more than I'm getting here. I can't afford to turn it down. I have a wife and family to support.'

'Do you want to leave us Bolter?'

'No. I don't think I do. I'm starting to get somewhere. At least I hope I am.'

'Good. I'm prepared to put your salary up to £3000 a year and you'll get further increases of £200 a year above any trade union rises for each of the next two years. You will have a new contract by the end of the week. What do you say to that?'

'Can I have time to think about it?'

'Think about it! Think about it! What's there to think about?'

'Well I'd like to speak to my wife first.'

'Go on then. I'll give you an hour to make your mind up.'

I skip along the corridor and ring Sheila.
'Hello. Something's come up. I'm not going to The Times *after all.'*
'Why not?'
'I'm staying on the FT.'
'What's gone wrong? Has The Times *withdrawn its offer?'*
'No. You're not going to believe this. The FT's putting my salary up
by £800 a year – £800! Twice the increase The Times *was offering. We*
can get a bridging loan if you like and you and the kids can come to
London as soon as we find a house.'
I keep a straight face as I report back to Sir Gordon with the news
that I'm staying. For perhaps the only time in my experience there's a
smile on his face. At least, I think it's a smile.

Sir Gordon Newton probably made his offer to me because he was annoyed that Rees Mogg and Vice, two people whom he had helped get started in journalism, were now daring to challenge him. As if it wasn't bad enough Rees Mogg and Vice recruiting Maurice Corina and Dennis Topping from the FT, they were now trying to poach recently recruited young hopefuls like me. Enough was enough.

Effectively I was number three in the industrial reporter pecking order on the FT, behind Tony Moreton, who was the industrial correspondent, and Michael Simmons. But within a year Tony was transferred to the news desk, where he eventually became deputy news editor, and Michael left the FT to join the *Guardian* as its East European correspondent.

This left me in prime position and very soon I was told that I was to become industrial correspondent and head up a small department as other young journalists were recruited from the provinces. Typically, however, Sir Gordon Newton moved swiftly to ensure that my elevation didn't go to my head. I was told that I was to join him and other colleagues on a promotional trip to Birmingham, where the FT was to throw a dinner for leading businessmen (for which read potential advertisers).

At the dinner I enjoyed being paraded as the new industrial correspondent of the *Financial Times* among my former contacts in Birmingham. The evening went well as I chatted with old friends, including Peter Cartwright, the FT's Midlands correspondent, who had been one of those who'd encouraged me to make the move to London.

As the wine flowed our guests were encouraged to tell us what they thought of the *Financial Times* and how it might be improved. The paper's City coverage received a fair amount of praise and a surprising number of people told us how much they enjoyed the arts coverage, Sheila Black's women's page and Trevor Bailey's articles on cricket.

'But what about the industrial coverage?' I asked, looking for compliments.

Sir Gordon pounced: 'Your job is to keep the advertisements apart,' he said. It wasn't a bad description of the journalist's job, I suppose, but it felt like a very public putdown.

Worse was to come from Sir Gordon, however, when I was given my first opportunity to write a feature for the paper, a role previously reserved for that happy band of men the Oxbridge recruits.

The designated subject for my first FT feature was British Standard Time, which the government was about to bring in for an experimental period of three years from March 1968 to October 1971. Under this new arrangement the time was to be moved to one hour in advance of Greenwich Mean Time throughout the year, instead of being one hour in advance of GMT in the summer (British Summer Time) and one hour back to GMT in the winter. It was argued that the new arrangement would mean there would be no need to change the clocks twice, which was obviously true, and that it would be more convenient in commercial dealings with Europe, which was more arguable.

As soon as the government announced its intention to change to British Standard Time the debate started. The change would mean people getting up in the dark. It would lead to more road accidents and it would push up the crime figures. Street lighting costs would go up. The education of our children would be affected. Outdoor workers such as postmen and building workers would be inconvenienced. And so on.

But the FT wasn't interested in such concerns. It wanted evidence of a positive business advantage. The new industrial correspondent was told to get on to his old contacts in the West Midlands and find out how much extra money businesses were likely to earn as a result of the UK coming into line with Europe. Each day there would be an extra hour of possible contact with their Continental counterparts to play with and that must be worth something, surely.

I did my best, ringing round many of the car and motorcycle companies as well as the trade associations and asking them to quantify how much additional income they expected to get as a result of the time change. None of them could come up with a figure.

The public relations officer of one company told me that he'd been given a flea in the ear when he'd asked the question of his overseas sales division. 'When you're after business in France or wherever you don't watch the clock. If it's necessary to come in early or leave late, that's what you do. The time change won't make a scrap of difference.'

I wrote my piece and handed it in to the features editor, aware that I hadn't found anything to support the central premise that added time meant added money.

I shared the office where I worked with eight other people. It was off the corridor which led to the editor's room and had port-hole windows in the two doors which led into it. If Sir Gordon Newton spotted someone he wanted to speak to, he simply walked in. His stock opening question was 'What are you on?' and it is said that one of my predecessors, reading a newspaper, had once replied: 'Page 17 – the house ads' and immediately regretted it. 'Read the newspapers in your own time,' Newton snapped.

On this occasion Sir Gordon pushed his way through the doorway holding sheets of paper in his hand, my feature on British Standard Time. He came over to me and threw the lot in the air. I looked on in amazement as the paper fell round my ears.

'I will not have rubbish like that in my newspaper,' he said angrily.

The room went quiet. None of my colleagues knew what to say and nor did I. I felt like crying or sinking under the desk and hiding away. Newton simply glowered at me and walked out of the room. I felt totally humiliated and very angry.

After I'd calmed down I picked up the pieces of paper and took them to the features editor's office. I told him what had happened and we discussed what Sir Gordon's objections to my piece might be. He had learned to interpret the Newton grunts. I learned from him that although the editor knew instinctively what was wrong with a piece he was quite incapable of articulating his reasons for taking this view.

I argued that it was a silly idea in the first place. 'It's the editor's idea,' I was told.

'I guess it's a good one then,' I said.

Still not sure of what was expected of me I rewrote the feature and handed it in for a second time. It still didn't make the paper, but I was told that

Sir Gordon thought it was much better written. Of course it was, given the time I'd spent on it.

A feature on British Standard Time was eventually published by the FT, written by one of the golden graduates. I didn't think it was any better than my rewritten piece, but who was I to argue.

A short time later Sir Gordon walked along the corridor with Samuel Brittan, the pre-eminent economic journalist of his generation, a god-like figure in the business world and Whitehall, who was later knighted. The two men did a detour into the room where I worked, to Sam's obvious surprise, and for no apparent reason stopped at my desk. The room went quiet again.

'Sam. I will not have rubbish like that in my paper,' the editor said, and threw the article onto my desk. Some of the pages fell to the floor.

Samuel Brittan, a shy, awkward man, looked visibly shocked that Newton should talk to him in this way – and in front of me and the others, mere news reporters, at that. It was Sir Gordon's way of saying to me: 'You see. If I don't like a piece it doesn't matter who's written it. It won't go in the paper.' It was hard on Sam, though.

The British Standard Time idea was quietly dropped at the end of the three-year experiment. It had failed to yield any noticeable dividends for British industry. I felt good about that, but didn't remind Sir Gordon Newton of my early scepticism.

Newton wasn't an easy man to work for. Most of us were more than a little afraid of him, but I guess that helped to keep us on our toes. His bullying, humourless approach to editing the paper was certainly successful. He was the editor of the FT for 22 years, from 1950 to 1972 and in his time the paper trebled its circulation. And that's the ultimate test of a successful newspaper man. The best editors tend not to be loveable in my experience.

With time I became more adept at writing features but I always found news reporting more interesting and rewarding. I have always believed that it is people who make news not numbers or things. Some people are more interesting than others, of course, and John Stonehouse MP was one of the most interesting men I met during my career at the *Financial Times*. He gave the impression of having supreme confidence in everything he did even when he must have been terrified of what he was getting involved in.

At the time I met him the General Post Office was one of the businesses

I tended to call my own, along with the major state-owned industries – coal, steel, electricity supply and gas. I left the other, less newsworthy, private sector industries to the junior colleagues who had joined me from the provinces. I was ambitious and obsessed with my by-line, which now described me as the paper's industrial editor.

John Stonehouse had just been appointed Postmaster General by the Prime Minister, Harold Wilson, whom I had come to know reasonably well, and found himself without a chairman for the Post Office. Undeterred Stonehouse decided to do the job himself, doubling up with his parliamentary duties as PMG, until such time as he could find a new chairman.

It took him five months to do it but eventually a press conference was called by the Post Office to introduce the new chairman. Stonehouse proudly announced that he had carried out the head hunting for the post himself and was proud of the outcome.

'Gentlemen,' the Minister said. 'A strong team is needed to run the biggest industry in Britain and you see before you an outstanding team leader. Viscount Hall is my personal choice to take the Post Office through to its next stage of development.'

We discovered that Viscount Hall of Cynon Valley, the son of a Labour peer, was a former naval surgeon who held 14 directorships in relatively unknown companies – obviously a man with connections. We also learned that he had no experience of the workings of the Post Office and wasn't in a position to tell us what he intended to do with it – a rare admission from the newly appointed chairman of a state-owned industry.

'Do you have any hobbies, Lord Hall?' I asked, getting a bit desperate for something to write about the man who knew nothing about the UK's vast mail and telecommunications empire, for which he was now to take responsibility.

'I have a boat which I sail on the Thames,' Lord Hall replied. 'I intend to lower the flag in salute every time I pass the big Post Office building on the river bank. Good for morale.'

It took a little time for the answer to sink in, for the listeners to realise that the cheroot-smoking milord wasn't joking.

I had visions of cheering Post Office workers lining the river bank as their chairman sailed majestically past, saluting them with a lowered flag and a cheerful wave, and had to fight hard to stop myself laughing out loud.

Not surprisingly perhaps, Lord Hall didn't last long as chairman of the

Post Office, which was in the process of being transformed from the General Post Office, a government department, into the Post Office Corporation, a nationalised industry supposedly separate from government.

Viscount Hall didn't like the government's plans for the transition and let this be known widely and publicly – a big mistake. He was sacked. Outraged at his dismissal Hall demanded that the Post Office's press office issue a public protest. Tom Dawson, the former business editor of *The Times* who headed the public relations department, refused, suggesting that his chairman should 'go quietly and preserve your dignity'.

The Viscount ignored Tom's advice and called a press conference at his Mayfair home. There he claimed that his sacking amounted to 'a monstrous rape of the Post Office Corporation' an interesting expression which didn't mean an awful lot but made a good headline. I never heard of Lord Hall again.

I didn't hear any more about John Stonehouse for some time either, at least not directly. His position as Postmaster General was abolished by the Post Office Act 1969 which established the Post Office Corporation, and he never held another public office. Without the extra money ministerial status would have brought, Stonehouse tried to make up for it by setting up various companies in order to augment his MP's salary. By 1974 these were mostly in financial trouble and he resorted to cooking the books.

When he discovered that the Department for Trade and Industry was beginning to take an interest in his affairs he decided to flee the country, adopting the identity of Joseph Markham, the dead husband of one of his constituents. The story of how John Stonehouse tried to fake his own suicide is too well known to repeat in detail. But for those unfamiliar with it he left some of his clothes on a beach in Miami and then scarpered to Australia, where he was joined by his secretary Sheila Buckley, who was also his mistress, with the intention of starting a new life.

He might have got away with it, too, but on Christmas Eve 1974 the police in Melbourne arrested him, thinking he was Lord Lucan, who was wanted for questioning over the death of his children's nanny. Eventually Stonehouse was extradited, charged with various criminal offences and imprisoned. He was released in 1979 and died eight years later.

John Stonehouse was undoubtedly a rogue, but a loveable one. On balance, I felt sorry for someone who probably meant well, who was certainly entertaining and who provided me with some very good stories.

Lord Hall's successor as Chairman of the Post Office was William Ryland, who should probably have been appointed ahead of Lord Hall. Bill Ryland had started working for the Post Office as a messenger and worked his way up through the ranks. He knew the business inside out. He took a particular interest in the press coverage which the Post Office received, insisting that his head of public relations scour the daily newspapers every day before breakfast and telephone him at home to tell him what was in them before he left for the office. One day the PR man, Reg Abbiss, a former BBC journalist, failed to ring him and an angry Sir William tracked him down at his home and demanded an explanation.

'There was nothing about us in the papers,' the poor man explained.

'No matter. I want to know when there's nothing in the papers as well as when there is,' Sir William said.

'But when I don't ring you that means there isn't anything in them.'

'Don't argue. Ring me. Every day.'

Within a year or so of joining the *Financial Times* I had become one of the best-known industrial correspondents in the country, not least because the paper had a very small staff of general reporters and a lot of pink space to fill. But that wasn't the only reason.

In his excellent history of the *Financial Times*, marking the paper's centenary, David Kynaston drew attention to just how busy I was at this time. Using a 'benchmark' issue, 30 October 1968, as an illustration he remarked on how far down the 'generalist' path the FT had come and how certain names kept cropping up, one of them Reginald Dale, the Common Market correspondent, who had contributed three stories that day.

'Even more prolific was Harold Bolter, who had recently come from the *Birmingham Post* and was to be an extremely able industrial correspondent for several years. On this particular day he had no fewer than five stories,' Kynaston wrote.

One story was about the road haulage industry being messed about by the government (nothing new there then). Another was concerned with British Overseas Airways Corporation (BOAC) redundancies. A third was about BOAC pay talks. In a fourth the building industry was said to be having difficulties going metric. Finally, I wrote a piece headed 'Too many amateurs in too many industries'. I'm sure I was right but goodness knows what that story was all about.

Throughout my eight years with the *Financial Times* Britain was in economic turmoil, no matter which political party was in power. Crisis followed crisis, accompanied by a succession of new government policies to deal with them, none of which seemed to work. The country was already operating a voluntary system of severe wage restraint, monitored by the Confederation of British Industry and the Trades Union Congress, when I arrived at the FT in 1967.

In January of the following year Labour Prime Minister Harold Wilson announced that pay rises would be limited to a 3.5 percent maximum for 12 months. A bare three months later he announced that wages would be frozen for a year. By the following year, 1969, the pay ceiling was changed to a range of 2.5 to 4.5 percent. And so it went on, during the Wilson period and that of Ted Heath.

It was my role as industrial editor to monitor the CBI's thinking during these talks, with John Elliott, the labour editor, watching over TUC attitudes and John Bourne, the lobby editor, keeping tabs on what the government was up to. My main contact, a good one, was Campbell Adamson, Director General of the CBI.

Those were the days when anyone could walk down Downing Street and one evening I was waiting in the rain outside No.10 for the talks to break up when a tall, distinguished-looking man in an opera cloak came striding down the street towards me. It was Lord Drogheda, chairman of the Covent Garden Opera House as well as the *Financial Times*. I'd never seen someone in an opera cloak before.

'Bolter. What are you doing here?' his lordship asks.

'The CBI and the TUC are meeting the prime minister, Lord Drogheda. The government's working on another prices and incomes initiative. I'm waiting for the meeting to end so that I can speak to Campbell Adamson to find out how they've got on.'

'I see. But what are you doing here, in the rain?'

'There's nowhere else for us to go. We have to wait till the meeting breaks up, then interview our contacts and phone a story over to the copy takers from one of the pay-phones down Whitehall.'

'What? That's disgraceful. Standing in the rain may be all right for reporters from the Daily Mirror *but it's not good enough for the* Financial Times. *I shall speak to the prime minister first thing tomorrow morning.'*

'Yes, Lord Drogheda. Thank you.'

The famous Downing Street door opens and one of the first people out of the building is Campbell Adamson. Lord Drogheda beats me to him and has a quick word with my contact.

'The meeting's adjourned. The talks will continue tomorrow,' Lord Drogheda calls out. Good of the chairman to do my job for me.

Two things happen the following day.

When I arrive in Downing Street to cover the resumed talks, one of the government's press officers directs me to a house at the top of the street, where a room has been put aside for the press. The room is equipped with beer and sandwiches and, wonder of wonders, a bank of telephones.

The same afternoon my daughter Helen, then 11 years old, answers the telephone at home and calls out to her mother.

'Mummy. Have we got a residence? There's somebody on the phone. I think he said he was a Lord something or other. He wants to know if this is the Bolter residence.'

Sheila takes the phone off Helen and finds herself talking to the FT's chairman, who has rung up to apologise for the conditions I've been forced to work in during the Downing Street talks.

'I have told the prime minister that it is simply not good enough and he has promised to do something about it.'

'Thank you Lord Drogheda.'

Ted Heath may have managed to do something about the working conditions of the journalists covering Downing Street prices and incomes talks that followed but he had no such luck with the trade union representatives attending them. He was at loggerheads with them throughout his three years as prime minister.

Six months after Heath became prime minister he threw down the gauntlet with the introduction of the Industrial Relations Act, which he claimed was designed to improve industrial relations. The legislation was based on the North American system of collective bargaining, in which the law plays a prominent part. It provided for pre-strike ballots and a cooling-off period before any stoppages took place, and established the National Industrial Relations Court, which was empowered to grant injunctions to prevent strikes and to settle a variety of labour disputes.

The intention may have been to improve industrial relations. In fact it had the opposite effect. The Trades Union Congress, led by Vic Feather,

Our wedding day. Sheila and I on September 3rd 1960. We don't look old enough do we?

Above: A relatively sober moment during my farewell party from the *Financial Times*. Left to right Michael Cassell, Ray Dafter, Rhys David, me and Tony Moreton.

Below: Me, looking somewhat tired and emotional, snuggling up to Elinor Goodman, then with the *F.T.* at my farewell party, while Jurek Martin looks on. Elinor went on to become Political Editor of Channel Four News, from 1988 to 2005.

Above: Prince Philip meets some of the staff at the opening of the Sellafield Visitors' Centre. I am by his side, right of the picture. (Photograph courtesy of the *Whitehaven News*).

Below: Preparing for the Royal Garden Party. Left to right: Roy Pilling, a good friend and fellow Board member, Margaret Pilling, my wife Sheila and me.

Above: The British Nuclear Fuels Board in the mid-1980s, shortly after Sir Christopher Harding became Chairman. Sir Christopher is on the left, arms folded, and the others seated are Jean Denton, later Baroness Denton of Halifax, Neville Chamberlain, Chief Executive, and Dr Bill Wilkinson. From left to right standing are Roy Dantzig (non-executive director), Dr Tom Marsham (non-exec), me, Alan Johnson, John Hayles, Roy Pilling, John Wills (non-exec) and Sir Norman Wooding (non-exec). Note the even division between executive and non-executive directors!

Below: Sir John Guinness (standing, wearing glasses) shortly after he became Chairman of BNFL. Here he is hosting a lunch party for company employees who received awards in the 1992 New Years Honours, including me. (I am semi-seated, left of picture, and my wife Sheila is seated on the left, in front of me.

Above: The summer 2009 get together of the *Financial Times* gourmets. Here we are pre-dinner at the Old Rectory, Farnham, in Dorset, where we stayed before we walked across the road to the Michelin recommended Museum Inn for another memorable evening. Standing left to right, David Walker, Ena Moreton, Tony Moreton, me, and Ray Dafter. Seated left to right, Anne Hand, Christine Dafter, Pat Walker and my wife, Sheila, wearing the dark glasses because of her dry eyes, a condition which is insufficiently researched. Unfortunately, Michael and Linda Cassell were unable to make it on this occassion. Here's to the next time!

Below: Not many state-owned industry directors dress (or undress) like this! Here I am in the role of the Kralahome, or chief minister, in 'The King and I'. In the foreground is Linda Townson, in the leading role of Anna.

Right: Strutting my stuff (right of picture) as Honore in 'Gigi' (the Maurice Chevalier part in the film) with my old friend Liam Sammon as Gaston, left of picture.

Below: My wife, Sheila, in the starring role of Madam Tiang, the King's No. 1 wife in 'The King and I', in which she was truly brilliant.

Above: Those were the days. Some of the former BNFL directors who served with Con Allday at one of their annual lunches. Left to right: Dr Bill Wilkinson, Roy Pilling, Sir John Hill, BNFL's (and my) first chairman, Alan Johnson, Con Allday, who succeeded Sir John as Chairman, Dr Donald Avery, John Hayles and me.

Below: My old friend Roland Gribben's take on my decision to resign from BNFL in March 1993. Roly was Business Editor of the *Daily Telegraph* at the time the story made every national newspaper and the main radio and television news bulletins.

BNFL director quits over house decoration bills

By Roland Gribben, Business Editor

A DIRECTOR of British Nuclear Fuels resigned yesterday after part of the bill for decorating work at his present and former homes was sent to the company for payment.

Harold Bolter, 55, company secretary and director of corporate affairs, said he was unaware the company had been billed for the work, carried out by a contractor, who also worked for the company, but added: "Ignorance is no excuse for what has happened."

He offered his resignation after an internal inquiry into the reasons for the bill. He told the inquiry he should have been more careful in checking what he thought was an attractive tender for the work.

Mr Bolter, a former Financial Times journalist, who joined the company 17 years ago to head up the public relations operation, is believed to have received a compensation package but his entitlement has been reduced. His salary was £80,000.

The company said the financial details surrounding his departure were confidential but added: "The terms which Mr Bolter receives will reflect the circumstances in which he is leaving the company."

Mr Bolter, described as the most important executive in the company behind Neville Chamberlain, chief executive, has played a key role in defending the company against nuclear and environmental critics and in opening Sellafield, the main nuclear reprocessing centre, to the public.

A colleague said: "He has behaved impeccably. He has operated an open and honest policy and has taken the view that as a director he has to be above reproach."

Mr Bolter, who was made a CBE last year, said he would fully reimburse the company.

The work was carried out by the contractor at his former home in Sale, Cheshire, and present home at Warrington, Cheshire.

He said: "As a director of BNFL I should have been wary about accepting an offer of assistance from contractors working for BNFL and more vigilant in checking the bills I received.

"In the circumstances it is right that I leave the company, which I wish well."

See City Comment

Harold Bolter: 'I should have been more vigilant'

Above: Jack Cunningham, MP, right with the umbrella, keeps his leader, Neil Kinnock MP, dry as they walk through Whitehaven town centre, in the heart of Jack's constituency in the 1980s. I met Kinnock on this visit and discussed Sellafield with him. Tim Knowles, then Works Secretary at Sellafield, is with the two MPs, who are now together again in the House of Lords.

Below: Meet the family. The day I was appointed a Commander of the Order of the British Empire (CBE). Left to right: my daughter Sarah, my wife Sheila, me, daughter Helen and son Matthew.

campaigned against the legislation when it was still at the Bill stage and there were a series of one-day strikes up and down the country in protest against the law being used against the trade unions as planned. The largest stoppage involved 1.5 million workers and had a particularly damaging impact on the motor industry, the docks and newspapers.

After the Bill received Royal Assent in September 1971 the TUC voted to require its member unions not to comply with its provisions – an out-and-out challenge to the authority of the government and, indeed, the law.

It wasn't only the trade unions who opposed Heath's Industrial Relations Act, however. Many employers felt it was unworkable.

Campbell Adamson, who had been Director General of the CBI for about two years when the Act came into force, always claimed that his biggest achievement in the seven years he was at the CBI was to persuade the Confederation's members to hold back price rises during 1971 and 1972, without which Heath's pay and prices policy would never have taken off. That is as may be. But some of us knew that Adamson was no supporter of the Industrial Relations Act and Ted Heath's attempt to control the trade unions through the legal system, which he regarded as socially divisive.

The mining industry was hugely important to the country's energy supply at this time. With 280,000 members the National Union of Mineworkers was also one of the most influential trade unions and the NUM was the first union to flex its muscles. In January 1972 the miners began a pay strike, picketing coal depots, open cast mines, ports and power stations, in defiance of the law – a foretaste of what was to come.

The Wilberforce Court of Inquiry effectively ended the strike with 22 percent pay increase recommendations, giving Ted Heath a bloody nose and convincing the chattering classes that the country was becoming ungovernable.

There was even discussion within the *Financial Times* hierarchy, led by Fredy Fisher, the man being groomed to succeed Sir Gordon Newton as editor, that it might be necessary to bring in the military to restore order. The name of Brigadier Sir Otho Prior-Palmer, a former Tory MP and father of one of the FT's golden graduates, was mentioned as a possible controller of the southwest of England, where he lived.

I was one of those counselling caution. Bad as the situation was, I thought we were in danger of over-reacting and making ourselves look silly. In the end the FT did not come out in support of the country becoming a military dictatorship.

Economically, the following year was not much different – more pay restrictions and another Bill to regulate prices, pay, dividend and rents, this time for a three-year period. And all the time, in the background, there was still the Industrial Relations Act which was so hated by the trade unions. Something had to give.

Once again it was the miners who brought the matter to a head when the NUM executive announced that the miners would hold a full-scale national strike, with no holds barred, to start from February 7th 1974.

Ted Heath immediately called a general election, to take place on February 28th, on the issue of 'Who Governs Britain?' The titles given by the two main political parties to their manifestos provided the electorate with a fair indication of the way they intended to go forward should they win the election. The Tories used the slogan: 'Firm Action For A Fair Britain'. Labour chose: 'Let Us Work Together – Labour's Way Out of the Crisis'.

The electorate chose the easier option, Labour's promise of more of those ineffective Downing Street talks – but it was a close-run thing.

In its eve of election editorial the *Financial Times* had fully supported Heath's decision to go to the country on the issue of 'Who Governs Britain?' arguing that it was the only way of avoiding either the misery of a long strike or the larger consequences of agreeing to the miners' demands.

I wasn't consulted. Had I been I would have asked whoever wrote the leader: 'And what do you do when the trade unions continue to defy the government and the law, declare a State of Emergency and bring in the military?'

Ted Heath resigned once it was clear that he couldn't form a government and blamed Campbell Adamson, Director General of the CBI, for the Conservatives' election defeat. Two days before the general election, Adamson had made a speech to the Industrial Relations Society at what he thought was a private meeting – a dangerous assumption. Asked what the Conservatives should do with the Industrial Relations Act if they won the election he replied: 'If I were them I would try to get close to the unions and hammer out something better.'

These words, which I reported, created a political sensation and Adamson was forced to tender his resignation, although he didn't withdraw his words. In the end his resignation was refused after extremely strong support was shown for him from senior members of the CBI staff, but he never had the authority among the CBI's members which he had previously enjoyed.

Campbell Adamson was knighted in 1976 during the Labour government's period in office, probably confirming Ted Heath's suspicions about him. He went on to become chairman of the Abbey National Building Society, where he had a major impact on the UK's building societies, effectively beginning the movement which saw most of them changing their status from mutual ownership to that of public companies.

Ted Heath returned to the back benches of the House of Commons, where he sulked for a quarter of a century.

Campbell Adamson had a highly successful career in the steel industry before becoming Director General of the CBI. He must have been a possible choice as chairman of the British Steel Corporation when the second steel nationalisation brought together 90 percent of the UK steel industry, with 268,500 employees, in 1967.

The man actually chosen was Julian Mond, later Lord Melchett, who had a merchant banker background. He had chaired the committee which planned the second steel industry nationalisation and was well aware that the industry was in a state of crisis when he took over the top job. The nature of steel making was changing rapidly – the Japanese were beginning to pose a serious threat to the European steel makers and there was no longer a need for over a quarter of a million steel workers.

Lord Melchett adopted a softly softly approach towards the problems of bringing more realism into the industry and had some success, although he sometimes showed his frustration about having five ministers to whom he was directly responsible.

When Lord Melchett died of a heart attack in 1973, after six years as chairman of BSC, he was succeeded by his number two, Sir Monty Finniston. Where Lord Melchett was urbane, cultured and subtle, Sir Monty was dynamic, confident and impatient to get things done. His long-term vision was of a state-owned steel industry which would employ around 50,000 workers, a fifth of the workforce he inherited.

The emphasis, of course, had to be on the long term. No government would countenance public discussion of a redundancy programme on that scale and certainly not a Labour government.

In 1974 Sir Monty set out his strategy for what he regarded as a gradual transition to a slimmed-down steel industry, one involving an initial reduction of around 20,000 in the workforce and another 20,000 redundancies later. Tony Benn, Secretary of State for Industry, didn't regard that as gradual and told Sir Monty to review the strategy.

Somewhat provocatively Sir Monty wrote to Mr Benn saying that the British Steel Corporation was losing £2.5 million a week and now needed to shed a further 20,000 workers if it was to remain viable – on top of the 40,000 jobs set to disappear in the Corporation's long-term strategy proposals. His letter was released to the press, including me.

At first the Secretary of State took Sir Monty's entry into public debate on the future of the steel industry rather well.

'As you well know I have always strongly favoured the rights of the Chairmen and Board members of nationalised industries to speak their minds openly and plainly on matters that appear to them to be of concern to their industries or to the public generally,' Mr Benn wrote in a letter to Sir Monty which was also copied to the press.

'You will know that recent reports of your statements have caused concern and anxiety to those who work in the steel industry and to the communities in which some of these plants are situated.'

This was an obvious reproof and Sir Monty couldn't resist replying, publicly of course.

'We are acutely conscious of the human and social problems involved, but the Corporation looks to the Government of the day to support us constantly in the essential strategy of producing a modern steel industry, for on this depends in the years to come the jobs and wealth of those in the industry and of the many more in the industries down-stream of them,' Sir Monty wrote.

Note the reference to 'the Government of the day'. Later Sir Monty was to make a more straightforward reference to the fragility of elected governments by stating that 'Government and Ministers come and go but the steel industry has to make decisions, the consequences of which will be felt for decades.'

Sir Monty also rallied support from other nationalised industry chairmen, 18 of whom – including Sir Monty and led by Sir Richard Marsh, Chairman of British Railways – met at BSC's headquarters and agreed to make a joint approach to the prime minister, Harold Wilson, to urge him to curb Whitehall intervention in the state sector.

Lord Robens, the former chairman of the National Coal Board, who had himself managed a sizeable redundancy programme during his time at the NCB, also weighed in on Sir Monty's behalf. The former Alf Robens, once a leading light in the Labour Party, described Tony Benn's decision to ask Sir Monty for an explanation for planned manpower cuts in the steel industry as 'unwarranted interference'.

'Unless you want nationalised industries run by fifth-rate rabbits you had better pay attention to the fact that men are free men and entitled to express themselves in any way they desire,' Lord Robens said, again in a published letter.

Sir Monty Finniston rang me at the office late one night, just as I'd finished typing up the latest episode in the Benn–Finniston slanging match.

'Harold. It's Monty Finniston here.'

'Hello Monty. What can I do for you?'

'I hope you don't mind, but if you're not too busy I'd like to talk to you about how you think things are going – off the record, as a friend.'

'I'm not sure I know what you mean Monty.' I like and admire Monty, *someone who also came from an impoverished background, but I haven't thought of myself as his friend.*

'Do you think we're managing to get our message over that there have to be redundancies if the industry is to survive and become viable long term? Is there anything else we should be doing?'

'I can't think of anything. The need for cut-backs is getting a lot of coverage.'

'What about the public debate with Tony Benn? How do you think that's going?'

'As far as I'm concerned it's great stuff. A public row makes great copy, great headlines. But is it what you want?'

'What do you mean?'

'Do you want to keep your job or is this row with Benn a sort of last hurrah?'

'Of course I want to stay at the Corporation. I've a lot to do.'

'Well, you're going a funny way about it. The simple fact is that Tony Benn is your boss. He is in a position to fire you. You are not in a position to fire him. Although he might exasperate Harold Wilson at times,

113

the PM is not going to sack Benn over this issue. He's getting a lot of flack himself from the steel industry constituencies.'

'But I'm getting a lot of support.'

'Mainly from other nationalised industry chairmen and a few news-paper leader writers. I think you've probably already gone too far with that stuff about ministers may come and ministers may go and the need for them to think and act in the long-term interest of the industries they're responsible for. They rarely do you know.'

'That's too cynical for me. Anyway Harold, thanks for being frank. Goodnight.'

Sir Monty Finniston left the British Steel Corporation shortly afterwards, to be succeeded by Sir Charles Villiers.

I didn't realise it at the time but my days at the *Financial Times* were numbered too, but in my case my departure was my own choice.

The writing had been on the wall from the time Fredy Fisher succeeded Sir Gordon Newton as editor on January 1st 1973. Fredy had a German-Jewish background and never lost his accent. It made him sound aggres-sive even when he was trying to be friendly. He's described in David Kynaston's centenary history as not the easiest of people to work with and I agree with that assessment. Kynaston provides the most telling descrip-tion of the Fredy Fisher I knew.

He came over as authoritarian and didn't seem very interested in other people's ideas. I suspect that he realised he could never emulate Newton, a recognition that translated into bombast.

Fredy's news editor was David Prior-Palmer, son of Sir Otho. I found him not dissimilar to Fredy – abrasive, opinionated and something of an empire builder. He persuaded Fisher that although I'd been running the industrial department without interference from Doug York for some years I should henceforth report to him.

Two events stand out as the catalysts for my decision to leave the FT. When Britain entered the Common Market I was asked by Prior-Palmer to go back to the West Midlands, interview some of the industrialists I knew, and produce a feature describing the effect they thought entry into Europe would have on their businesses.

It all sounded a bit like the brief I was given when asked to write about the British Standard Time experiment. Nevertheless, I set up the interviews and booked into a Birmingham hotel. A few days before I was due to set off on my travels I received a telephone call from Robert Mauthner, the FT's Paris correspondent.

He explained to me that he had been asked by David Prior-Palmer to go to the West Midlands and produce a feature on how industrialists there regarded entry into the Common Market, from the perspective of a journalist working on the continent. Could I let him have a list of my contacts please?

I was furious. The idea for the feature was a perfectly good one, but replacing me with Mauthner, which would involve me telling my contacts that someone else would now be talking to them, most certainly was not. I tackled Prior-Palmer and was brushed aside.

'I don't have to explain my decisions to you any more than I do to any of the other reporters on this paper,' he said.

'Well I think you do. I'm not just any reporter. I am industrial editor and that should mean something, even to you,' I replied.

But I knew that Prior-Palmer was right. He was the coming man. I was probably the one that was going to have to go.

The event that finally convinced me to look for a job elsewhere was a brief conversation that I had with Fredy Fisher.

'Harold,' he said. 'This man David Walker who works for you. I have just found out that he has a First and is a Scholar of St Catherine's College, Cambridge. He is wasted as an industrial news reporter. I am going to move him to the features desk. I see him as a future features editor.'

I realised then that the FT would return to its old ways, with the emphasis placed on the feature writers, and the news reporters merely tolerated as unfortunate necessities.

If Fredy had bothered to ask me what post I thought David Walker was best suited to fill I would have told him that he should be doing the job which had been given to David Prior-Palmer, that of news editor.

Eventually, in the late 1970s, David Walker did become news editor and a very good one. Kynaston's history describes him as 'the very reliable David Walker, who possessed a complete grip on detail and valued clear, lucid, unjargonised reporting'. That is precisely what I would have expected from him.

It took me a little time after these two incidents to find the post that I thought would suit me. My options were to switch to another national newspaper, if a post became available or could be engineered, to branch out as a freelance journalist, or to move into public relations, selling your soul as most reporters think of it.

It took a lot of thought and a remarkably encouraging interview with Con Allday, Chief Executive of British Nuclear Fuels, who told me that he saw me as a future director of his company, to help me make up my mind.

Fredy Fisher tried hard to persuade me to stay with the *Financial Times* but I'd reached my decision. I sold my soul – and got a very good price for it.

9

The Nuclear Salesman

I started working for British Nuclear Fuels Limited two weeks before the company began to pay for my services. That may seem generous of me, but I was moving to BNFL for a salary increase of 50 percent and my future employer obviously needed help. Billions of pounds worth of business was potentially at stake.

It was the morning of Tuesday 21st October 1975 when my elder daughter Helen appeared in the bedroom carrying a copy of the *Daily Mirror*. I'd been working late on a story for the *Financial Times* the night before and was trying to have a lie-in.

'Mummy thought you should see this straight away,' Helen said. 'It's about your new job.'

The *Mirror*'s front page lead was headed 'Plan To Make Britain World's Nuclear Dustbin'. The story attacked BNFL's proposed construction of a £3 billion thermal oxide reprocessing plant (THORP) at Windscale, now known as Sellafield,

As soon as I read the *Mirror* piece I realised that it was dynamite and that I was in for an explosive start to my new role as Director of Information at BNFL. My concerns were confirmed when I took a telephone call from Brian Potts, who described himself as a press officer. I later learned that he wasn't just any old press officer, he was the only press officer BNFL had at the time.

'It's Brian Potts here Mr Bolter. Have you seen the Mirror*?'*

'Yes. I've got it in front of me. Incidentally, you'd better call me Harold if we're to work together.'

'Okay. Con Allday asked me to give you a ring. He wonders if you

can give us some advice on how to deal with the Mirror *story.' Con Allday, BNFL's Chief Executive, is the man who recruited me.*

'Fine. But let's discuss the piece first Brian. What do you know about it? Why isn't there a BNFL comment in it? Tony Benn's quoted as welcoming the story as a valuable contribution to public debate about nuclear power. They obviously had time to get a quote from him.'

'They didn't ask us for a comment. Ronnie Bedford, the science editor, rang me at home to warn me about the story. He said he knew it was nonsense but there was nothing he could do to stop it. He was only consulted after the first edition had been put to bed.'

'What do you know about Stanley Bonnet – the reporter who wrote it?'

'Even that's not certain. It's all a bit mysterious. Ronnie Bedford thinks Bryn Jones may be behind it.'

'Bryn Jones? The industrial reporter? I don't get it. Never mind, let's leave that for later. Have you drafted a response statement yet?'

'No. I thought I'd speak to you first. I've had a lot of calls from other papers already. And the television people. The Express *seems keen to shoot the* Mirror *piece down.'*

'Surprise, surprise. Now what I want you to do is to draft a statement setting out the arguments for THORP – if you haven't got something drafted already.'

'No, we haven't. We've never faced anything like this before.'

'Okay then. Draft something and come back to me. I'll be at the FT. Talk about the tremendous benefits THORP will bring to the engineering and construction industries, the jobs it will create in an area of high unemployment, the export earnings it will draw in, the value to the UK electricity utilities of us building a plant of an optimum size ... You know the sort of thing.'

Con Allday has talked to me at length about THORP at my job interview so I know quite a bit about the arguments for the plant.

'By the way Brian, do you have anything on reprocessing which can be sent out quickly to the press and the people we believe support nuclear power – something in lay terms? If you have I'd find a copy useful.'

'No, we don't have anything like that. Only publicity material.'

I came off the phone feeling confused. The adrenalin was flowing and I was looking forward to starting my new job. But I also felt concerned. From my short conversation with Brian it was clear to me that I had a great deal to sort out at BNFL.

I agreed the statement prepared by Brian Potts later that morning. A shortened version of it appeared in the *Financial Times*. My old colleague David Fishlock, the paper's science editor, was quick to point out that the *Mirror*'s story was not a new one and that he'd written about THORP months earlier. The trouble was that where David saw THORP as a success story, the *Mirror* saw it as a public disgrace and a threat to health, safety, the universe and goodness knows what else.

The 'dustbin' story was followed up by every national newspaper and a piece was carried on all of the radio and television news bulletins. It was open season on BNFL and Windscale, and the media weighed in with a mixture of serious analytical stories and a few pieces of absolute nonsense.

One of the tabloids ran a story about blackberries as big as cricket balls growing in a lane near the site because of the effects of radiation. It didn't pinpoint where these freaks of nature were growing, of course, and there were no pictures of them either.

Another ran an interview with a councillor from the north east, on holiday at Cockermouth, who had popped across to look at the Windscale site and been horrified to find the trees nearby withered and stripped of all their foliage.

'Where was this?' I asked the paper's reporter.

'He says it's just outside Whitehaven, up a steep hill, overlooking the rugby league ground,' came the reply.

'The man's an idiot. That's Marchon, Albright and Wilson's detergent factory. The effects of its chemical discharges are well known in the area. Marchon's at least ten miles away from Windscale.'

'Oh. I see.' But no apology and no correction.

Gradually I pieced together how the *Daily Mirror*'s attack on THORP came about. There were three men behind the piece and the flood of adverse publicity which followed in its wake. The unlikely trio consisted of a 'Friend' who was no friend of nuclear power or, in my view, of the environment either, a *Daily Mirror* reporter who was too shy to put his name to a front page lead story and the government minister responsible for nuclear energy, who was meant to be its main defender in the Commons but seemed determined to kill the industry off.

The Friend was Walt Patterson, the chief anti-nuclear spokesman of

Friends of the Earth. He'd written a pamphlet some months earlier which claimed that THORP would make Windscale 'One of the World's Most Radioactive Nuclear Dustbins'.

Walt was later to admit that he was embarrassed by the headline put on his piece. He prided himself on his scientific knowledge and knew very well that it had never been BNFL's intention to dump spent nuclear fuel from the UK and overseas nuclear power stations at Windscale. The plan had always been to reprocess, or recycle, the fuel.

FoE's real concern was that as part of reprocessing a small amount of plutonium would be separated out from the spent fuel. In the case of BNFL's overseas customers this would be returned to them. The FoE was opposed to the shipment of separated plutonium around the world because of the possibility of it being released into the environment as a result of an accident at sea. It was also afraid that plutonium might be stolen by terrorists or pirates and made into crude weapons or used for blackmail purposes.

Those are perfectly legitimate concerns, it seems to me, but they don't justify the 'nuclear dustbin' tag which has dogged the Sellafield site on and off for the last 30 years.

The *Daily Mirror* journalist involved was Bryn Jones, as Brian Potts had suspected from his conversation with Ronnie Bedford. I found out later that Bryn had strong environmentalist views and realised that his name on the story would discredit it. He'd therefore persuaded Stanley Bonnet, the *Mirror*'s education correspondent, to put his by-line on the piece.

Bryn Jones was someone I knew from my days writing about industry for the FT. He'd simply taken Walt Patterson's pamphlet and the headline put on it and worked it up into an 'exclusive' front page splash for the *Daily Mirror*. The story was a straightforward crib from the Friends of the Earth article and so was the headline.

For some time I thought that Walt and Bryn had been working together in an attempt to halt the THORP project, but now I'm not so sure. In later years Walt Patterson complained that Bryn Jones's version of what he had written was 'augmented with numerous technical errors'.

Bryn Jones left journalism not long after his 'dustbin' coup and joined the environmental group formed and financed by Anita Roddick, of Bodyshop fame, as a full-time campaigner. His career move came as no surprise to me.

The government minister who welcomed the *Mirror* story despite its 'numerous technical errors', as Walt Patterson put it, was my old friend Tony Benn, the Secretary of State for Energy. Until the *Mirror* piece appeared, most of the people who worked for BNFL thought that Benn supported nuclear power and the company's aspirations to become a leading player in the world-wide nuclear fuel and reprocessing industry.

'I don't understand him,' Brian Potts said in one of our early conversations. 'It's not so long ago that he came to Risley and begged people not to leave BNFL to take up better paid jobs in the States.

'He used a pipe-smoking analogy. He said that the industry might not sell many pipes, the nuclear reactors of the business, but it could sell plenty of tobacco, the fuel. It was all very reassuring.'

Benn's performance in the wake of the *Mirror*'s 'dustbin' story was far from reassuring. In fact it seemed to me to be downright antagonistic. I've no idea to this day what changed his attitude to nuclear power so quickly. Was it a developing concern about the safety of nuclear power? Was it his obvious delight in public debate? Was it a straightforward preference for coal-fired power stations, despite their effects on the environment, which were recognised even then?

Or was it simply that the National Union of Mineworkers lobbied him with their concerns about the growing role of nuclear power in the energy mix and what they saw as a threat to their industry? At that time the NUM was a power in the land and had considerable influence within the Labour Party, which Benn hoped one day to lead.

What I do know is that largely because of the actions taken by Tony Benn after the *Mirror* piece appeared I was kept busier than I'd ever been in my life. First of all I had to get to know and understand the strange culture of the industry I had joined. British Nuclear Fuels was formed out of the production group of the United Kingdom Atomic Energy Authority in 1971, four years before I was recruited, and was still bedding down.

Its attitudes were those of the civil service, from which it had emerged. People were addressed by their surnames, with or without the Mr, and there was a preoccupation with job grades. 'Jones is only an SEO you know.' Titles such as CA, CO, EO, HEO, SEO, Banded and Senior Staff were common currency in everyday conversation.

The work ethic was different, too. I was used to working whatever hours were necessary. My new colleagues were used to working the hours agreed with the civil service unions, which had been carried over into BNFL. Fridays were known as 'POETS Day' the polite version of which is 'Push Off Early Tomorrow's Saturday'.

My first positive action when I took up my new post as a public relations man was to write the lay person's guide to reprocessing which was so sadly missing when I joined BNFL. I did it by doing a straightforward reporting job, interviewing the company specialists – at least those prepared to talk to me – and knocking out a piece which I understood and that other lay people might therefore be expected to understand.

When my finished effort was circulated Con Allday thought it was exactly what was needed and agreed that it should be sent out to all MPs – including Tony Benn – as well as members of the House of Lords and all the company's main contractors, the businesses which stood to benefit from THORP going ahead.

At it simplest, when uranium-based nuclear fuel is taken out of a reactor it consists of 97 percent unused uranium, some of which can be used again. Up to 1 percent is plutonium, which can be used as a fuel in fast reactors or mixed with uranium to make fuel for conventional reactors. The remaining 2 to 3 percent is fission product waste. Reprocessing separates these products out.

It was obvious to me that one of the MPs whom I should meet as quickly as possible was Dr John Cunningham, the MP for Whitehaven, who had Windscale in his constituency. I asked Arthur Scott, BNFL's Company Secretary, to whom I reported, what was known about Dr Cunningham, who is known in Cumbria as Jack.

'I think he's against us,' Arthur said. 'We're just getting over a strike at Windscale and he supported the workers' pay claim in public.' Arthur had personnel as one of his briefs as well as the new public relations department which I headed.

'Well of course he supported the workers, Arthur,' I replied, the surprise in my voice. 'He's a Labour MP for goodness sake. Most of the Sellafield workforce probably vote for him and some of them will work for him in his constituency.'

I was astonished to learn that no one of any seniority in the company had ever met Jack Cunningham to discuss his views on nuclear power. I saw Con Allday and suggested that he and I had dinner with Jack, who was and is a true friend of nuclear power. And a true friend of mine, too.

The three of us went to the Boulestin restaurant near Covent Garden, an old haunt of mine from my days in journalism. Con, Jack and I got on very well from the start and it was an extremely successful – and convivial – working dinner.

We found that Jack, with a chemistry degree and a PhD, understood the nature of nuclear power and reprocessing in particular far better than most people outside the industry – and certainly far better than his boss, Tony Benn. Jack was Minister of Energy, a position in which he could obviously be very helpful – but he had to tread carefully.

As part of my programme of education for MPs and the general reporters who were now covering BNFL's affairs in place of the science writers I took a party of journalists up to Cumbria to see the existing reprocessing plant at Windscale. This one dealt with spent fuel from the first generation Magnox power stations.

Like them I found our tour around the plants involved with radioactive materials distinctly eerie. We walked round to the accompaniment of the insistent bleep of the permanent alarm system, which echoed through the cavernous buildings.

'What the hell's that?' one of the reporters asked me.

'It's the alarm system.'

'Why are we still here then? Shouldn't we get out?'

'No, no. The time to get out is if the bleep stops. While it's bleeping we know that the alarm system's working properly.' The reporter seemed far from convinced.

As they went in and out of the various plants the journalists had to don white overalls and put protective plastic covers over their shoes. Both were handed in as they left a particular area – to be washed, in the case of the overalls, and taken away to be treated as low-level radioactive waste, in the case of the shoe covers – just in case they'd picked up tiny bits of radioactive material.

As they went in and out of the plants the reporters passed through barriers with installed monitors checking that they didn't have anything nasty on them. Some of them seemed concerned about the process but they all put a brave face on things. So did I – I was new to all of this too.

After the tour round Windscale I took the party on to Barrow in Furness, the home port of the ships used for transporting spent fuel from the Magnox reactors which the UK had sold abroad and which BNFL supplied with fuel. At Barrow the transport flasks containing the fuel were unloaded and transferred to the railways for the short journey up to Windscale. By coincidence Fishers, the company operating the ships on behalf of BNFL, was expecting the arrival of a ship from Italy within days.

Stanley Bonnet, the man who'd lent his name to Bryn Jones's 'dustbin' story was on the trip I organised. He confirmed that he'd had nothing to do with writing the piece with which he'd been credited and seemed to find the whole thing a huge joke. I told him that in my opinion Bryn, with his help, had stitched up his own newspaper.

The ship bringing spent fuel from Italy for reprocessing at Windscale was several days late arriving in port because of engine trouble. Stanley kept teasing me that he was going to write a piece saying the ship was missing, possibly sunk. He didn't do so. A continuing supply of scotch may have helped to calm his fevered imaginings.

Media interest in BNFL's reprocessing operation gradually died down and I thought it would be possible for me to relax and take stock of what I'd inherited by way of a public relations department. Tony Benn had other ideas.

Bernard Ingham, then a Labour Party supporter and Director of Information at the Department of Energy, warned me that his Secretary of State would not be satisfied until there'd been a widespread public debate about the future of the THORP project.

In an attempt to meet Benn's wishes I set up a series of debates and lectures in town halls, church halls and leisure centres throughout West Cumbria, places where it seemed to me that people had a legitimate interest in the issues raised by THORP. I found that there was as much interest in the plant's potential for creating jobs as in its safety.

People in that part of the world had lived with atomic energy for nearly 30 years by then and many of them didn't take kindly to the idea of 'off comers' from Friends of the Earth telling them what they should be worried about.

The dozens of meetings which I organised in that isolated part of Britain were not enough for Tony Benn, however. I was advised by Bernard that his boss wanted a set-piece public debate in London. He came up with the idea of BNFL organising – and paying for – a debate at Church House, Westminster.

At Bernard's suggestion Tony Benn was invited to introduce the debate, which was chaired by Sir George Porter, and he kindly agreed to do so. Getting him to stay away might have been more of a problem.

The BNFL speakers were Con Allday, BNFL's Chief Executive, and Peter Mummery, then General Manager of the Sellafield site. Walt Patterson, from Friends of the Earth, and Dr Paul Smoker, someone I'd never heard of, represented those opposed to reprocessing.

The debate took place on Thursday January 16th 1976 and lasted all day. I sat through speech after speech and question after question and was possibly the only person in the hall to do so. It was tedious and repetitive, but it did the trick as far as Tony Benn was concerned.

On March 12th he announced that the government had decided that BNFL could take on reprocessing work for overseas customers, subject to the negotiation of satisfactory terms, including the option to return radio-active waste to the country of origin – which was always the intention anyway, as Benn well knew.

The following month Friends of the Earth tried to breathe some life back into its anti-THORP campaign by chartering a British Rail train and taking supporters up to Cumbria to debate the issues yet again with BNFL management and trade union representatives. I decided to treat the event as a positive PR opportunity.

To their surprise we welcomed our visitors with open arms, arranging a platform and microphones for the speakers just outside the Sellafield site's perimeter fence. Local caterers were tipped off about the potential business and sold the protestors food and hot drinks during slack moments. I even had a special issue of the company's newspaper, *BNFL News*, published, welcoming the protesters to Cumbria and explaining what reprocessing was all about. I suspected that some of them had no idea what they were protesting against. Copies were placed on the seats of the train for them to read on their return journey to London. I didn't want to antagonise them by handing out the paper while they were still near the security fence in case they tried to storm it.

Just in case there was trouble we had UKAEA policemen hidden from view behind a canteen building while the interminable debate went on – well hidden because I didn't want a pitched battle to break out in front of the television cameras.

The event went so well from our point of view that Martyn Lewis, then the northern correspondent of ITV, reported for ITN News that he wasn't sure whether the Friends of the Earth protest was a pro-nuclear or anti-nuclear demonstration.

The press gradually lost interest again and BNFL was able to put in a planning application for permission to build THORP to Cumbria County Council. After a lot of prevarication the council found a way to duck the issue and pass the proposal back to the government for consideration by the Department of the Environment.

The company came very close to getting a quick and favourable decision from the Cabinet but the Windscale management somehow contrived to turn a relatively small incident on the site into a political hot potato. The incident involved a leak of mildly radioactive material from a clapped-out plant which the site management tried to cover up.

'Clapped-out' may sound like a harsh description of the condition of nuclear plants which the public expect to be kept ultra safe but it was an accurate one at that time. The dictionary definition of the expression says that it means 'worn out from age or heavy use' and there is no denying that some of the buildings and equipment at Windscale fitted the description.

Shortly after I joined BNFL, the company's then chairman, Sir John Hill, briefed Tony Benn about the state of the Windscale site and the site's history. Later he discussed their conversation with me. Sir John apparently reminded Benn that Windscale was established as a weapons site and that its early task was to produce plutonium for the atomic bomb. With the Russians thought to be poised to march on Berlin and then on to Britain, speed was of the essence and site safety was a secondary consideration. If and when mistakes were made and radioactive material was spilled it was simply covered up where it fell.

Then there was the famous Windscale fire of 1957 – the UK's biggest nuclear accident – when one of the plutonium-producing reactors caught fire. Sir John, who played a major role in dealing with the aftermath of this incident, reminded the Secretary of State that the fire had been put out with 300,000 tons of water, which went right through the stricken plant and into the ground, carrying radioactive debris with it.

I have no doubt that Sir John's intention was to underline the case for the government funding the massive clean-up of the Windscale site, in preparation for it to become a major civil nuclear power facility. I'm not sure that Tony took the point however. Sir John's impression was that his main reaction was one of horror.

It wasn't only the old military plants which were in a poor state either. One of the clapped-out plants which so concerned Sir John Hill was the one that was found to be leaking just as I thought THORP was on the point of being approved by the Cabinet.

It was an old concrete silo containing the magnesium oxide cladding removed from spent Magnox fuel before the fuel itself was reprocessed. This cladding had to be kept under water in the silo, known as B38 (B stands for Building) because of the danger of spontaneous combustion and an explosion.

Water from the 12-year-old silo had leaked and was leaking. Nobody knows how long this had been going on, but when the Windscale management stumbled on the problem it was leaking at the rate of over 100 gallons a day – hardly the seepage which the site told me I could call it. It's probable that tens of thousands of gallons of mildly contaminated water had soaked into the ground.

The leak was discovered by accident on October 10th 1976 when the site management was excavating ground near the old silo with a view to building a new one next to it. It took a fortnight for the management to inform regional officials of the Nuclear Installations Inspectorate of the event. Their counterparts at the Department of the Environment were told even later. These are the health and safety and environmental protection agencies responsible for monitoring the operation of nuclear plants.

But the NII and DoE still heard about the leak long before I did. I didn't hear about the problem for another two months – and neither did Con Allday.

I learned about it from Jack Cunningham who rang me to ask what I knew about a leak at Windscale. He'd been told about it by Denis Howell, one of his MP colleagues, who'd picked up a rumour in the House of Commons. I told Jack that I doubted whether the rumour could be true as I hadn't heard about any leak.

It was only too true, of course. Tony Benn was told about the incident on December 8th and BNFL issued a public statement, virtually an apology, which I wrote. The Secretary of State was furious with Con Allday for not telling him about the leak and wanted heads to roll. Con wouldn't tell him that he'd been kept in the dark about the incident himself. It would only have added to the pressure for someone to be sacked. Con's sympathies were with the people struggling to manage a site bedevilled by problems left behind by the early nuclear pioneers as Britain raced to get to the atom bomb.

Within days Tony Benn, still furious with Con Allday, issued an edict that in future any nuclear incident 'however apparently trivial' had to be reported to him. He would then decide whether to make the matter public. No private sector company would have stood for it, but BNFL was state owned and had to do what it was told.

I persuaded Con that Benn's instruction would leave the company too vulnerable to the views of the Secretary of State on the importance of an incident and to him choosing the timing of any subsequent public announcement. He might well have a different agenda, I argued, influenced as much by politics as considerations of the country's energy needs and BNFL's future viability.

We agreed that the company would issue a press release about every event reported to Tony Benn and the Department of Energy. Within BNFL the policy was known as 'boring for Britain' and it was still in place when I left the company.

A more serious consequence of the silo leak was that BNFL's planning application for THORP was made subject to a public inquiry, causing a delay which the French reprocessing company COGEMA seized upon. Instead of £12 billion of overseas earnings BNFL was lucky to keep half the business.

After the inquiry was announced, but before it began, there was a further complication for BNFL to take into account as it prepared its evidence. President Jimmy Carter announced that the Americans were going to wind down their reprocessing operations and stop work on the fast breeder reactor.

The Dounreay fast reactor in Scotland used plutonium as a fuel and it was one of the arguments for retaining reprocessing in the UK which was being worked up for the inquiry. Tony Benn wanted to comment on the US policy change but was forbidden to do so by Prime Minister Jim Callaghan. I assume Benn would have welcomed the US initiative if he'd been allowed to do so, embarrassing the government and BNFL.

What Jimmy Carter didn't say when he announced that reprocessing was to stop was that he was only talking about the US's civil reprocessing programme. The US carried on extracting plutonium for its weapons programme in its military plants and made up any shortfalls in quality material by buying it from the UK.

The Windscale Inquiry opened on June 14th 1977 and was conducted by Mr Justice Roger Parker, assisted by two independent technical assessors. It lasted 100 days. In the end BNFL received approval for the construction of THORP, much to the disappointment and anger of Friends of the Earth and the half dozen other anti-nuclear organisations which sprang up in the wake of the dustbin story, all of whom found ways to pay the not inconsiderable fees of the barristers who represented them.

This is not the place to delve into the detail of the myriad issues raised at the Windscale Inquiry, beyond saying that the proceedings were exhaustive and exhausting. My memories of the inquiry are more personal than technical.

I sat through every day of the proceedings. My main self-imposed task was to take a view on what had excited the press each day and feed this back to the lawyers and the BNFL technical team who were beavering away in a portable building at the back of the Whitehaven Civic Hall, where the inquiry was held.

In addition I produced notes on what I regarded as interesting bits of by-play between the lawyers, as though I was writing for, say, the Press Association or the *Daily Telegraph*. In fact I did write for the PA and the *Telegraph* occasionally as media interest in the inquiry started to flag. I also covered for other newspaper reporters who wanted to slip out from the Civic Hall for extended lunches or early evening assignations.

If the local freelance journalist meant to be covering the inquiry for the Press Association couldn't get to the Civic Hall I would put together a piece for him. He would then phone it through to PA for transmission to the nation's media. He was paid for the piece and I got the press coverage I wanted – not strictly ethical, but there you are.

Rather than leave a reporter up in Cumbria on the off-chance of something interesting happening, the *Daily Telegraph's* science editor Adrian Berry asked me to telephone anything I found interesting over to him in London. In effect I was the *Telegraph's* correspondent and several stories sourced by me duly appeared in the paper, as though written by an impartial news reporter. For this to work, of course, I had to be careful to report on evidence which was detrimental to the company's case from time to time as well. But it will be no surprise that the overall balance of my stories favoured approval being given for the construction of THORP.

My final memory of the Windscale Inquiry is of the camaraderie which built up among the people who were regulars at the inquiry and living away from home – BNFL staff, environmentalists and officials from the government departments sent up to Cumbria to provide administrative back-up for the inquiry. Barbecues, treasure hunts and quiz nights were organised and a five-a-side football league formed at the Whitehaven leisure centre. I played for BNFL as a somewhat immobile striker and apart from scoring a few goals I managed to tackle Walt Patterson rather heavily a couple of times as he ran past me.

But all good things must come to an end and the participants finally packed their bags on November 4th 1977 and left West Cumbria. Both sides were convinced that they had had the better of the argument.

Two weeks after the inquiry finished, Friends of the Earth threw a party in London to celebrate its end. Tony Benn, effectively the owner of Windscale, as Energy Secretary, and with an interest in the financial success of THORP, went along to it.

The word I was getting from within the Department of Energy was that the Secretary of State was very impressed with the performance of Walt Patterson and Tom Burke, FoE's director, at the inquiry and thought there was every chance that the THORP project would be turned down. He didn't seem too worried about it either.

Tony Benn might have thought that FoE had done very well at the Windscale Inquiry but Mr Justice Parker and his technical assessors did not. Nearly three months after the inquiry ended Mr Justice Parker recommended approval for THORP.

He did so in remarkably lucid and unequivocal terms and in language which could be readily understood by a lay readership. Tony Benn had expected the report to be more ambivalent, leaving scope for the government to order the THORP project to be delayed or abandoned. The chances are that with the man responsible within government for the nuclear power industry showing no great sympathy for the project, it would founder.

Con Allday threw a party for the BNFL staff who had been involved in the Windscale Inquiry at Cottons hotel near Knutsford. It was quite a celebration. Tony Benn wasn't invited to it. I doubt if he'd have come if he had been.

Predictably, the anti-nuclear groups didn't like the Parker report and a month after it appeared Friends of the Earth organised an anti-Windscale demonstration in Trafalgar Square. Tony Benn couldn't resist popping round to see and hear what he could, but at least he had the sense not to speak. He must have felt very frustrated.

Arthur Scargill, the leader of the National Union of Mineworkers, did speak, however. I found it quite extraordinary then – and still do – that Friends of the Earth was prepared to allow someone representing workers in probably the most polluting of the energy industries to share their platform. At the demonstration Scargill called for a programme of civil disobedience to 'Stop Windscale'. One might have expected the Secretary of State for Energy to frown on a call for people to flout the law and shut down a state-owned asset. Far from it.

Months later I learned that on the night of the 'Stop Windscale' rally Arthur Scargill, a great fan of Tony Benn whom he saw as a future leader of the Labour Party, had joined him and his wife Caroline for dinner at Benn's home, along with some sympathetic journalists. I'm sure it was a fun occasion but Windscale was not shut down.

Soon after the Parker report appeared, BNFL's Company Secretary, Arthur Scott, to whom I reported as Director of Information, announced his retirement. I received a tip-off from Arthur's secretary, the estimable Joan Byrne, that I was in the running for Scott's job but that if I wanted it I'd better show an interest. Joan was my secretary when I first joined BNFL but had joined Arthur on promotion when his secretary retired.

Comparing what it was like to work for the two of us Joan said that the difference between us was that Arthur Scott was a real gentleman. Clearly she didn't regard me as being in the same league in the gentlemanly stakes, but she still wanted to see me become company secretary.

Joan told me that there was a rumour that Peter Mummery, pulled back to Risley from Windscale after the B38 silo incident and then put in charge of the back-up team at the Windscale Inquiry, was being touted for the company secretary post by the Personnel Manager, Arthur Riddle. He was arguing that because I was doing a good job, and my post as Director of Information would be difficult to fill, I shouldn't be moved.

Con Allday asks to see me and Joan says it might be about Arthur Scott's job. Her friend Dorothy Ashurst, Con's secretary, isn't sure, which is unusual. Between them Dorothy and Joan usually know more about what's going on at Risley than the directors. They were both born in Leigh, not far from Risley, and are known as the Leigh mafia.

Con seems to be in an affable mood when I join him in his office. I take it as a good sign.

'Harold. I have a few ideas I want to discuss with you about the press office,' he says.

'Oh. I thought you wanted to talk about Arthur Scott's replacement. Rumour has it that it's a choice between me and Peter Mummery.'

'I wonder where you got that from,' Con says knowingly. He is aware of the Leigh mafia, too.

He gets up from his desk and walks across to the window, his back to me. He doesn't speak for a minute or so and I wonder if I've put my foot in it. I decide to prompt him – in for a penny, in for a pound.

'According to what I've heard, Con, you've decided not to make me company secretary because I'm doing too good a job where I am. I don't think that's fair. As I understand it you were sales director before you became chief executive and I'm sure somebody must have said that you couldn't be spared from the sales job, too.

'If BNFL's the sort of company that only promotes people who can be easily replaced, or who are going spare for some reason, then it's not the company I want to carry on working for.'

Con turns away from the window and smiles. He's obviously made his mind up.

'Right. Arthur's job is yours. But you'll have to continue to be responsible for public relations as well. I'm going to leave it up to you to find your own replacement and whoever you get will report to you.'

I leave the room, feeling pleased with myself. We've both forgotten what we were supposed to be talking about.

One of the departments which reported to me when I became company secretary was personnel. Arthur Riddle, who'd pushed Peter Mummery's candidacy, came to congratulate me soon after I took over. 'You were always my choice you know Harold,' he said.

The man I chose to succeed me as director of information was Jeffrey Preece, a former colleague of mine from my early days with the *Birmingham*

Post. Strictly speaking Jeff chose himself – he volunteered to join me when he heard about the job on the journalistic grapevine.

Jeff was ten years older than me and had worked for *The Times*, the BBC and the Central Electricity Generating Board as well as the *Post*. He was vastly experienced and a first-class communications practitioner. I was lucky to have him working with me as I eased my way into my new post.

With THORP finally approved and under construction I thought my fire-fighting days were over and that I could settle down with Jeffrey to work out a longer-term strategy for improving BNFL's public image and get to know the other departments for which I was now responsible as company secretary. It was not to be.

In March 1979, less than three years after excavation work had revealed the B38 silo leak which led to the THORP inquiry and less than 12 months after BNFL had been given permission to build THORP, they went digging at Windscale again.

This time they discovered that for at least eight years highly radioactive acid had been leaking into the ground from pipework in a building known as B701 which was supposed to have been shut down 21 years earlier. It was one of the clapped-out buildings Sir John Hill must have had in mind when he briefed Tony Benn about the state of the Windscale site.

'People forgot the building was there and they shouldn't have,' Con Allday told the *Financial Times*, somewhat ruefully.

Con and I were attending an overseas conference on the day the discovery was reported to Whitehall and he was meant to be addressing a plenary session next day. A Department of Energy official tracked Con down and told him Tony Benn wanted him to get back to London on the next available aircraft and meet him to discuss what had happened. Con was obviously in for another telling off.

'You'll have to make the speech tomorrow Harold,' Con said.

'You mean read it?'

'No. I mean make it. I haven't finished writing it yet. We'll sit down together after dinner and work something up.'

'What about George Inglis or Alan Johnson? They're board members. I'm not – and I'm not technical or scientific either. You know that. It's the plenary session remember. There'll be questions at the end. I could be made to look very, very stupid.'

'You'll cope. George is responsible for fuel manufacture and Alan for enrichment. They're not involved in reprocessing and they haven't been involved in the arguments over Sellafield and the THORP business. You have. You've learned a lot since you joined us.'

The next morning Con left for his meeting with Tony Benn and I made my way early to the hall where the conference plenary session was to be held, to be briefed on what was expected of me. I was told that a seat had been reserved for me on the front row and that when my name was called I was to make my way up a cat-walk onto the stage, where a lectern and microphone awaited me. I was to be the third speaker.

By the time the session began there were well over a thousand people in the hall. When I was called to speak it was explained that I was standing in for Con Allday. I made my way gingerly up the ramp to the platform. I was extremely nervous.

Con and I had worked up a vigorous case for reprocessing and THORP, and it turned out to be just what the audience, largely made up of nuclear scientists and engineers, wanted to hear. The response to what I had to say was very supportive.

I was followed by a speaker from the American nuclear industry, who tried to defend Jimmy Carter's decision to end civil nuclear fuel reprocessing. His heart didn't seem to be in it and he was not well received. Most of the questions at the end of the session were aimed at him and I was given an easy ride, thank goodness.

I left the conference as soon as I'd made my contribution to it in order to get back to the UK to find out what the B701 incident was all about and what had happened at Con's meeting with Tony Benn.

I was told that the ground contamination had occurred when radioactive acid leaked through the cladding of B701. Rather more than 100,000 curies of radioactivity, contained in 10,000 litres of liquid, had leaked into the ground over a period of at least eight years. Nobody noticed.

Less than one-millionth of a curie of radioactivity can be lethal, if the wrong sort of activity affects the wrong part of the body. This time there was no attempt to play down the seriousness of the incident, as there was at the time of the B38 silo leak. The company acknowledged that over the years there had been several errors of judgement and departures from proper safety standards.

The B701 leak was discovered just before the 1979 general election, which Labour lost. It was probably just as well for BNFL, Windscale and the THORP project that it did. Tony Benn had become an increasingly vocal critic. In a speech made during the election campaign he expressed his concerns about nuclear safety following a reactor accident at the Three Mile Island power station in the US and the B701 incident at Windscale.

He revealed that he'd asked the government's chief nuclear inspector to consider whether all or part of the Windscale site should be shut down. I learned from Jack Cunningham that Benn was also pressing for a public inquiry into the B701 incident.

Jack pre-empted the matter by issuing a statement demanding an investigation of the incident by the Nuclear Installations Inspectorate. He knew that this would take place in private and be far less damaging than a full-scale inquiry carried out under the gaze of the media. The Windscale management didn't understand the ploy at all and asked me why Cunningham had turned on them. I gave them a brief lesson in practical politics.

Prompted by the B701 incident, and without waiting to hear what it might be told to do following the NII investigation, BNFL examined all the plants on the Sellafield site to make sure that old buildings and equipment were safe and that there had been no further leaks. Everything seemed to be in order.

Con Allday also divided the vast, sprawling Windscale site into two more manageable parts – one responsible for the older plants, which he called Calder works, and the other responsible for the newer ones and projects under construction such as THORP, called Windscale works. The two works each had general managers, who reported to a site director.

Together the two works formed what Con called the Sellafield site, the name by which it is known today and which I will use in future. I could see the logic for the change but warned Con that the company would be accused by the press of trying to bury the name Windscale, because of its connection with a spate of recent incidents.

'It's our site not theirs,' Con said, and the structural change was made.

As we expected Jeff Preece and I found ourselves being derided for what the media regarded as a particularly inept piece of spin doctoring.

The safety checks carried out on old plants and the management reorganisation weren't enough to satisfy the incoming Conservative government. Soon after the general election Michael Heseltine, the newly appointed Secretary of State for the Environment, visited Sellafield. He gave Con

Allday a roasting about the state of the site, having been briefed by his officials to make a detour to some of the worst plants during his works tour rather than accept the carefully selected itinerary suggested to him by BNFL.

Mr Heseltine chose the lunch associated with the visit to give Con a dressing down in front of his senior Sellafield managers. Con took it in silence. He could hardly answer back. It seemed to me to be most unfair.

In my experience at BNFL it was the incidents which had the potential for causing damage off-site which attracted most interest, as one would expect. Couple that with the suggestion that children living near Sellafield might have contracted leukaemia as a result of the site's activities and you have the makings of some sensational headlines and compelling television.

The interest aroused by a Yorkshire television programme, 'Windscale: The Nuclear Laundry' which was broadcast nationally on the ITV network on Tuesday November 1st 1983, was truly phenomenal. YTV hadn't yet come to terms with the name Sellafield.

It was based on research into the incidence of cancer in coastal areas of West Cumbria that had been commissioned by Greenpeace, which had taken over as the main anti-nuclear organisation from Friends of the Earth. It paid particular attention to Seascale, two miles south of Sellafield, where many of the site's employees live. YTV discovered a small cluster of leukaemias in these villages and alleged that it might have been caused by discharges of radioactivity from Sellafield.

At the last minute YTV asked BNFL to put someone up to be interviewed live by Jonathon Dimbleby, the programme's presenter, at the end of the filmed report which carried the allegations. Despite the short notice, I decided that we must do so because of the damaging impression given by the 'empty chair' approach sometimes taken by TV, on the lines of 'we asked BNFL to provide someone to answer these important questions but the company declined to do so'.

Peter Mummery, by now director of health and safety, was put up as the company's spokesman, as much as anything because we didn't know what the programme might contain and were worried that non-scientists such as Jeffrey Preece or myself might be wrong-footed.

Peter was treated appallingly by the programme makers. When he arrived at the YTV studios in Leeds they refused to tell him anything about the allegations he would face. They then kept him waiting for nearly two hours in a small room with only a BNFL press officer for company before they took him into the studio for questioning.

Peter Mummery was clearly agitated as he watched the filmed material and waited for Jonathon Dimbleby to start his inquisition. There were several shots of Peter's fingers drumming the table where he sat, an obvious sign of nervousness. His voice had that edge of frustration and annoyance about it which might be expected from someone messed about as much as he had been. It's fair to say that the interview was a disaster.

The YTV programme caused another political and media furore. It also set in train a major government inquiry, headed by Sir Douglas Black, and over a dozen new pieces of academic research which kept Sellafield in the medical, legal and media spotlights for over a decade.

To make matters worse, a couple of weeks after the 'Nuclear Laundry' programme had been broadcast there was another incident at Sellafield, one which effectively closed local beaches for six months along a 25-mile stretch of the West Cumbrian coastline.

It's the late afternoon of Friday November 18th 1983 and I'm thinking of going home when the telephone rings.

'Harold. It's Roy Pilling here.' Roy is Sellafield's site director. He doesn't often ring me. I'm worried.

'Yes Roy.'

'I'm looking out of the office window and I can see what looks like an oil slick on the surface of the sea. There's a sort of sheen to it and the sun is being reflected off it.' Roy sounds almost lyrical.

'What's happened? Has a ship sunk or something?'

'No, no. Nothing like that. It's a mixture of solvent and crud from the factory. It's starting to come ashore.'

'What's crud?'

'It's chemical solvent – used solvent, with radioactive material in it.'

'I see. It sounds as though you've had time to analyse it. Is it a routine discharge or what?'

'No. It's not routine. We're still trying to sort out what's happened. It would probably have dispersed by now but the sea's been unusually calm for days.'

'Is it anything to do with the claim by Greenpeace earlier this week

that a rubber dinghy was contaminated while they were taking samples off the end of the pipeline and trying to block it?'
  'No, we don't think so.'
  'Have you told Con Allday?'
  'Yes. He's coming up to the site tomorrow. He wants you with him.'
  'I see. Okay Roy. See you tomorrow then.'

When Con Allday and I arrived at Sellafield's emergency control room on Saturday morning we learned that the incident had its roots in something which had occurred eight days earlier when the Magnox reprocessing plant was being washed out during the annual maintenance shut down.

As a result of a management error, about 4500 curies of radioactive liquid was transferred to one of the sea tanks where low-level waste is held for a final check to be made on its radioactivity content before it's discharged. Because of further procedural mistakes most, if not all, of this material was pumped out to the Irish Sea.

The site's management tried a variety of ways to recover the situation and convinced themselves that there was no reason to tell anyone at company headquarters about the incident, even though they'd told local inspectors from the Department of the Environment and the Ministry of Agriculture, Fisheries and Food something of what was going on.

Once again Con Allday and I were kept completely in the dark. It was only the solvent slick which forced the management to take us into their confidence.

Some members of the site management team seemed to feel that they'd just been unlucky. If the sea hadn't been unusually calm for a week the solvent and crud would simply have vanished in the vastness of the sea and no one would have been any the wiser. I found myself wondering whether this sort of thing had happened before.

In discussion with the management I prepared the formal reports for ministers and the press statements which were sent out over the weekend. Those first statements were inaccurate and far too reassuring, but I don't entirely blame the management for that. It can happen in any industry when people are put under pressure to comment quickly on a developing situation.

When a clearer picture of what had occurred emerged the Department of the Environment advised the public to 'avoid unnecessary use' of the beaches. It kept this warning in place for six months, until the middle of May the following year, extending the area it covered as contaminated rubbish continued to be washed up further and further away from the Sellafield site. The warning was finally withdrawn after Giles Shaw, a junior minister at energy, took a 15-minute swim off the Seascale beach to demonstrate his confidence that the problem was over.

His boss, Peter Walker, the Conservative government's Secretary of State for Energy, reacted much as Tony Benn had when serious incidents happened during his time in office. He called for heads to roll.

Once more Con Allday remained loyal to his staff at Sellafield. His logic was that it would be wrong to get rid of Roy Pilling, the site director, who'd been on holiday at the time the first mistakes were made. The next possible candidate for the chop, Roy's deputy John Doran, who was responsible for Windscale works and the sea tanks, was close to retirement and to dismiss him would have been a pretty empty gesture. Going further down the line would almost certainly not satisfy the Secretary of State and would send out the wrong signals about loyalty and support to younger men whom the company would need in the future.

Con asked me what I would do in his situation. I told him that I'd sack somebody, no matter how unfair it seemed, and do what I could to get a decent pay-off for them from the Treasury. I would do so, not so much because of the incident, but so that Sellafield finally understood that he would no longer tolerate managers keeping him (and me) in the dark.

'This could cost you your own job you know Con,' I said. 'If you're not prepared to give Peter Walker the scapegoat he wants, all you have left is the equivalent of the three-card trick. Create confusion, move people around – the more the merrier. First you see them, then you don't. Look busy.'

That is what Con did, and to an extent it worked. Nobody was sacked, but the company's management structure suffered as a result of unplanned management moves. Roy Pilling, already a board member, was pulled back to Risley, as Peter Mummery had been after the B38 incident, and a new role had to be found for him in a hurry. Gordon Steele, General Manager of BNFL's fuel-making factory at Springfields, near Preston, was sent up to Cumbria to take over responsibility for Sellafield, and his deputy promoted to take over from him at Springfields.

I don't think I was part of this management merry-go-round as such but it was around this time that I was appointed to the Board of BNFL, with the somewhat cumbersome title of Company Secretary and Director of Corporate Affairs. I was as proud as punch at having been made a director of one of Britain's largest state-owned industries – even if it was one of the most controversial.

Despite BNFL being in bad odour with Peter Walker and other members of the Cabinet I was persuaded by Geoffrey Tucker, a former publicity director of the Conservative Party, that the company should have a presence at the 1984 Tory Party Conference in Brighton.

Because of the beach incident the company's public and political image was at an extremely low ebb and I hesitated for a long time before agreeing to hold a reception at the conference. I thought we might come in for some flak and that the event could turn out to be counterproductive.

Geoffrey Tucker had been appointed as a consultant to BNFL by Con Allday on the advice of Sir William McAlpine, whose company had major interests in nuclear power, and who was and is a staunch supporter of the industry. His appointment was also supported by Lord Whitelaw, the prime minister's deputy, whom I came to rely on a great deal for political advice subsequently.

We organised the BNFL reception at the Grand Hotel, the main conference hotel, for the evening of October 11th 1984. It was meant to run from 7 pm to 9 pm, leaving plenty of time for the delegates, journalists and even a few environmentalists who popped in to say hello plenty of time to move on to other meetings and parties. In fact it went on till around 11 pm and was a thoroughly convivial occasion. There was no flak.

As I prepared to leave the Grand to walk to the Metropole Hotel next door, where I was staying, I was waylaid by a small group of old friends from the media in the lobby and joined them for a night cap in the ground floor bar at the front of the hotel. I turned down an invitation to accompany them to yet another reception at the Grand and got to bed just before midnight, ready for a quick getaway the following morning to drive back north.

I was fast asleep when the bomb went off at the Grand Hotel Brighton at 2.54 am on October 12th. The noise was tremendous, even in the Metropole, and woke me up. I had no idea what was happening, of course, but soon found myself caught up in the panic and confusion which surrounded the attempt by the Provisional IRA to kill Prime Minister Margaret Thatcher.

The fire alarm went off in the Metropole as I came out of a deep sleep and to this day I don't know whether it was set off by the shock waves from the explosion at the Grand or whether the police had ordered the hotel management to clear the Metropole in case there were further bombs in the hotels close to the Grand.

I could hear other guests running along the corridor outside my room and joined them, wearing an overcoat over my pyjamas and a pair of shoes with no socks. I probably looked a sight.

As I stepped outside the hotel ambulances were racing to the scene, their sirens screaming, and there was general clamour as the Metropole guests tried to find out what was going on. The Grand was already cordoned off and we were kept well away from the scene, although it was obvious that there was considerable carnage.

Eventually the guests were allowed back into the Metropole and I returned to my room, shivering. I didn't sleep much. I thought of ringing Sheila to tell her that I was all right, but decided that if I rang her in the early hours of the morning, waking her up, I would only frighten her. I had no reason to think she would learn about the Brighton bombing until the morning and then only if she had heard the news on the radio or television.

Instead I rang my secretary, Joan Byrne, at around 8.30 am, the time she normally got into the office, to ask her to ring Sheila and assure her I was OK. In fact it was Sheila who told Joan what had happened in Brighton that day. Sheila had caught the news bulletins and was terrified that I might have been staying at the Grand Hotel and had telephoned Joan at her home. As I was only staying in Brighton for one night I hadn't bothered to tell Sheila which hotel I was in, but Joan was able to inform her that although I had been shaken by what had happened I had been staying at the Metropole and not the Grand and that I was fine.

We now know that five people were killed that night at the Grand, including a Conservative MP, Sir Anthony Berry, and Roberta, the wife of John Wakeham, the Treasury Secretary, whom I was to get to know in later years when he became Secretary of State for Energy. Several other people including Norman Tebbit's wife Margaret were left permanently disabled.

But by some miracle the Prime Minister and her husband Denis escaped injury, even though the bathroom in their suite of rooms was damaged. At four in the morning the indomitable Mrs Thatcher gave an interview to John Cole, the BBC's political editor, an old friend of mine, informing him – and the IRA of course – that the show would go on.

By the time the conference opened, the Prime Minister had re-written her planned speech, attacking the IRA rather than the Labour Party. Whatever anyone thought of her politics nobody could question the courage of the Iron Lady, who was to continue as prime minister for another six years.

In my view she would have gone on for longer than that if it had not been for the singularly inept campaign run by her Parliamentary Private Secretary, Peter Morrison, during the 1990 election for the leadership of the Conservative Party involving Mrs Thatcher and Michael Heseltine. I must say I was amazed that the Prime Minister had given the campaign job to Morrison, whom I had met three years earlier when I accompanied Christopher Harding, the recently appointed Chairman of BNFL, to discuss a strike at Sellafield with him when he was Energy Minister.

Christopher and I thought we had been called in for a grilling by the minister about the dispute, which was hitting the headlines. Instead, when we were shown into his office we found his conference table covered with dozens of toys – and it was them he proceeded to talk about. It turned out that he was a keen collector of clockwork soldiers and the like.

We didn't really discuss the strike, Sellafield, or anything else to do with nuclear power. I found Peter Morrison terribly laid back and, I have to say, distinctly odd, not at all the sort of man to look to for inspiration and drive during a hard-fought leadership contest.

Con Allday was 63 at the time of the beach incident and would dearly have liked to stay on as part-time chairman of the company after his normal retirement age of 65, passing on his full-time duties as chief executive to another executive board member, Bill Wilkinson, who was responsible for THORP and the other major engineering projects. That didn't happen, and I believe that Con's consistent refusal to give government ministers of both of the main political parties what they wanted when things went wrong played a large part in that.

His cause wasn't helped by the publication of Sir Douglas Black's report on the inquiry he had led into Yorkshire Television's leukaemia scare programme, which had taken him and his inquiry colleagues two years to produce. The report was published in December 1985, the month Con Allday was due to retire.

The report concluded that the mortality rate in West Cumbria was near to the national average, which everybody knew from previous studies, but that this did not preclude the existence of local pockets of mortality at levels which were higher than expected, which YTV had already shown. Then – surprise, surprise – the report recommended that further research should be carried out, including four separate epidemiological studies into various aspects of the problem apparently identified by Yorkshire Television.

YTV invited Sir Douglas Black to take part in a follow-up to the original 'Nuclear Laundry' programme and asked for a BNFL representative again. This time I nominated myself.

When I arrived at the studios I was asked to wait in a side room. I refused. I left the building, leaving the press officer who had travelled with me to talk to the programme makers while I went off to a local café for a coffee. They were not going to mess me about like they had Peter Mummery.

I am sure that the programme wasn't at all what YTV wanted. It was flat and rather boring. Jonathon Dimbleby repeatedly put it to me that there was a possibility the tiny leukaemia cluster its researchers had found near Sellafield might have been the result of the site's activities.

In turn I kept putting it to him that there could be other causes and that the number of deaths identified in the original programme was so small that it could be argued that they were not statistically significant. Sir Douglas Black agreed with me.

Then I pointed out to Dimbleby that the Black report had confirmed that in West Cumbria as a whole the death rate from leukaemias was close to the national average. Within an average there would inevitably be highs and lows. In some villages close to Sellafield the incidence of leukaemia was lower than expected. Was this due to radiation perhaps? Could it be that small doses of radiation were beneficial?

'You can't have it both ways Mr Dimbleby,' I said.

Shortly after this programme was transmitted, Roger Marsh, who was responsible for security in the company, reporting to me, came to see me.

'Harold,' he said. 'I have to tell you that there is some concern that you may be in danger, because of all the television you've done lately. We think there's a possibility that some sort of threat may be made against you. There's nothing specific, but because it's always you defending the company on television you have become a well-known public figure. We think there's a possibility that somebody might identify you as a target for some sort of action.'

I pushed the possibility to one side, refusing to believe that people with genuine concerns about nuclear power would turn to violence in support of their cause.

Later, when animal rights activists unleashed campaigns involving intimidation, hate mail, malicious phone calls, hoax bombs, arson attacks and property destruction, I was less sure. Roger Marsh and his security team continued to monitor the possibility of a personal attack on me throughout my career at BNFL.

The second Yorkshire Television programme did little to damage the reputation of Sellafield and BNFL further, but it was unfortunate that the Black report had appeared just as Con Allday was about to leave the nuclear industry.

I worked for Con Allday for 10 eventful years, during which my own stock had risen considerably. He had fulfilled the promise he made to me when I joined BNFL that if I did well I could make it to the board. I felt grateful to him for the chances he'd given me and sorry when he left BNFL. I also felt – and still feel – that his contribution to the nuclear power industry had not been properly recognised with the knighthood he so richly deserved.

Nevertheless, I couldn't help starting to wonder what the future held for me with a new chairman and a new chief executive about to be put in place. The hell with it, I thought. My career isn't everything and I've had little enough chance to enjoy myself lately. It's time I did.

For some time Sheila had pressed me, fairly gently, to join her as a member of Sale Operatic Society, a first-class amateur group which put on musicals at the Garrick theatre in Altrincham. I'd always enjoyed the performances I'd been to see there and decided to take up Sheila's suggestion. It was something we could do together.

It must have been a bit of my father, the old ham with a love of brass bands and male voice choirs, coming out in me.

10

The Leading Man

I was eight years old when I made my first stage appearance. It took place in Dartmouth Park, which had a bandstand with a small stage and a semi-circular auditorium. From time to time a brass band played and occasionally there would be a strangulated tenor or a shrill soprano belting out 'Velia' or some other aria from light opera, usually with tremendous gusto and vibrato.

Some of the singers sounded like the noise made by a gleed under a door, as my father put it. A gleed was a fragment of coke and when it became wedged under a door it screeched when the door was opened, setting the teeth on edge.

One Sunday afternoon the people responsible for organising events at the bandstand decided to hold a children's talent contest, with prizes. I spotted the posters advertising it and persuaded Marina and Beryl, the sisters closest to my own age, to take me. Marina didn't want to know about taking part but Beryl and I did.

My turn came and I stepped out on to the stage. A man holding a microphone by its stand awaited me. The microphone and its stand were taller than me. The man lifted me up and placed me on a box so that I could be heard, and asked me my name.

'Harold Bolter.'
'What can you do Harold?'
'Well, I can whistle and sing a bit.'
'What can you sing?'
'I can sing the sixpence song.'
'What's that Harold?'

'It's a song my dad sings. I'll show you if you like.'
'Very well then. Sing the sixpence song for us.'
There's a piano on stage but the lady playing it doesn't know the sixpence song. I'm on my own.

'I've got sixpence,' I begin. 'A jolly, jolly sixpence,
I've got sixpence to last me all my life.
I've got tuppence to lend and tuppence to spend,
And tuppence to take home to my wife.
No care have I to grieve me. No pretty little girls to deceive me,
I'm happy as a lark believe me. As I go rolling home,
Rolling home, blind drunk. Rolling home, blind drunk . . .'

'That's enough of that I think,' the man says quickly. 'Your dad's got the words wrong. I think we'd better hear you whistle. What do you want to whistle Harold?'
'What about the sixpence song?'
'Oh, all right then.'

The whistle came out in a breathy, sibilant rush but I pride myself that it was in tune. I suspect it didn't matter. I was given a prize, to muted applause. The man probably wanted to get me off the stage as soon as he could. My prize was a penknife. I didn't stay to see what the contest winner was given. A machete, perhaps? I lost the penknife within a few days, anyway. I don't know what Beryl sang or what her prize was. I was too embarrassed to stay and listen.

A few years later I made my second public appearance. This time it was at the Salvation Army citadel near West Bromwich town centre. My father had decided that I should sing a duet with my sister Marina. He'd written some new words to Brahms' Lullaby. Despite Marina's misgivings we rehearsed the piece under Dad's tutelage and all seemed set for the big day.

The Army band struck up and I began my father's take on the Cradle Song, as the Lullaby is sometimes known. 'Never fear, never fear, for the saviour is near. He will guide you, walk beside you and make your way clear,' I sang

But where was Marina? I glanced sideways and there she was, her mouth firmly shut, her eyes wide open and a look of terror on her face. No help there then. I pressed on and somehow reached the end of the piece. There was no applause. I suppose it was because the intended duet was part of a religious service. I hope so anyway.

My contact with the public performance of music was somewhat intermittent after that, although there was plenty of music played and listened to at home.

Encouraged by my father I joined the Salvation Army band shortly after I started grammar school. He saw it as a cheap way for me to learn to read music and play the cornet. I even appeared on the streets dressed in the Army's famous red vest on a few occasions. Truth to tell I wasn't very good and ducked out of some of the trickier passages.

My time with the Army lasted a few years but eventually I lost interest in the B flat cornet. I was becoming more interested in girls and the Salvation Army wasn't too well blessed with them. A particular Methodist chapel, on the other hand, had a fine selection of attractive young ladies.

I joined Guns Lane Methodist Church. Apart from the pretty girls the church had a thriving youth club and choir. Guns Lane also put on concert parties and an annual pantomime and I became involved in them. On one memorable occasion I was cast in the lead as Prince Charming in a pantomime – unusual for a boy. I was persuaded to dress up in a white satin-like suit, much against my better instincts. I felt like an idiot and from the photographs of the occasion I looked like one.

Track forward a quarter of a century, a period taken up with National Service, marriage, children and building a career in Birmingham and London, and I renewed my interest in the performing arts. By then Sheila was singing with Sale Operatic Society.

In the bar of the Garrick Playhouse in Altrincham where the Sale amateurs strutted their stuff I met Derek Hurdwell, occasional chorus member of the society and permanent tickets secretary, along with his wife Anne. All of the amateurs find it easy to get female chorus members and extremely difficult to persuade men to perform. Sale was no exception.

'Why don't you join the chorus?' Derek asked me after I'd told him how much I enjoyed the shows I'd seen at the Garrick, which is a delightful little theatre.

'I've been thinking about it but I can't guarantee getting to rehearsals.'

'You don't have to make all of the rehearsals. You'll enjoy it. Give it a go.'

So I did. I joined the chorus for the next show, *Oklahoma*, and allowed myself to be kitted out in a cowboy suit. I have rather a large head, but somehow the cowboy hat hired for me was far too big for it – more of a fifteen-gallon hat than the normal ten gallons. Sheila stuffed it with crumpled newspaper but I still felt that if I spun round too quickly the hat would remain where it was.

Although this was my first musical I was given a line of dialogue. To be precise I was given two words to shout out during an auction scene where the cowboys bid for the girls' picnic baskets. It was the first bid so I couldn't really fluff it. My immortal line was 'Two bits!' I was word perfect.

The Sale society put on two shows a year and somehow I managed to organise my working life so that I could take part in at least one of them. For several years I was content with appearing in the chorus or in small cameo roles. Then I became ambitious.

I headed straight for the deep end and put myself forward for the role of Honore in the stage version of Lerner and Loewe's *Gigi*, the part played by Maurice Chevalier in the film version which starred Leslie Caron as Gigi and Louis Jourdan as Gaston. Sheila thought I'd taken leave of my senses.

'You do realise that the Chevalier character has more songs than anyone else in the show?' she asked.

'No,' I said, standing on my dignity. 'But don't worry. I'll cope. I only have to sing "I'm Glad I'm Not Young Any More" and another song I've forgotten.'

'Typical. The song you've forgotten is "Ah Yes I Remember It Well". It's a duet which Honore sings with his old girlfriend. And in the show he sings four songs, not two, including another duet with Gaston.'

'Oh God, not two duets,' I said, thinking back to the Sally Army fiasco with Marina.

'I suppose it will be all right,' my wife said thoughtfully. 'You won't get the part anyway.'

What my wife didn't know was that I'd been secretly preparing for the audition. I was a main board director of BNFL by this time and also on the board of several of its subsidiaries and associates. One of them was Nuclear Transport Limited, a tripartite company with French and German as well as British directors. Its role was to organise the transport of spent nuclear fuel around Europe.

One of the French directors of NTL, a Monsieur Indoudjian, spoke English with the sort of accent which Maurice Chevalier employed to such effect and I found I could do a reasonable impression of him – Indoudjian I mean. By the time the audition came round I'd learned the dialogue and the words to the two songs and was raring to go. I found that I really wanted the part. And to nearly everyone else's surprise I got it.

I learned later that it was a close-run thing. There were five people on the audition committee, drawn from the society's membership, and the director, Mike Donohue, was there to advise them. He apparently insisted that I was his idea of Honore and talked them into ignoring my lack of experience.

When I did my week-long impression of M. Indoudjian doing his impersonation of Chevalier in *Gigi* Sheila was in the chorus, twitching away each time the chorus struck up at the start of one of my songs, far more nervous than I was. She had neuralgia throughout the week, brought on by her concern about what might happen to me. Meanwhile, I loved every minute of it and wondered what all the fuss was about.

Christopher Harding had recently taken over from Con Allday as chairman of BNFL and he thought it was hilarious that one of his directors was treading the boards in his spare time. Christopher insisted that the other executive directors of the company should join him at one of the performances of *Gigi* unless they had a good excuse for not doing so.

After the show some of them professed to have enjoyed it and Christopher loved it. He told me it was much more his scene than the chamber orchestra concerts he attended as a duty with Lord Marshall, the chairman of BNFL's largest UK customer, the Central Electricity Generating Board – 'Can't stand all that scratchy music.'

Modesty apart, I was pretty good in *Gigi*, although I did mess up 'Ah Yes I Remember It Well' one night during the week's run by starting the song on the second verse. My co-star and fellow duetist, Judith Plaster, muttered 'not *that* well' under her breath but somehow we got through the song. Nobody seemed to notice.

I went on to become the definitive Von Trapp in *The Sound of Music* (at least in my eyes) and managed a passable George Sanders impression as Cosmo Constantine in *Call Me Madam*. While Sale was still my home society I also appeared by invitation with the Radcliffe St Thomas and Urmston societies.

As a result I was cast as both the drunken jailer Frank and the nervous lawyer Blind in Johann Strauss junior's *Die Fledermaus* – not in the same production, of course, and not for the same society. Both of them are comic characters and made a change from the elderly roués and charmers I'd played hitherto.

Appearing in *Die Fledermaus* with Radcliffe St Thomas was a wonderful experience. I loved the music and the challenge of singing difficult music. One song, which translates as 'Brother Mine', involved holding a line against four others in five-part harmony – and to think I was once nervous of duets!

One of my smaller, cameo roles with Sale was that of Sir Dinadan in *Camelot*. There wasn't too much dialogue, no solo singing and not much interaction with the leading players. *Camelot* was also produced by Mike Donohue, the best director of amateur shows in the north west that I have met. Mike earned a living working for one of the electricity utilities but his real life, then as now, was directing musicals. I have no doubt that if his life had taken a different course he could have made it as a director in the professional theatre.

Mike Donohue could be over-ambitious at times though. The Lerner and Loewe libretto calls for the opening scene of *Camelot* to be set in a snow storm somewhere in England and that's what Mike wanted. This was a bit of a challenge for Sale Operatic Society's properties manager, Colin Barker, but he came up trumps. He hired a machine which blew clouds of steamy soap suds across the stage. With a bit of imagination the audience might take it for snow.

At the final rehearsal for the show, a week before we were to be introduced to Colin's snow machine, Mike marked out the places where the cast were to stand as the snow drifted over them during the overture. I was positioned next to a new member of the chorus, Wally Throsby. Mike explained that we were all to stand perfectly still until the overture was over and we could get on with the performance.

The dress rehearsal was on the Sunday preceding Monday's opening night. I assumed my immobile stance near centre stage next to Wally, dressed in a short tunic and tights. I really don't have the legs for tights. I look like Max Wall. I felt silly, but not nearly as silly as I did when Colin Barker's snow machine clanked noisily into life, threatening to drown the overture and my wife, who had to sing over it.

The soapy snow flew up into the air and drifted over the stage before coming down again, much of it onto the top of my head. A pyramid of soap suds built up as I stood perfectly still – one inch, two inches, three, four – forming a near perfect ice-cream cone on top of my head. I couldn't take any more and started to edge to one side, away from the flow. Mike Donohue spotted me.

'Stand still,' he shouted from the front row of the stalls. 'Make a note,' he ordered his assistant, Muriel Coakley, a talented choreographer whose job at the dress rehearsal was to make sure nothing was forgotten when Mike carried out his inquest later, commenting on things which had gone wrong and trying to put them right.

Along came Monday and opening night and we all moved into our pre-arranged positions for the overture. 'Wally,' I said to my new companion. 'What are you doing there? You're in the wrong place. Mike swapped us over at the end of the dress rehearsal. Weren't you listening?'

Uncertain of himself, the new boy exchanged places with me and for the next couple of performances it was Wally who suffered the humiliation of the soap suds building up on his head. Mid-week he was tipped off about what was going on and shuffled closer to me. Mike didn't even notice.

Amateur theatre, particularly musical theatre, has many magical moments like that. With time I became chairman of Sale Operatic and even, briefly, its president. I tried to instil the sense into the society's performing members that there was a difference between being amateurs and being amateurish.

But when things went wrong it wasn't always the fault of the players. The lighting and sound systems at the Garrick had to be hired from the people who ran the theatre and operated by their members. We suspected that they weren't always as concerned about the fate of the Sale Operatic shows as they were about the Garrick's own productions.

In my early days with Sale Operatic the society liked to put on a golden oldie from time to time, Novello's *King's Rhapsody*, Lehar's *The Merry Widow*, or *The Song of Norway*, which draws heavily on the music of Edvard Grieg, that sort of thing. It gave the chorus a chance to have a good sing and the leading ladies the opportunity to dress up in extravagant costumes.

In Novello's *King's Rhapsody* (or King's Raspberry as some of the more irreverent male chorus members called it) there's an important dramatic moment when the king and his courtiers await news of the birth of a child to the queen – a 21-gun salute for a son and a mere 18 if it's a girl.

The Garrick's sound man assured me, as Sale Operatic's chairman, that the 21-gun salute was in place. It had been recorded on tape and all would be well. It was, too, right until the Saturday matinee. I wasn't in the show but stood at the back of the theatre as the cast waited to hear whether a son and heir had been born.

'She loves you, yeah, yeah, yeah. With a love like that . . .'

The Beatles song rang out. I ran upstairs to the sound box and berated the Garrick's sound engineer, who had played the wrong side of a double-sided tape. He turned the Beatles off and for a brief moment there was silence on stage. But not in the audience, which consisted mainly of pensioners. They found the whole thing hilarious.

With great presence of mind, Bill Lawson, who was playing the lead role of King Nicki and who bore a striking resemblance to Ivor Novello, began to ad lib with Fred Wood, another old trouper. Fred cupped his ear as though listening hard for the guns: 'Thirteen, fourteen, fifteen,' he intoned, joined by Bill, until they reached 21. Bingo! And the show moved on.

Another of my favourite moments came during a production of *Carousel* in which I played the minor role of Mr Bascombe, the local businessman whom Billy Bigelow, the leading character, tries to rob.

The attempted robbery scene only takes a few minutes so it was relatively easy to fit rehearsals for the part of Bascombe within the confines of an increasingly busy working life at BNFL. Other than this small scene all that Bascombe has to do is to reappear at the end of the show. Betty Farmer, an attractive blonde lady and a talented singer, if a little dizzy at times, was to be my partner for the 'who's best' sequence of the show, as the performers call the curtain calls.

The two of us were meant to carry chairs onto the stage in darkness after the penultimate scene, which is set in a garden and features the Snow family and Billy Bigelow's widow, Julie, the leading lady. The finale which follows takes place in the schoolhouse yard where the daughter of Billy and Julie receives a school prize watched, among others, by the ghost of her dead father. Very dramatic, if slightly absurd.

'Come on,' Betty shouts through the doorway of the men's dressing room. *'We're on.'*

'Are you sure? Nobody else is moving.'

'Come on. We'll be late'

We get in position and pick up our chairs from the back of the wings.

Betty runs on to the darkened stage carrying her chair, hotly pursued by me with mine. We place the chairs carefully in position stage right and sit down. The lights come up. We are in the garden not the school-house yard. We've invaded the stage prematurely.

'Oh my God,' Betty whispers. 'What are we going to do?'

'Sit still and smile,' I say between gritted teeth. 'Pretend to talk to me as if nothing's happened. I'll think of something.'

'Should we pick up the chairs and get off?'

'No. No. Do that and everybody will know we've dropped a clanger. Anyway we'd have to carry the bloody chairs back on again in a few minutes' time. That would be a dead giveaway. Sit still and smile.'

Off stage I can see Mr Snow preparing to make his entrance into the garden, accompanied by a crocodile line of his and Mrs Snow's many children. They look surprised to see Betty and me waiting for them.

'Got it,' I whisper. 'When they come on we'll stand up. I'll doff my hat to Mr Snow as he walks past us and then we'll walk off.'

'With the chairs?'

'No. Not with the chairs. We just walk off quietly, as though nothing's happened.'

And that is what we did.

After that night's performance my wife was talking to her good friend Jean Wood.

'I don't remember Harold and Betty being in the garden scene,' Jean said. Sheila explained what had happened.

'Oh,' said Jean. 'I assumed Mike Donohue had decided to dress that side of the stage. It was a bit empty.' Good old Jean.

I thoroughly enjoyed my involvement in amateur operatics, although the name Sale Operatic Society was rather misleading. The group is now called the Sale and Altrincham Musical Theatre which more accurately describes the shows it performs. Gradually, I found I was enjoying the opera more than the musicals I appeared in.

My first contact with opera, which has become the musical love of my life, came as a result of my work as industrial editor of the *Financial Times*, where I wrote about the nationalised industries, including the then British Steel Corporation.

In the late 1960s the international steel industry held a conference in Brussels and I went over to cover it for the FT. Midway through the conference the organisers arranged for the delegates and the gentlemen of the press to attend the opera and I found myself sitting next to Bob Scholey, who was then deputy chairman of the BSC.

Bob had risen from management positions within the steel industry in Sheffield and had a reputation for toughness. He was known as Black Bob and cultivated his persona as a horny handed son of toil. But Black Bob had another side to him.

Before the performance began Bob and I began to discuss the opera we were about to see. I confessed that it would be my first opera. Bob then explained the plot to me and also told me that I was about to hear possibly the world's finest diva sing the role for which she was best known.

That night as Elisabeth Schwarzkopf sang the role of the Marschallin in Richard Strauss's *Die Rosenkavalier* I sat enthralled with her voice, her timeless beauty and the poignancy of her acting, particularly the scene where Octavian leaves her for a younger woman, the fool. I fell a little in love with Schwarzkopf I think and I certainly fell in love with the opera, which remains one of my favourites. Black Bob, sitting next to me was clearly just as affected. I think we regarded each other in a different light after that evening of shared emotion.

It was my move to BNFL and the north west of England which enabled Sheila and me to progress our developing interest in music and the theatre, in their several forms. At my instigation BNFL decided that it should get more involved in the performing arts, as part of the strategy which I was developing to show that the company was here to stay and determined to be part of the wider community.

We started in a relatively small way by sponsoring a one-off search for new musicals at the lovely little theatre at Buxton, in Derbyshire, close to Chatsworth. The search lasted a week and wasn't a total success, but Sheila and I enjoyed watching excerpts from musicals based on plays and films such as *Goodnight Mr Tom* and *Frankenstein*.

Later I was persuaded, without too much difficulty, that BNFL should take over the sponsorship of one of Britain's finest brass bands, following the decision by Leyland Daf to discontinue its association with the band, and the BNFL Band was formed. My father, with his lifetime involvement in the brass band movement, would have been proud of me. Within a year the BNFL Band had become the 1992 All England Masters Champion, with a truly wonderful competition performance of Philip Sparke's specially written 'Cambridge Variations'.

The company also agreed that we could give a small amount of sponsorship to the Warrington Male Voice Choir. Once more I felt my father pulling the strings.

But much as I loved the concerts given by the brass band and the choir my love for the opera was developing fast and I persuaded my BNFL board colleagues that we should invite key customers and community leaders to occasional performances by companies visiting the Opera House in Manchester, including the touring Glyndebourne company.

My first corporate booking was for Giuseppe Verdi's *Attila*, not an opera I knew and not one that's performed very often. I didn't know what to expect, but assumed it would have fearsome hordes of blood-thirsty warriors, led by the rapacious monster who has gone down in history as Attila the Hun.

How wrong I was. This Attila is a lovesick softy, easy prey for Odabella, the Italian amazon leading a gang of female cut-throats, who is determined to kill him. It isn't the most plausible of plots but the music is superb, which is more than could be said for the costumes and scenery. They were extremely drab, deliberately so I guess, given the period in which the opera is set. With time I've forgotten the names of the singers taking the parts of Attila and Odabella but I remember them as very large people indeed, particularly the lady, and that both of them had very fine voices. The fact that they were overweight made not a scrap of difference. I found Attila's lusting for Odabella entirely credible and loved the opera, as did my wife. Not all of the people invited to join us felt the same about it though.

George Inglis, a former colleague on the board of BNFL, had moved on to Marlow as managing director of Urenco, a European associate company, and Urenco had managed to obtain a block of tickets for several performances at Glyndebourne each season. I suspect his board was having second thoughts about the cost of the enterprise and he approached me to see if BNFL would be prepared to take the tickets for one of the performances each year, whatever the opera. I quickly found space in the public relations budget.

For several years Sheila and I hosted a party at one of the Glyndebourne operas. Those invited varied over the years but several became regulars. I think particularly of Bernard Ingham, then with Margaret Thatcher at 10 Downing Street, and his wife Nancy, David Fishlock, the FT's science editor and his wife Mary, Neville Gaffin and his wife Jean Caines, both of them top government press officers and Jim Corner, of the British Nuclear Forum, and his wife Christa.

One year Jack Cunningham, Labour MP for Copeland, accepted an invitation to attend one of the operas with his wife Maureen. The opera was one of Benjamin Britten's, who has never been one of my favourite composers, but the weather was glorious and the interval meal in the old Middle Wallop restaurant was fine.

I was acutely aware, however, that Jack and Bernard seemed a little uncomfortable, although they knew each other well and had worked together as part of Tony Benn's team at the Department of Energy. But that was before Bernard became a Tory and Margaret Thatcher's press spokesman.

The problem was that there were cameras flashing away in the bar where we met before the performance, during the interval and at the end as we wound up the day. I guess that both Jack and Bernard had visions of a picture of the two of them enjoying each other's company getting into one of the tabloids. Fortunately, it didn't happen.

For me Glyndebourne was a tremendous learning experience. I encountered operas that I had never heard of before and sometimes, having suspected that a particular opera would not be for me, I found myself sitting enthralled in the sweaty old theatre which preceded today's wonderful auditorium.

One of the operas which affected me in this way was Peter Hall's acclaimed 1982 production of Gluck's *Orphée et Eurydice*, in which Dame Janet Baker made her last stage appearance as Orphée, which is quite often played by a woman. The opening of the piece was pure magic as the chorus, perfectly synchronised, moved slowly, solemnly down-stage as they mourned the death of Eurydice. It was an inspired production and I felt privileged to be there. I felt much the same way about Trevor Nunn's 1986 production of George Gershwin's *Porgy and Bess*, starring Sir Willard White, with its mainly black cast.

Since our Glyndebourne days my wife and I have seen as much opera as we can, in this country and elsewhere in Europe. I would particularly recommend the opera staged in Menorca in January each year at the lovely theatre in Mahon, the capital, if you can get tickets, which are like gold dust. We saw a production of *Tosca* there which suited the relatively small theatre admirably.

We accompanied good friends of ours, Francisco and Elise Gomila Mascaro. Before travelling to Menorca I'd asked Francisco whether members of the audience wore evening dress. '*Si*,' he said. He seemed a little uncertain and to ensure I'd understood him correctly over the phone I asked: 'Do the men wear evening suits, Francisco?' The reply came in English: 'Yes, we wear evening suits. Don't worry.'

When I picked Francisco and Elise up at their home in Alaior on the way to the theatre Elise was in her finery. Francisco, on the other hand, was only wearing a lounge suit. I was resplendent in my dress suit. 'You said the men wore evening suits,' I protested. 'This is the suit I wear in the evenings for special occasions,' he said.

I was the only man in the audience wearing evening dress that night. The only other men so attired were the members of the orchestra.

The musicians and the leading singers were all professionals, but the members of the chorus were amateurs, very gifted ones. During the interval they moved into the audience to chat to their friends and relatives. I was introduced to a lady chorus member, probably a cousin of Francisco, who has many cousins in important places in Menorca. She seemed surprised to discover that I wasn't playing in the orchestra. It was all very relaxed but somehow it made not a scrap of difference to our appreciation of their highly charged dramatic performances on stage.

Our delight in the Menorcan *Tosca* was in sharp contrast to our reaction to the *Tosca* we saw at the famous Verona amphitheatre in Italy. I have a cautionary tale to tell about Verona.

More than a million people attend the annual opera season at the 2000-year-old amphitheatre. Not all of them know what to expect. We certainly didn't. On our visit there with our good friends Rita and Jimmy Johnston we stayed in Lake Garda for a couple of weeks and had booked tickets for three operas, *Tosca*, *Nabucco* and *Aida*, in advance. We saw one and two thirds of the three operas.

They call them the gradinata, the stone steps where the Romans once sat in the Arena Di Verona and watched the Christians being fed to the lions. From personal experience I can say that the spectacle must have been extremely painful to all concerned – with the possible exception of the lions.

The company through which we booked the holiday also reserved our opera tickets for us, to be collected when we arrived in Italy. The only 'seats' on offer were those on the gradinata, the steeply sloping shelves which climb into the Veronese sky.

The first opera, three days after our arrival, was to be *Tosca* and we were all very much looking forward to it, although I sensed that something might be wrong when we were asked to report for the coach which was to take us from the hotel to the arena at 5.45 pm – a full three and a half hours before the performance was due to begin.

The second hint that there might be trouble ahead came on the coach when the courier warned us that there would be a full house that night, with 20,000 spectators in the arena. Anyone with tickets for the gradinata would be well advised to get into the stadium as quickly as possible, he said.

Quickly was not possible. Sheila and I and our two friends joined the flying wedge formation of would-be opera goers who battled their way into the arena and up a steep and winding stone staircase. Finally we broke out into the evening sunlight – to find that at least 19,900 others had beaten us to it and were claiming territorial rights.

Pushing aside our natural English reserve my wife and I eventually elbowed ourselves into place on the stone steps, about eight rows down from the summit of the gradinata. Jimmy and Rita made it to the top, which was quite an achievement. In the distance, far below us, beyond the serried ranks of seething humanity, the stage hands were still putting the enormous slabs of scenery together, like ants trying to move a dining-room suite.

I am six feet tall and my limbs have never been particularly flexible. This proved a problem for me, for those perched precariously in front of me and for those threatening to fall on me from behind. Wriggle forward, to ease the flow of blood to the small of the back and the young woman in front of me felt the full force of my knees. Ease back and I received the same treatment from the rather large and somewhat rude German lady sitting behind me, who thought I was trying to break her legs. My wife, just over five feet tall, had no such problems.

Then there were the vendors, forcing their way along their chosen routes to push the sale of programmes, ice cream, sandwiches, soft drinks and wine or offering to rent out cushions to those who felt they could rise to the occasion and slip one beneath them. Sheila and I were on one of the favourite runs and seemed to get trampled on about every five minutes.

Somehow we survived and the orchestra struck up the overture to *Tosca*. I have to say, though, that our two-hour ordeal wasn't the best way to prepare for an opera as sensitive and intensely dramatic as that one.

The Mexican wave which rippled around the arena shortly before the overture made me wonder what we were in for by way of audience participation, too. Glyndebourne was never like this. Pushing such elitist thoughts to one side I settled down to enjoy the opera. The problem was that I could hardly see or hear any of the action from up in the eyrie. Even the largest of the principals looked like a pigmy as she whispered her first aria.

What I could see very clearly was the flickering light of the torch which the young woman in front of me used to illuminate her copy of the libretto, switching it on and off as though signalling to a confederate as she reached for her binoculars. I was reduced to watching the real performance – the opera, that is – from over the top of my jacket, which I placed strategically in front of my face to hide the torchlight.

The Verona arena is made for enormous spectacles, of the lions-eat-Christians kind, with a large, if continuously dwindling, cast. It is not made for the intimate opera which *Tosca* undoubtedly is. *Tosca* has some wonderful arias and occasional duets but it has hardly a chorus number to speak of or any other form of grand distraction.

To make matters worse, someone seems to have convinced those staging opera in the arena that its natural acoustics will largely suffice and that only a minimal sound system is necessary. They are wrong. Anything less than fortissimo drifted off into the night before it reached us up there in the gods.

The first act interval came just in time. I creaked to my feet and stretched, convinced that hip replacement surgery was an inevitable consequence of what I had been subjected to. (And, as both hips have now been replaced, I may have had a case.)

Gluttons for punishment, Sheila and I decided to stick it out. Somehow we made it to the second act interval, although our minds were more on our aching bones than on the fates of Tosca and Cavaradossi. It was then that we decided enough was enough and signalled our intentions to leave to Jimmy and Rita. Battered and bruised, we fled the scene, or rather we stumbled from it, stepping carefully over the bodies and carrier bags which littered the way to the exit far below us. That is how we came to see two-thirds of an opera.

As we left the arena a young girl tripped over an outstretched leg and pitched forward onto her knees. Fortunately, she wasn't badly injured. The only way we could stay upright was by grabbing some part of a total stranger's anatomy. The arena is not a place for anyone suffering from vertigo.

As we left the arena a lady attendant offered to stamp the back of our hands with some mysterious sign which would enable us to get back for the dramatic final act. We declined gracefully and went out into the square, breathing sighs of relief. We sat at a little bar until our friends joined us at the end of the performance. I didn't even complain about being ripped off over the price of the drinks. There is a price to be paid for bliss.

Jimmy and Rita were more stoical than us. Before leaving the UK we had booked for a performance of *Nabucco* to follow *Tosca* on the following evening – to be enjoyed from the gradinata steps, of course. They went. We didn't.

They kindly offered to try to sell our tickets and to our delight they succeeded, although we did feel slightly guilty, knowing what the purchasers had let themselves in for. *Nabucco* was a triumph, apparently, a tremendous spectacle and beautifully sung. Our friends teased us that we'd missed a treat. We had absolutely no regrets.

During the following day conversation turned to the issue of the performance of *Aida*, which was still a week away. To go or not to go, that was the question. 'Not if it means sitting on the gradinata,' I said. 'Not on your life,' my wife echoed.

Through the tour company's representative we managed to upgrade our tickets and joined the middle-class patrons in the gradinata numerata – numbered metal seats, paying an extra £40 or so each for the privilege. Twice as much would still have been money well spent. Because we now had numbered seats we didn't have to enter the arena until 20 minutes before the performance began, which meant we had time for a very pleasant dinner at a quiet restaurant. Inside the arena we didn't have to fight for space, we were near the action, which we could see and hear, and the vendors kept to the aisles.

Aida was also more suited to the auditorium than *Tosca* had been – a vibrant mixture of opera, music hall and circus, with superb scenery, a cast of hundreds, trumpeters and flaming torches up in the ramparts and prancing horses joining the grand parade.

As we left we decided that next time – if there was a next time – we would do fewer operas and sit with the grand ladies and gentlemen in the poltrone or even the poltrinissime, the front and second row stalls. The Duke and Duchess of Kent sat in the poltrinissime gold seats, the best of the best, the night we saw *Aida*, holding up the start of the second act after retiring for drinks. They were sitting on proper theatre seats. If it's good enough for them, I thought, it's good enough for me.

11

The Royal Dinner Guest

Christopher Harding was hosting a 'meet the new chairman' party for senior staff at BNFL's head office when the radioactive cloud from Chernobyl reached the UK. It was Friday May 2nd 1986 and Sheila and I were looking forward to a pleasant evening with colleagues, followed by a quiet weekend on our own. It was not to be.

The Chernobyl disaster had happened six days earlier. Since then there'd been considerable speculation about whether the cloud moving across the continent would drift over to Britain from the Ukraine, and if so where it would deposit its potentially lethal contents.

It was still the early evening and Christopher's party was just getting going when one of the waitresses told me I was wanted urgently on the telephone. The duty officer at Sellafield wanted to speak to me. I feared the worst. I usually did if Sellafield contacted me outside normal office hours.

We were just getting over a period of intense press and public interest following a run of four incidents in less than a month at Sellafield. All of them were relatively minor but together they gave the impression of a site which was out of control. The last thing we needed was a fifth incident.

When media interest was at its fiercest I'd received a request from Peter Sissons, then covering industry for Channel Four News, for permission to take a television crew up to Sellafield. Peter also asked if Walt Patterson, my old adversary from Friends of the Earth, could join him on the visit and if he could film inside the plutonium store, something no other television programme maker had been allowed to do.

On my advice Con Allday agreed to all of Peter's requests. This helped to overcome opposition from the company's security advisers, who were worried that the Channel Four film might identify for potential terrorists where the plutonium store was sited. It was Con's last major decision in the public relations area before his retirement.

The twenty-minute programme segment in Channel Four News which came out of Peter Sissons's visit convinced me that we were on the right lines with the 'open and honest' policy towards public information which Con Allday and I had agreed was essential, even if the people running Sellafield opposed it.

Introducing the programme, Sissons described Sellafield as the most controversial nuclear power plant in the world, which it was. But he also said that after thirty years of near total secrecy things were changing and that he'd been invited to film anywhere he wanted, subject to the protection of national security. The programme explained reprocessing concisely and effectively – providing excellent archive film for the future – and the position of the plutonium store was not identified. At the end of it Walt Patterson said that he believed BNFL was now trying to be more open and honest.

The Channel Four News slot was something of a coup for the company and for me. But it came at the end of an exceptionally tiring few weeks, involving me in a lot of time away from home and a succession of radio and television interviews. I felt a little edgy as I left Christopher Harding's party to answer the phone call from Sellafield.

'Hello. Harold Bolter here. What's the problem? Don't tell me you've had an another incident . . .'

'No. Nothing like that. It's the Chernobyl activity. It's here,' the Sellafield duty officer says. 'The fixed alarms at the gates are picking up signals from cars coming on to the site, would you believe. Alarms are going off all over the place.

'One of the environmental monitoring people has a Geiger counter at his home in Cockermouth and he's phoned in to say that he's measuring activity there. I guess he thought we might be having a problem on site.' As the wind blows or the crow flies, Cockermouth must be a good 20 miles from Sellafield.

'Are you sure you haven't got a problem on site?' I ask suspiciously.

'Absolutely certain. The activity's on the clothes of some of the workers when they get here. We're having to decontaminate them before they can start work. I've never seen anything like it.'

'Okay I believe you. But if it's all down to Chernobyl why do you want to get involved? What can Sellafield do about it? It's somebody else's problem.'

'We think we're the first place in the country to measure the activity. We want to put out a press statement – to show how good our environmental monitoring equipment is.'

'Hang on a minute. I'm not sure that's a good idea, given what's happened at Sellafield over the last few weeks. I want you to prepare a report for Whitehall and a draft press release. Neville Chamberlain and I will decide whether you issue a press release or not.'

Neville Chamberlain has just taken over as chief executive of the company, having been appointed by Christopher Harding, another new boy, over the heads of more senior people. He's never worked at Sellafield and hasn't been involved in the various alarums and excursions there over the years, as I have.

'Producing the drafts you've asked for will take time,' I'm told.

'Fine. There's no rush.'

A delay will suit me very well. The first editions of the national newspapers will soon be put to bed and I don't want them speculating that there might have been some sort of disaster at Sellafield. That could happen if BNFL announces that it's the first nuclear site in the country to find some of the Chernobyl activity. Let someone else be first.

Half an hour or so later, while monitoring the news bulletins on the radio, I heard that the United Kingdom Atomic Energy Authority site at Winfrith in Dorset, the other end of the country from Sellafield, had announced the arrival of the Chernobyl contamination, claiming to be the first to spot it. Good for them.

I then rang the Sellafield duty officer and asked where the drafts I'd asked for were. He said I would have them soon – and sounded a little peeved that having prevented the site from moving quickly I was now pressing for action.

I don't know whether the Chernobyl fall-out landed in West Cumbria before anywhere else in the country but I do know that it was identified at Sellafield before they spotted it at Winfrith. In a small way I may have changed history.

I didn't see much of our new chairman's 'getting to know you' party and nor did several other staff members. We were too busy conferring with Whitehall about what sort of activity we were picking up in Cumbria and near the company's other sites in Cheshire, Lancashire and the small reactor site at Chapelcross, just over the Scottish border.

Our wives and partners seemed to enjoy themselves though. When I popped into the dining room where the party was being held to brief the new chairman and chief executive on the progress of the Chernobyl cloud, there were about half a dozen women sitting in a circle around Christopher Harding. They appeared to be laughing at something Sheila had said. On our way home I asked her what she'd been talking about.

'I told your new chairman that as you've been away for most of the last few weeks I wasn't at all surprised that you were otherwise engaged tonight,' Sheila said. 'In fact I told him that I see so little of you nowadays that I ought to be compensated for the loss of my conjugal rights.'

For the rest of Christopher Harding's time with BNFL he greeted my wife with the words: 'Hello Sheila. How are your conjugals?' The answer varied somewhat.

Chernobyl had a chastening effect on the world-wide nuclear power industry. Morale plummeted in the UK and the reactor operators were particularly subdued. The Chernobyl disaster involved a power station incident not an accident at one of the international reprocessing centres, as some of us at BNFL were quick to point out. The reactor operators had become increasingly critical of BNFL during the spate of incidents which had occurred at Sellafield. Now it was their turn to face the glare of a hostile media.

A working party was set up by the industry to consider what action should be taken in the light of Chernobyl, led by Lord Marshall, the chairman of the Central Electricity Generating Board and a former deputy chairman of the UKAEA. I was one of the two BNFL representatives.

Lord Marshall was a larger than life character in every sense – physically, vocally and emotionally. He was extremely bright and a great favourite of the prime minister, Margaret Thatcher – herself a supporter of nuclear power – but he could get carried away by his own rhetoric and quicksilver mind at times. Marshall's first public reaction to what had happened at Chernobyl was to issue a statement that it was a disaster which had been waiting to happen. Typically, he went on to say that he'd warned the Russians repeatedly that reactors such as that built at Chernobyl would not be considered safe enough to be licensed in Britain.

The trouble with that stance, it seemed to me, was that although Walter might well have told the Russian nuclear czars that their reactor design was fundamentally unsafe he had done so privately, scientist to scientist. To have any chance of having an effect he should have shouted it from the rooftops.

As media interest in the implications of Chernobyl for the UK continued unabated, Lord Marshall persuaded himself that the only way to calm things down would be to shut one of the country's older Magnox nuclear power stations. Mischievous as ever, he suggested that the oldest one, Calder Hall, opened by the Queen 30 years earlier, should be sacrificed. Calder Hall just happened to be owned by BNFL, not the CEGB.

I reminded Walter that Calder Hall provided the Sellafield site with its steam and electricity supplies. Shutting it down would mean that reprocessing would be brought to a halt – and that was not only going to cost BNFL a great deal of money but its customers, the generating boards, as well. Lord Marshall then began to think of other potential targets, including some of the CEGB's own Magnox stations.

We discussed Walter's reactor shut-down idea at one of our internal BNFL executive meetings and came to the conclusion that it was another non-runner. I was briefed to tell him that in our view the industry would be making a big mistake if a nuclear power station in the UK was shut down because one in the Ukraine, of a totally different design, had exploded.

To shut down a safe reactor would imply that there was something wrong with it and we knew that wasn't the case. Moreover, shutting down one reactor was likely to have a domino effect, bringing the operation of all the Magnox stations into question as fuel and reprocessing costs were spread over fewer and fewer stations. The economic argument prevailed and the Magnox stations stayed open. Calder Hall continued to operate for a further 17 years – safely.

Nevertheless, I found the discussions of Chernobyl's effects at Walter Marshall's meetings a considerable shock to the system. They made me question whether I wanted to continue working in an industry where such an horrendous accident could happen and I'm sure that many others began to have doubts, too.

I was forced to consider my position quickly as I was committed to speaking at a conference on nuclear power to be held at Lancaster University a few weeks later. This conference, intended for local authority representatives, had been planned months before the Chernobyl disaster happened and I'd already written my speech for it. Following Chernobyl I threw the speech away and wrote another one describing what I thought would happen in the wake of the accident there.

I came to the conclusion that nuclear power would continue, despite the public clamour for it to be halted, because it was needed. Those countries which were heavily dependent on it, such as France, Japan and, incredibly perhaps, the Soviet Union and its then Eastern European satellites, would certainly not give it up. I have been proved right.

I also expanded on the argument that even if the illogical decision was taken to shut the UK nuclear industry down because of an accident elsewhere in the world involving a form of technology not used in the UK, the shutdown process itself would have to be carefully managed if it was to be done safely.

I think I persuaded a few of the local authority delegates that there was some sort of future for nuclear power, but I failed miserably with a group of student demonstrators who had heard that I was on the campus and invaded the conference. Effectively, they took over the meeting. I was asked whether I minded but it was made obvious to me that there might be trouble if I objected to their presence.

As I spoke the students moved slowly around the hall, their faces painted white and some of them carrying babies. From time to time a few of them would fall to the floor, simulating what they imagined were the death throes of someone dying from radiation. It made rational discussion impossible. All I could do was plough on.

Although I was convinced that nuclear power would continue I wasn't 100 percent certain that I wanted to be part of it. In the end, however, after much soul searching I came to the conclusion that I did. The reasoning process I went through at that time remains valid today.

My former career as an industrial journalist had convinced me that there was no such thing as a totally safe industry. Even the so-called 'green' alternatives to nuclear power involve manufacturing processes which carry risks. I'd visited steel works and rolling mills and watched men sweating it out in front of ferociously hot furnaces. I'd seen them grapple with molten metal, poking and prodding it as it snaked along the channels which contained it. I'd been down a coal mine and seen what was then the new technique of retreat mining, the coal falling behind the miners as the equipment they were using carved huge slices out of the roof as they went along. The dangers were self-evident.

I had watched the fishing boats come into the harbour at Hull in the early hours of the morning after days and nights out fishing. I'd talked to the fishermen about the risks they faced and about friends and relatives who'd died at sea. I'd been round some of the biggest chemical works in the country and was aware of the dangers of some of the poisonous products made and stored in them or transported up and down the country in road tankers or railway trucks. Some of my scientific colleagues had pointed out chlorine tankers moving along the M6 as we travelled north to Sellafield and explained the dangers posed by them should there be a catastrophic motorway crash.

The danger from chemicals had been underlined only 16 months earlier. In the early hours of December 3rd 1984, there had been a disaster which in terms of its effects was even worse than the nuclear accident at Chernobyl. It happened at a Union Carbide subsidiary producing pesticides in the heart of the city of Bhopal, in the state of Madhaya Pradesh in India. A holding tank at this plant overheated and released 40 tons of methyl isocyanate gas into the environment. Being heavier than air, the gas rolled along the ground through the surrounding streets, killing and maiming people as it enveloped their homes and wrapped itself around them.

There is still some controversy about how many people died as a result of Bhopal. Some put the figure at between 2500 and 5000. Others estimate that more than 20,000 people were killed – and that there are more deaths to come.

According to the Bhopal Medical Appeal organisation, which is still trying to raise funds to help people affected by this tragic incident, more than 120,000 people still suffer from ailments caused by the accident and the subsequent pollution at the plant. These ailments include blindness, respiratory problems and gynaecological disorders.

By contrast, 56 people died as a direct result of the Chernobyl explosion according to the International Atomic Energy Authority and the World Health Organisation and there may be another 4000 extra deaths eventually due to cancer among the 6.6 million people most highly exposed to the fall-out. This is clearly dreadful, but the fact remains that the Bhopal chemical catastrophe led to the deaths of more people than the Chernobyl nuclear disaster.

When the Chernobyl accident occurred I was faced with a public relations dilemma as well as an emotional one. For close on two years BNFL's advertising agency had been working on a TV and newspaper programme which looked very promising and which we were ready to launch. But would it be right to do so with the media still covering horror stories from Chernobyl?

A media myth has developed that BNFL's new chairman, Christopher Harding, was responsible for the advertising and associated Sellafield visitors' centre concept and its timing. This is simply not true and, as far as I'm aware, he never made such a claim. Both the press and TV advertising and the idea of an exhibition centre came from me while Con Allday, Christopher's predecessor, was still chairman. The advertising had been in the making long before Christopher Harding became chairman and we had a visitors' centre, of sorts, up and running before Con left the company.

If anything, Christopher's appointment delayed the advertising campaign launch. Con was ready to agree it if he'd been allowed to stay on as chairman but when it was decided that he had to go he thought it more appropriate that my proposal should go to a board meeting chaired by Harding.

I met Christopher a couple of months before he took over as chairman and gave him a thorough briefing on the advertising campaign concept and planned expenditure on it. His response was interesting.

'I like the idea of the campaign,' he said, 'but are you sure it's going to work?'

'I can't give you any cast iron guarantees,' I replied. 'But my gut feeling is that it's going to work very well indeed. All our focus group research suggests that people are waiting for a signal that we've stopped being secretive.'

'Okay Harold, but if things go wrong on your head be it.'

My proposal for a £3 million spend on advertising went to the first board meeting chaired by Christopher Harding and after a bit of a struggle it was approved. As I expected, some of the external directors thought it was a lot of money to spend on advertising and Walter Marshall let it be known that the CEGB wouldn't help to pay for it through our reprocessing tariffs.

The attitude of the external directors is best described as the bicycle shed syndrome. They could get their heads around relatively small sums of money like £3 million and argue the toss about it for hours given the chance. But when a capital expenditure proposal relating to a massive engineering project costing ten or a hundred times that amount came to them for approval it often as not went through on the nod.

The advertisements which formed the main plank of our 'open and honest' campaign were developed by Young & Rubicam, the agency which I had chosen in consultation with Jeffrey Preece and Bob Cartwright, BNFL's advertising manager, who liaised with the agency.

John Banks and Toby Hoare, the Y&R executives handling the BNFL account had persuaded me that we stood no chance of influencing the attitudes of people who were extremely anti-nuclear through advertising so we shouldn't waste money on trying to do so. We had to concentrate on three groups of people who might listen to what we said and whom we might convince that we had a case worth supporting.

The first of these groups was categorised as the 'mainstreamers', people best thought of as Mr and Mrs Average – home centred, patriotic, the core of our society. They might not fully understand the issues, but worried about leaks and accidents and how these might affect their own well-being.

The second target group was categorised as the 'succeeders' – business people who were generally well informed and confident, and represented the commercial thrust of society. They could be expected to want Britain to be at the forefront of a world technology such as nuclear power.

Finally, there were the 'reformers' – highly educated people who were more concerned with social and moral issues than other people – *Guardian* readers, if you will. That may seem surprising, but we felt that these people would be interested in such issues as the effect which burning fossil fuels had on the environment. This was over 20 years ago, remember, but some people were already aware of the dangers.

Through advertising we wanted people to come to accept that BNFL was not trying to hide anything, rather that it was going to great lengths to provide facts and information to the public. We also wanted to show that the company was confident that once people had all the facts they would be reassured about the professionalism, safety and benefits of the work which BNFL did for Britain.

The strategy we settled upon was straightforward. For 'mainstreamers' we intended to use television to communicate the 'open and honest' concept in a simple way. For 'succeeders' and 'reformers' this would be supported by a press campaign designed to fill in more detail, recognising their place in society as influential opinion formers.

To a considerable extent the nature and subject of the launch commercial for television was dictated to us by the then Independent Broadcasting Authority (IBA). The IBA's code of advertising standards and practice at that time stated that 'no advertisements may be inserted by or on behalf of any body, the objects whereof are wholly or mainly of a political nature and no advertisement may be directed towards a political end'.

The IBA took the view that a company producing fuel for nuclear power stations and dealing with it when it came out of the reactors had a political objective. It was ridiculous, particularly when it was prepared to allow Tory government advertisements pushing the privatisation of whole swathes of British industry to get onto TV.

The IBA remained intransigent for over a year, but eventually Young & Rubicam wore it down. It came out with a new edict, as illogical as earlier ones, but which nevertheless opened up a window of opportunity for us. It insisted that to meet its rules advertising must be associated with the sale of products and should not be used to influence attitudes. As BNFL didn't have a product which was for general sale, it would not be allowed on television.

But BNFL did have a product which was generally available to members of the public – the small exhibition centre near the perimeter fence of Sellafield which I had managed to get built when I first joined BNFL. It wasn't the most attractive place in the world. At the insistence of the Sellafield management it had been built over the top of a dental surgery close to the perimeter fence. But it was a tourist attraction of sorts – and other tourist attractions were being advertised on television.

The IBA could wriggle no further and agreed that we could advertise a tourist venue. Fortunately, using the visitors' centre as a focus for our TV advertising fitted in remarkably well with the results of our research.

We had tested advertisements which sought to explain the benefits of nuclear power and others which discussed the risks, trying to put them into the context of everyday risks, and they simply didn't work. BNFL's credibility was so low that nobody believed what we said. The only message which did register favourably with our test audiences was the one that invited people to go to Sellafield to see what went on there for themselves.

The launch commercial which Young & Rubicam developed was to the point. Against a backdrop of the Cumbrian countryside, beautifully filmed, an open invitation was extended to people to visit the Sellafield visitors' centre. This was accompanied by press advertisements containing a similar message, which were placed in a selection of Sunday newspaper colour supplements and other magazines.

A formal invitation card was attached to the press advertisements – a new technique 20 years ago. When the card was removed it revealed a picture of Sellafield, looking at its best on a sunny day in the Lake District.

After a lot of agonising we launched our advertising campaign six weeks after Chernobyl. I convinced Christopher Harding that because of the disaster members of the public wanted more than ever before to understand nuclear power. They would either throw it out as a result of the concerns raised by the world's worst nuclear incident or come to terms with it.

Christopher was clearly nervous about what we were about to do, but told me that he would support my decision to launch the campaign as long as I realised that if anything went wrong I would take the blame. I agreed.

The launch couldn't have gone better. The first television advertisement by any company in the nuclear power industry was carried as a news item on virtually every BBC and commercial television and radio bulletin and in every national newspaper. The BBC incorporated the fifty-second ad into its main TV news programme. It was the first time it had carried an advertisement for anything other than its own programmes or publications.

We calculated later that the advertisement generated more than £2 million of free advertising in newspaper editorial columns and radio and television news slots, plus a wider range of spin-off newspaper articles and visits to Sellafield by journalists and TV news crews.

Our message to people to visit the exhibition centre did more than reinforce our message that we wanted to be open and honest, although we know from follow-up research that it worked very well in that context. The important thing was not how many people actually went up to Sellafield, which is not very accessible, but that most of the population knew that they could go there

Later we found that the television advertisement also carried a subliminal message on safety which we hadn't anticipated. People began to say that Sellafield must be safe or BNFL wouldn't have dared to invite people to visit the site.

Greenpeace, which had taken over from Friends of the Earth as the leading anti-nuclear organisation, was silly enough to object to the advertisement campaign. It complained that the ads were a waste of public money which should have been spent on safety. That gave us the chance to respond with a press release showing how much we had spent on safety and the environment, and pointing out that far from wasting public funds BNFL had paid a dividend to the Treasury every year since the company was formed.

We went on to tweak Greenpeace's tail further by taking two facing pages in most of the national newspapers. On the left-hand page we ran these words: 'For one side of the argument about nuclear energy British Nuclear Fuels urge you to write to this address:' We then gave BNFL's address. On the opposite, right-hand page we ran exactly the same words – and gave Greenpeace's address, using their logo.

The message was clear – we believed that our arguments were more persuasive than theirs and were prepared to take our chances in an open and honest debate. Again, Greenpeace responded rather petulantly, complaining that we had used their name and logo without permission. All that did was draw more attention to the advertisement, giving us even more free publicity.

As a result of the advertising campaign the number of visitors to Sellafield increased dramatically, from just under 30,000 visitors in 1985 to 65,000 in 1986. By 1987, the first full year of advertising, they had reached 104,000 and the tiny exhibition centre over the dentist's surgery was bursting at the seams. At the weekends we had people queueing to get in.

In May 1987 I received permission from the board to build a new Sellafield visitors' centre at a cost of £5 million, split roughly equally between the fabric of the building and the display materials inside it. The new centre was opened by HRH Prince Philip, Duke of Edinburgh, in June 1988. The number of visitors soared to 160,000 over the next year and in 1989 the centre and BNFL's overall 'open and honest' public information policy won the top Institute of Public Relations award, the Sword of Excellence.

The Sellafield visitors' centre was updated in 2003 and has attracted around three million visitors since Prince Philip formally opened it. It's doubtful if any owner of Sellafield – and responsibility for the site seems to change hands fairly regularly – will ever be able to shut it down, because of its 'open and honest' symbolism.

Prince Philip's decision to open the Sellafield visitors' centre was undoubtedly influenced by the fact that for several years BNFL – at my prompting – had sponsored the Lowther Horse Driving Trials, in which he competed with his carriage and four.

In August 1987 Christopher Harding, my wife and I were invited by the Earl and Countess of Lonsdale, the owners of the Lowther estate, to join Prince Philip and other guests for dinner at Askham Hall, where they lived, during the Trials.

There were perhaps a dozen people there and as we mingled before dinner and were presented to Prince Philip, Lady Lonsdale offered me some fudge which she told me she'd made herself. I declined, explaining that I didn't have much of a sweet tooth.

After dinner, as we drank our coffee in the drawing room, the Countess came round again, offering what I took to be more of her home-made fudge. This time I decided that it would be politic to take a piece. It was cube sugar.

'I simply love cube sugar,' I said as I ate a lump of it, to the considerable surprise of Lady Lonsdale.

Dinner itself was dominated by Prince Philip, as one would expect. Everyone deferred to him. As soon as he finished whatever he was eating Lady Lonsdale rang a small glass bell and the servants removed the dinner plates. That may have been fine for everybody else but Sheila is a slow eater. She left Askham Hall feeling hungry.

My personal stock was extremely high following the success of the advertising campaign and the visitors' centre opening by Prince Philip. I was approached by Geoffrey Tucker, a former publicity director of the Conservative Party who had become a consultant to BNFL in Con Allday's time as chairman, to see if I would be interested in taking charge of publicity at the Channel Tunnel Company, later to become Eurotunnel. The tunnel project was in trouble financially and getting a very bad press, and Lord Pennock, the Channel Tunnel Company's chairman, thought I was the man to work up a strategy to restore its reputation.

He offered me the post of Director of Corporate Affairs and placed a financial package on the table which would have made me much wealthier than I could ever expect to become working in the public sector for BNFL. In addition to the basic package there was a compensation clause in it to cater for the possible early ending of the project – a sure sign of how precarious the Channel Tunnel Company's finances were at the time and how close the tunnel came to not being built.

I decided to take the job and saw Christopher Harding, still the relatively new chairman of BNFL, and handed in my notice. He asked for time to see if he could win approval from the mandarins in Whitehall for a counter offer. I told Harding that it would take a salary increase of around 40 percent to keep me at BNFL and I doubted very much if he would be able to obtain permission to pay me that sort of money.

In the event the offer was below 40 percent – but not too far below. As a result I became the highest-paid director in the company, with the exception of Christopher himself, with a total salary and bonuses package worth over £100,000 a year. This was considerably more than the newly appointed chief executive was being paid.

I also managed to negotiate an improvement in my pension terms. It was agreed that every year I worked for BNFL in future would be worth two years in terms of my pension entitlement.

Christopher and I also came to an agreement that I should receive a CBE in recognition of my services to the nuclear power industry. That took longer to bring about, mainly because Christopher wanted Neville Chamberlain and my very good friend John Hayles, the man who negotiated the Japanese THORP contracts and who was about to retire, to be so honoured before me. But it happened in the end.

Despite the positive publicity the company was getting, reinforced by a chairman who had a natural gift for making himself liked by all sorts of people, even some of the nuclear industry's opponents, BNFL and Sellafield still had serious problems.

One of the four epidemiological studies commissioned as a result of the Black inquiry into leukaemias in the Sellafield area in 1985, started when Con Allday was chairman, was one led by Professor Martin Gardner, of the Medical Research Council's Environmental Epidemiological Unit at the University of Southampton. His report appeared early in 1990, and shook the company and the Sellafield workforce to the core.

A few days before the Gardner report was due to be published, Dr Roger Berry, the company's Director of Health and Safety, came to see me. Recruited six months earlier by Neville Chamberlain, Roger had previously been Professor of Oncology in the Middlesex School of Medicine of University College, London. He hadn't worked in industry previously and had a bit of a professorial air about him.

Roger told me that he'd received a copy of the Gardner report and thought it might lead to considerable press interest, but because it had been given to him on a confidential basis he couldn't give me any details. I told him that was ridiculous. What was I supposed to do about a report I wasn't allowed to see? I pleaded with him to give me some idea of what was in it but he refused. I was extremely annoyed with him.

Eventually I received a copy of the Gardner report a bare 48 hours before it was published and was forbidden to brief the workforce or trade unions on its contents by the terms of the embargo placed on it. Dr Berry informed me that the Gardner study was an impeccable piece of scientific research and that it was unchallengeable.

The Gardner report's main finding, which Dr Berry supported, was that the external radiation received by fathers during their employment at Sellafield was associated with the development of leukaemia among their children.

It suggested that men who received a cumulative total of more than ten rems of radiation before the date of their child's conception, especially if they had been exposed to one rem or more in the six months immediately prior to conception, stood six to eight times the chance of fathering a child with leukaemia than other men.

The indications were that radiation exposures at these levels affected the germ cells of the workers concerned, producing a mutation in their sperm which led to leukaemia in their children.

It was the stuff of nightmares. The report was launched at a London press conference and we hadn't been allowed to warn employees about what it contained, although I'd asked Dr Berry to press Gardner to speak to the Sellafield workforce before his report appeared. Professor Gardner had declined to do so. As a result, employees had to face up to headlines speaking of 'Sellafield's Deadly Inheritance' or stating as fact that 'Dads Passed Cancer to Babies'.

Some of the employees who had children with leukaemia were in despair and the company was suddenly faced with thousands of worried families seeking advice, comfort and reassurance. I felt near to despair myself. The scenario painted by the Gardner report was simply horrendous – and totally unexpected.

The Gardner hypothesis was based on very small numbers – only ten cases of leukaemia over a period of 36 years, from 1950 to 1985 – and it is a sad fact that around 1200 children develop leukaemia every year in the

UK. But those ten cases attracted more attention than all of the others put together.

Given Dr Berry's insistence that the Gardner hypothesis was based on sound science, and his belief that the link between radiation exposure and leukaemia had been proved, the company's public response to it had to be muted and anodyne. All we could say was that we would take the Gardner report extremely seriously and review all of its implications for the health and safety of our employees and their families.

Then, nearly a week after he had launched his report in London, Professor Gardner was finally persuaded to go to Sellafield to explain his report to the workforce. Roger Berry went with him. The meeting took place in the canteen, one of Sellafield's largest indoor meeting areas, which was packed with employees and their wives and partners. Jeffrey Preece attended on my behalf.

What happened was a public relations disaster. After a lively meeting, in which feelings ran high, Professor Gardner held a news conference, supported by Roger Berry. As soon as it ended Jeffrey Preece was on the phone to me.

'Harold. We're in big, big trouble. Roger Berry's told the press up here that the company is thinking of advising the Sellafield workforce not to have families, in order to avoid the risk of fathering a child with leukaemia. The union people are hopping mad and they're contacting their national leaders.'

'I'm not surprised! What exactly did Berry say?'

'Hang on. I made a note. Here you are: "It may be that the proper advice is, if you are so worried, then maybe the advice is that you do not have a family."'

'I don't believe it. Well, yes I do. A few days ago he suggested that we should ask younger employees who worked in the active areas to stay celibate or use contraceptives. Honestly! Then he came up with the idea that the company might establish a sperm bank or call for radiation volunteers from among the older men. The man's a loose cannon.'

'Harold. That's all very well, but what am I supposed to say here, now? The Press Association is about to put out a story that Roger's warning men not to have sex with their wives. PA's pushing for a response from us. They'll run the story without a response if we don't get a move on.'

'Where is Roger Berry? Get him to the phone.'

'I can't. He left for home as soon as the press conference ended. He's got a two and a half hour drive ahead of him.'

'Okay, Jeff. Tell PA I'll phone them with a company response within the next half hour. I'm going to have to disown Roger Berry. He won't like it but there you are. We have no choice. We can't forbid workers to have sex for God's sake.'

I rushed out a statement that what Dr Berry had said was not company policy. I went on to say that BNFL would offer a programme of medical counselling by the company's doctors for all employees at Sellafield who wanted it, on an individual, personal basis. We would emphasise to them that the Gardner report was a hypothesis, not proven fact, without playing down what the risk might be to them if its conclusions were confirmed. We would also commission further research of our own.

'Ultimately, it is for each individual worker to reach a decision, not for the company to advise on one course of action or another. If an individual worker asks to be removed to a different area of work to reduce his radiation exposure, the company will give sympathetic consideration to the request,' I said.

Once again I had been forced to make company policy on the hoof, as it were, under pressure. There was no time to consult anyone or to get approval. I didn't know what the chief executive or chairman's reaction would be, although I was sure Roger Berry wouldn't like what I'd said.

In the event Neville Chamberlain and Christopher Harding supported me 100 percent, which was a relief. Roger Berry felt badly let down. I tried to explain to him that what I'd said was the only way to protect the company – and probably his career as well for that matter. He never accepted this.

As it was he was pilloried by some of the tabloids. As soon as the story broke, reporters managed to find out where he lived and camped outside his home in Cheshire, waiting for him to return from Sellafield. Roger and his wife, Valerie, didn't have children and this became known, too. One of the papers tried to link this to Roger's advice about not fathering children. I felt desperately sorry for both of them.

My statement didn't end the matter, of course. Following the Roger Berry episode, the trade unions stepped up their pressure on the company to decide what it was going to do. Waiting for the results of further research was no answer to the immediate problem of a workforce which had been completely stunned and demoralised by the Gardner hypothesis, they said. They were obviously right.

Jack Dromey, of the Transport and General Workers Union, was particularly incensed at what he saw as the company's lack of action and warned that some trade union members were threatening to stop work. Matters were brought to a head on the morning of Friday February 23rd 1990, when the trade unions demanded an immediate meeting with Neville Chamberlain.

Fortuitously, Neville, Roger Berry, Grahame Smith, the Sellafield site director, and I were at the Hilton Hotel, near Manchester airport, for a senior management group conference. Instead of the conference, Neville agreed to meet the union leaders that afternoon at the Heathrow business centre. Then the four of us sat down to work out what we were going to say to them. Neville turned to me first.

'What do you think Harold?'

'In my view it doesn't matter what reservations we might have about Gardner – and I know we have plenty – we have no alternative but to treat his hypothesis as though it's correct. Roger thinks Gardner's got it right, remember – and he is the company's director of health and safety.

'To do nothing will be tantamount to telling people that if they continue to work at Sellafield they can either take their chances on fathering children with leukaemia – or stop having sex. It's not on. We have to bring radiation doses down to the levels Gardner reckons are safe.'

Roger Berry remains quiet, as he does throughout the meeting. Grahame Smith, on the other hand, explodes.

'What are you trying to do Harold, ruin the reprocessing business, finish Sellafield off? This is crazy. I don't care what Gardner says – and I don't care what Roger says either. The Gardner hypothesis doesn't stack up with what we know from experience.

'There's something wrong with it. It's flawed. Roger might think Gardner's right but the health and safety people at Sellafield don't believe a word of it. The cost of trying to put into practice what Gardner's recommending will ruin the reprocessing business. We can't do it.'

'Grahame,' I say, 'we're seeing the unions this afternoon. We can't tell them that although the man responsible for health and safety in the

company, a cancer expert, thinks the Gardner report is correct Grahame Smith, the site director, doesn't so we're not going to do anything. It won't wash.

'It's all right you saying it will ruin the business but how do you know that Grahame? You haven't done the costing exercise yet. Ignoring Gardner could be worse for the business than acting on his recommendations. We could be in for a long drawn-out strike. If that happens we'll have to reduce doses in the end anyway, to get the men back. Doing nothing isn't an option.'

Neville Chamberlain announces his decision. 'I agree with you Harold. Get something typed up and we'll try to get the unions to use it as a framework for discussion when we meet them this afternoon.'

And that is what happened. I wrote a position paper committing the company to working with the unions on a programme designed to ensure that no workers received more than the one and a half rems of radiation a year recommended by Gardner. It was agreed that I would present the paper at the Heathrow meeting with the trade unions, leaving Neville Chamberlain to arbitrate if things went wrong.

When Neville and I arrived at Heathrow we were greeted by the television cameras and a dozen or so newspaper reporters, obviously alerted by the unions. We promised the journalists that we'd make a statement after we'd met the trade unions and went into the meeting with an agitated group of trade union officials.

It was quickly apparent that Jack Dromey, married to Harriet Harman MP and with young children of his own, was very upset about what the Gardner report contained and what Roger Berry had said. He had to be calmed down by Jimmy Airley, the chairman of the trade union side of the Company Joint Industrial Council, before it was agreed that my position paper should be used as the focus for our discussion.

My paper was agreed in its entirety and the reporters attending the press briefing, who had been expecting a row, were amazed – and disappointed – to find the two sides in total agreement about what had to be done in the light of Gardner.

At that time no fewer than 285 of the 6500 radiation workers at Sellafield received doses above Gardner's recommended control level. It took nearly four years of hard work and a great deal of money but the Gardner figure was achieved. Whether such a drastic reduction in radiation doses was necessary is arguable but with feeling running so high at that time I think we had no alternative but to agree to it.

I am convinced that as a result of what we agreed with the trade unions that day at Heathrow the operations carried out at Sellafield are now as safe as in any comparable industry – and safer than most. That must be worth something.

Equally, I don't think there's much doubt that Grahame Smith's instinct that the Gardner report was flawed was correct. Later test cases in the courts confirmed as much. That was certainly the view of Mr Justice French, who cleared BNFL of causing cancers in two women, daughters of men who had worked at Sellafield, in test cases brought in the High Court on their behalf by Martyn Day, a solicitor who took a particular interest in radiation effects.

Mr Justice French said that the Gardner hypothesis stood alone, unsupported by any other studies. He also said that criticism of the Gardner theory by BNFL's witnesses all had validity and diminished confidence in its conclusions. Case dismissed.

I'd left BNFL by the time these cases ended in October 1993 and so had Christopher Harding. On his departure he was awarded a well-deserved knighthood for his services to the nuclear industry. Christopher was a personally charming man who mixed easily. He always did his homework on the people he was about to meet, which is very flattering, and always dropped them a note to thank them after the meeting, which also went down well. He established himself in the minds of national and local politicians and most sections of the media as someone who could be trusted. It was he who insisted that at least half of BNFL's monthly board meetings should be held close to one of the company's operating sites or its headquarters at Risley and that on the evening before them a dinner should be held for local community leaders. Previously most board meetings were held in London, to suit the convenience of the non-executive directors.

All told, Christopher was a great networker, with an engaging personality, and he was a good chairman to work for, even though he obviously knew far less about nuclear power than his predecessor, the incomparable Con Allday.

Christopher was succeeded as chairman by John Guinness, the Permanent Secretary at the Department of Energy, when the department was wound up by the Energy Secretary, John Wakeham, a distant relative of his. It was a convenient appointment, no doubt, but it was opposed by all of the BNFL executive directors, who felt that it was a retrograde step to put a civil servant in charge of the company.

Shortly before he arrived at BNFL, Neville Chamberlain told me that he'd been asked by Guinness to find out from me whether I would be more likely or less likely to stay with the company if I was given my long-awaited, and promised, CBE. I wasn't sure what the point of the question was, but I assumed Guinness wanted to be sure I stayed with the company.

I hesitated a lot. At the time I was considering an excellent offer from Pilkington, the glass company, to become its PR director and felt very tempted. At BNFL I had a reputation for being 'a safe pair of hands' and as a result I was overloaded with work. I was a director not only of BNFL itself but of BNFL Inc, an American offshoot, Nuclear Transport Limited, an Anglo-French-German company, UK Nirex, the organisation seeking to find a disposal site for nuclear waste, the West Cumbria Development Association, of which I became chairman, and the British Nuclear Forum, the industry's trade association, which I also ended up chairing.

Within BNFL itself, I had my formal role as company secretary and was also responsible for public relations, the personnel function, the company administration and legal departments, the security and safeguards organisation, which looked after site security and ensured that plutonium was properly safeguarded, and the UKAEA police force. There were probably a few other things, which I've forgotten.

As I was to discover, the problem with having a safe pair of hands is that you spend so much time protecting the company's interests you forget to look after your own.

Despite feeling beleagured. I told Neville to tell the new chairman that I had no plans to leave BNFL. It was the right answer and in 1993 I finally received my CBE from Her Majesty the Queen at Buckingham Palace. It was a memorable and thoroughly enjoyable occasion and a matter of great pride to me. I suppose the lower the starting point in life the greater the enjoyment of some public recognition of success if and when it arrives.

Because only three members of the family were allowed to be present, Sheila and our two daughters, Helen and Sarah, were there for the investiture. Matthew, my son, is the kindest of people. He immediately volunteered to let the girls fill the places. 'No problem, I know a pub the Beatles used to go to. I'll see you at Beoty's for lunch.'

Apart from the actual investiture by the Queen, which I was too excited to remember much about, the big day was made for me by a couple of conversations I had with Michael Caine, the actor and film star, who received his CBE at the same time as me.

The honours ceremony was wonderfully choreographed. On our arrival the recipients were quietly arranged into three different groups – those to be made a Member of the Order of the British Empire or an Officer of the Order, those to be made Commanders, and those to be made Knight Commanders. The three groups were then corralled into separate parts of the room where we waited to be called forward.

One of the ladies who was to receive a CBE could hardly contain herself when she found herself in the same group of people as Michael Caine.

'Do you think he'd mind if I went to speak to him?' she asks.

'I wouldn't think so.'

'But I couldn't just walk up to him and start talking. I wouldn't know what to say.'

'Well come with me then and I'll introduce you.'

'Are you sure? You don't mind?'

'No, of course not. I'd like to meet him myself. It will be interesting to see what he's like in real life.'

Michael Caine is standing on his own, wearing a lounge suit. The rest of the men in the room are wearing morning dress, probably hired from Moss Bros like mine.

I cross the room with the nervous lady and make the introductions. The two talk briefly while I listen and look on. Then she moves away, satisfied.

'So what are you getting an award for?' Michael Caine asks me.

'Services to nuclear power.'

'Oh my God – and I've just shaken hands with you,' he says, laughing.

'It's okay. I haven't been up to Sellafield for over a week. The radiation's worn off by now with any luck.' He takes it as the joke it's meant to be.

'Anyway, can I ask you something? Why are you the only man in the

room wearing a lounge suit? – a very nice lounge suit, of course, but nevertheless a morning suit it is not. And I was told morning suit.'

'I've been working. Haven't had time to organise a morning suit.'

'I don't believe you. If you'd wanted a morning suit the wardrobe people at the studios would have found you one straight away. You just want to be different.'

From his laughter I know that I'm right.

The awards are made to people in alphabetical order and I precede the film star into the ballroom where the Queen is making the investitures, to the background sound of a brass band playing songs from the musicals, which seems appropriate. Our families are in the balcony, close to the band, watching us.

The instructions we have received are precise. Walk to the centre of the room when your name is called. Stop. Turn to the left and face the Queen. Take three steps forward and stop again. The Queen will then place the medal with its ribbon round your neck. She will say a few words to you and you'll know when to leave her presence. You then walk backwards three steps. Stop. Turn right and walk off.

I get the moves right. No problem. I am very much in awe of Her Majesty. She must think I'm a tongue-tied fool – me, with all my recent radio and television experience.

Michael Caine is the next to walk the walk. I've already left the room but Sheila tells me later that he makes a mess of the drill. Instead of walking backwards after receiving his medal he turns round and walks away with his back turned to the Queen.

I catch a word with him in the courtyard later as we meet up with our families again and wait for our cars to arrive

'You of all people – getting the moves wrong,' I say.

'The trouble is I'm used to several takes,' he says with a laugh. 'Anyway, where are you going for lunch?'

'Beoty's. Top of St Martins Lane, over the road from Moss Bros. It's my favourite restaurant in London. Before lunch I'm going to change out of this morning suit at Moss Bros. and return it. It's a bit conspicuous. Where are you going?'

'Langan's.'

'I should have known. You own the place, you mean devil.'

More laughter and we break off to return to our families and our respective restaurants. Whenever I see him in a film I still say: I like Michael Caine.

While I am proud of my CBE – and wish there were more occasions when I could decently show it off – I must confess that there are times when I question the system that brought it about. My award didn't come out of the blue, it formed part of a pay rise package. That turns the 'cash for honours' debate on its head, surely. Can a system which allows for honours in lieu of cash be any more right than one in which honours can be bought with cash?

When John Guinness asked whether I was more likely or less likely to stay at BNFL if I received an award he was making a very clear point, it seems to me. He was demonstrating that as a former top civil servant he was in a position to stop the promised award if I didn't do what he wanted me to do. So much for the agreement I'd made with Christopher Harding five years earlier, which I'd been told had been cleared with the Department of Energy where Guinness then worked.

In all, it seems to me that the ability people of influence have to with-hold honours is as important as their ability to push them through the system. I don't just mean the civil service mandarins, the Whitehall warriors as Willie Whitelaw used to call them, but also their generals, the govern-ment ministers who are supposed to be in charge of the warriors but all too often end up as their followers.

And we mustn't forget the honours dished out or withheld by the prime minister of the day – an obvious form of patronage. How many people are in the House of Lords simply because the PM wanted them out of the way to make way for someone else in the Commons? How many of the prime minister's friends and acolytes are rewarded?

At a lower level we must also remember the influence which the leading politicians and officials in our local authorities and regional government offices can have. They can effectively stop richly deserved honours going to members of the teaching and other public sector professions who have upset them somewhere along the line simply by not putting forward cita-tions for them.

Within BNFL it was a tradition, started by Christopher Harding, that recipients of honours – at all levels – should be invited to join the chairman for a single celebratory lunch at Risley, accompanied by their partners.

John Guinness, BNFL's new chairman, followed tradition after I'd been awarded my CBE but seemed to find the occasion difficult. The conversation round the table was desultory and stilted. Eventually it got round to the problems caused by negative equity. One of the factory workers prompted the discussion when he said that his son might have to sell his house at a loss because he couldn't afford to keep up his mortgage.

'I know exactly what you mean,' the chairman said. 'My family once had to sell hundreds of acres of land in Norfolk which they had bought for £3 an acre at a knock down price of £2 an acre . . . Mind you, it was 300 years ago.'

I don't know whether the numbers are right, but that was the import of John Guinness's remark. Its relevance to the plight of a young man struggling to keep his family housed at that very moment wasn't immediately obvious. To me it was snobbish and patronising.

I didn't really know John Guinness before he joined BNFL but when it was announced that he was to become our new chairman my old friend Roland Gribben, the *Daily Telegraph*'s business editor, described him as 'the waspish John Guinness'.

I looked the term up in the dictionary. Waspish, it said, sharply irritable. Synonyms: irascible, irritable, snappish, testy, touchy, venomous. I didn't like the sound of that.

12

The Fraud Suspect

My nightmares began some years ago. They've been diluted by time and occur intermittently now, but they are always there, waiting to appear, unbidden. In the worst of my dreams I am about to stand trial for a crime I didn't commit. In the best I'm preparing for my retirement from the company I left under a cloud and in a blaze of publicity.

There is to be a proper farewell this time, with the regulation dinner in the penthouse suite at the Café Royal. I will be presented with the silver salver which directors receive when they retire, suitably inscribed. A few kind words will be said about the contribution I've made to Britain's nuclear power industry and I will respond, briefly and graciously.

This goodbye will not involve a Serious Fraud Squad investigation into my conduct as a director of British Nuclear Fuels, ordered by a government minister, Michael Heseltine. There will be no front page headlines and no reporters, photographers and television cameramen surrounding my house, door-stepping, hoping to snatch a picture of me looking suitably contrite.

This time I will not be driven to contemplate taking my life.

'Kafkaesque' is a much-abused term but as I understand its meaning it describes all too accurately the surreal situation which led to my resignation as BNFL's Company Secretary and Director of Corporate Affairs.

It's been said that there is a senseless, disorienting, often menacing complexity and sense of impending danger to be found in Kafka's works. That is what I felt as I was forced to wait for nearly two years for my position to be resolved, kept in the dark about what was going on, left to imagine what it all meant and where it would end.

In his novel *The Trial* Kafka also describes the intentional distortion of reality by powerful but anonymous bureaucrats, who treat a lack of evidence as an irritating inconvenience. That sounds familiar, too.

In a typically Kafkaesque way my torment can be traced back to something simple and unthreatening: the decision Sheila and I took to move to a smaller property when the children started to leave home for university or marriage. We found a bungalow which a developer hadn't quite finished developing but which was more or less right for us and in the right location. It needed a breeze-block wall built to separate the central heating boiler from the garage where it had been placed, contravening fire regulations. We also decided to have an en suite bathroom installed in the main bedroom. For good measure we decided to replace all of the internal doors, which weren't to our taste. We chose a style we liked from a catalogue and agreed that the doors should be stained a mahogany colour.

Day-to-day site maintenance at Risley was in the hands of Malcolm Lees, a relatively junior administrator who managed a running contract with a local contractor for decorating and minor repair work, drawing on the services of other local firms, such as gardening contractors, when necessary. He learned of my problems with the new bungalow from someone and offered to arrange to get the work done. I jumped at the offer and agreed a price.

There was nothing unusual about contractors working for BNFL employees as well as the company, and there were no rules against the practice. Several of the directors and other members of staff had work done for them by contractors during the 18 years I worked for the company – at Risley and at the sites.

The work on the bungalow was done. New doors were fitted and a workman applied a mahogany-coloured stain to them, or so I thought. The existing doors, which were also new, were taken in part exchange. I paid my bill and life moved on. I didn't think any more about the matter.

Several years later BNFL ran into a problem over the implementation of its emergency procedures. These place a legal requirement on the company to set up a central control room at the company's headquarters in the event of a serious emergency at one of the operating sites and to act as the focus for communications with Whitehall.

As company secretary I was responsible for establishing the control centre. I also had to ensure that others, such as the chief executive, the board member in overall charge of the division involved in the incident and the director of health and safety, made their way to it as soon as possible.

Unfortunately, head office was on the far side of the Manchester ship canal from where most of the people with a designated role in an emergency lived, in places such as Knutsford, Wilmslow, Altrincham and Sale.

It was announced that the Thelwall viaduct section of the M6, the normal route across the canal, was to be repaired and expanded. This work would take several years to complete and we were warned to expect considerable delays. The only alternatives to the viaduct were a swing bridge and a toll bridge, both calling for detours and both expected to be subject to delays as they took the extra pressure.

One day Neville Chamberlain and I were discussing this situation and I mentioned that I was thinking of moving house, downsizing once more following the departure of our last child Sarah to university and my 93-year-old mother-in-law's move into a care home. Matthew would be the only one left with us and he was showing signs of leaving.

One option, I said, was for us to move closer to the office. This would have advantages for the company in relation to the emergency procedures and would also mean that I didn't have to face years of traffic jams on the way to the office.

There was a new housing development at Culcheth, a village within a few minutes' drive of Risley, which Sheila and I rather liked, I told Neville. If the company agreed to move us under the financial terms which applied to employees moved in the company's interest I would consider buying one of the houses. It seemed to make sense all round. Neville agreed.

Malcolm Lees came into the picture again because we had a last-minute hitch on the sale of the bungalow and I needed a new furniture removal company in a hurry, literally within days. He found one. I was grateful to him.

With the finance provided by BNFL Sheila and I thought we could get our new house just how we wanted it. The inside of the house was painted the usual magnolia and we decided to brighten things up by having the walls of all the rooms papered. We also wanted someone to fit the electric lights.

Malcolm Lees offered to help and we left the choice of the contractor or contractors to him. I made no secret of what was going on. Any time Lees wanted to talk to me or I wanted to check progress with him an appointment was arranged through my secretary, Christine Taylor, who had replaced Joan Byrne when she was poached by Neville Chamberlain.

My office could only be reached through a large, open-plan room containing a central pool of secretaries and typists – not somewhere where visitors went unnoticed. Dozens of people knew about the Bolters' bungalow project. Our choice of wallpaper and paint was even discussed with Lees by some of the girls.

I wasn't there when the work was carried out. The workmen usually came in after I'd left for the office and had gone by the time I got home. Either that or I was out and about on BNFL's business, in the UK and abroad.

I made it clear to Lees that I would buy all of the materials required and pay separately for labour. I would rely on him to keep a careful check on how many hours the workmen were putting in for us and ensure that a full record was kept.

Alwyn Ellis was the man to whom Malcolm Lees reported and late one Friday afternoon he asked to see me on a personal matter. When he entered my office he looked concerned and slightly embarrassed.

'It's Malcolm Lees,' he said. 'There's an internal audit going on and discrepancies have been found. It looks serious and there's a suspicion that some sort of fiddle has been going on, involving Lees and the Risley site contractor.

'Your name has come up in the investigation. It seems that the company has been charged for work done on your new house.'

'That's ridiculous,' I replied. 'I don't know whether you know it or not but the company is paying for my house move and has given me a lump sum. I suppose Lees could be confused about who's paying for what but he shouldn't be.

'Anyway the work on my house isn't even finished yet. The last I heard it was going to take another couple of weeks at least. I haven't received my bill and no money's changed hands.'

After Alwyn left I sent for Malcolm Lees. He arrived with a man he introduced as the manager of the contractor firm, not someone I knew. Lees was full of bonhomie, as usual, and said that it was normal for the internal audit section to turn their attention to the administration costs of the Risley site from time to time. There was nothing special about this one.

From what Alwyn Ellis had said I wasn't convinced, and said so. I also told Lees that while an internal audit was being carried out into his activities I would not discuss my project or anything to do with the audit with him and he must not try to see me.

'I've no idea what you've been up to and I don't want to know,' I said.

'Just be clear that the work you've organised for me has nothing to do with the Risley site maintenance contract. The work for me should have been finished ages ago. Get it sorted. How much is it likely to cost me anyway?'

'I won't know till all the work's done. I think it's going to be around the £3000 we estimated at the start,' Lees replied.

'Okay. This is what I'm going to do,' I said. 'I'll pay £2500 on account now – as a sort of stage payment – and the rest when the work's finished, whenever that is. I hope that will make it clear that this is a job I'm paying for, not something that is to be charged up to the company. Right? I don't want there to be any confusion.'

'No problem,' Lees said. It was a favourite expression of his.

I gave the contractor a cheque for £2500 there and then and the two men left.

I then saw Peter Roberts, the engineering director who had taken over responsibility for Risley site management from me a year earlier after I'd complained about work overload, and briefed him on the position. He seemed happy enough.

Weeks and months went by and the audit dragged on. I suspect I was the last person to be seen by Brian Brewer, the man carrying it out on behalf of the Finance Directorate. I found Brewer a bit garrulous and full of himself but he gave the impression of accepting what I told him about my situation, even seeming sympathetic.

For some reason Brewer told me about his marriage break-up and how he'd once thought of joining the police force as a detective. He told me he loved the job he'd been given in internal audit. He struck me as a lonely sort of man who needed someone to talk to. I'm a good listener and let him talk.

All work on my property had been halted when the audit began and I could see no likelihood of it getting finished in the near future. Eventually I decided to call it a day and finish the job myself or bring in another painter and decorator.

I asked Peter Roberts for a detailed justification of the bill for £2500 which I'd paid, not expecting to pay any more as no more work had been done. I was presented with a bill for £7720 – more than three times what I'd expected.

I thought that this was outrageous and went to see the Chief Executive to discuss it. Neville Chamberlain persuaded me to pay the bill, indicating that this would be the end of the matter. 'Get it out of the way Harold.'

It was in that spirit that I paid up, having asked for a breakdown of the bill, a request I repeated intermittently for several months. The size of that bill made me wonder whether the bills presented to me for the earlier work on the bungalow had been correct.

Rumours started flying around the Risley site about what Malcolm Lees and his contractor mates might or might not have done, fanned by Lees's absence from work, authorised by his GP. Brewer told anyone who would listen that Lees was simply stalling, trying to evade the questions which would face him on his return.

It was the day of the company executive meeting, which took place a week before the monthly board meeting, in order to agree papers to go to it. The meeting was attended by the executive directors, divisional directors and other senior personnel. I was sitting next to Neville Chamberlain, who was chairing it, my usual place. Joan Byrne knocked the door and entered with a message for him.

He turned to me. 'You'll have to carry on with the meeting Harold. There's something I have to attend to.' Although I wasn't formally his deputy the Chief Executive used me in this capacity when necessary, as I was the senior director.

I wondered what could be so important that Neville hadn't been able to wait till lunch-time to deal with it. I soon learned when the meeting broke up.

'The press office has picked up a rumour that you've resigned over the Malcolm Lees business,' Neville said. 'They're asking if it's true. What's it all about?'

'I've no idea. Who the hell's putting that sort of thing around? Is it just press office tittle-tattle or have they had calls from the newspapers?'

'I don't know. You're not leaving and that's fine by me. Forget it Harold.'

I found that easier said than done. Despite my determination not to be forced out by gossip I began to think of leaving the company. I asked Alex Milroy, the personnel officer responsible for the salaries and conditions of the directors, for a confidential assessment of what terms I might expect if I was granted voluntary early retirement.

Even without the extra pressure created by the audit and the Risley rumour machine I found working for the company increasingly unpleasant.

As if the volume of work piled on to me wasn't enough, the atmosphere in which I had to operate was extremely wearing. It was obvious that Neville Chamberlain and John Guinness couldn't stand the sight of each other.

When he was chairman, Christopher Harding had instituted an annual get together for senior people, with representatives from every site, about 30 of us in all. The event began with a welcome dinner at which Christopher spoke, supported by Neville Chamberlain, and continued during the following day, which was when the real work took place. Christopher left the working sessions to Neville.

The new chairman decided to continue the tradition. We'd been led to expect that Neville Chamberlain would be at the dinner as well but he found a prior engagement. I wasn't surprised. At the end of the meal, John Guinness rose to his feet. I was sitting opposite him.

'I've been told by Neville Chamberlain that I'm expected to say something tonight,' he begins. 'Is that right?' looking to me for an answer.

'Only if you want to, Chairman.'

'Right. Well, I don't know what sort of things my predecessor used to talk about on these occasions but I can tell you that I intend to be a very different chairman to Harding. I do not intend to spend as much time on public relations matters as he did. I don't regard that as the be-all and end-all of this company.'

So that's Christopher Harding put in his place. And me.

'I intend to turn BNFL into a company which can compete in the real world.

'From what I've seen there's scope for reducing the labour force of the company by at least 30 percent. That is my objective.'

So that's Neville Chamberlain, chief executive for the last six years, put in his place, too. It doesn't say much for the divisional directors and site general managers who are sitting around the table either. Their new chairman clearly thinks they've let manning levels get out of control.

John Guinness continues in this vein for perhaps ten minutes, haranguing the most senior people in the company. He seems to be enjoying their discomfiture.

Christopher Harding and Con Allday before him treated these occasions as a chance for some serious bonding and morale building – and as an opportunity to get to learn things about the company which they might not otherwise get to know. They were both aware that a convivial evening can loosen tongues.

By contrast, John Guinness seems to want to alienate his new colleagues, to keep them at a distance. What is he up to?

In any case, what does a career civil servant, only recently out of Whitehall, know about appropriate manpower levels in a highly scientific industry, one with fierce health and safety constraints? What does he know about public relations for that matter?

At the end of his speech John Guinness sits down. Some of my colleagues look angry. Others look embarrassed. A few of the younger ones, with careers to make, look scared and smile thinly, looking for a lead from someone. There is no applause.

'Any questions?' our new chairman asks. Silence.

'Have none of you got anything to say?' Silence.

'Harold Bolter. You're the senior director here. You say something.'

'I don't think it would be appropriate, Chairman.'

'I want you to say something,' (getting annoyed now.) 'Go on, say something.'

'It wouldn't be right.'

'I am telling you to speak. Asking you,' (correcting himself).

'Okay then,' I say, rising to my feet, everyone's attention on me, conscious that I've probably had one or two glasses of wine too many.

I am annoyed at being placed in this position. Chamberlain should be here. I don't need this on top of everything else that's going on in my working life.

'I will make the speech I thought the chairman was going to make,' I hear myself saying. Now my colleagues perk up.

'I believe that we're in better shape than we were when we met 12 months ago,' I begin.

'Reprocessing is going pretty well and the new waste plants are coming up to speed. As for the engineering construction programme, although the THORP project's late there's every sign that we've got a grip on things at last.

'For what it's worth I believe that we're winning the battle for public acceptance, too. People are beginning to recognise the need for nuclear power. If anything, this is the time to increase our public relations spend, to take more interest not less.

'It's no use throwing money around in a blind panic when things go wrong. The time to spend on public information is when people are prepared to listen to the message.

'The other parts of the business – enrichment and fuel manufacture and the reactor operators have all had a good year and we're heading for a reasonable profit from these divisions.

'But that doesn't mean that we can be complacent. The energy market is getting more and more competitive and we can't expect much help from the government.

'The chairman's right to say that there's scope for efficiency improvements. There always is. Whether he's right to say that a 30 percent reduction in manpower levels is possible I wouldn't know. I don't know where that figure comes from, or whether it applies to all or parts of the business.

'I think we have to do the work, undertake a thorough manpower study, beginning in the most obvious places, which I guess are Sellafield and Risley, and then reach a considered view on what can be done to get numbers down.'

I sit down to enthusiastic applause. John Guinness doesn't join in. After a few minutes of desultory conversation with the man sitting next to him he stands up, makes his excuses and takes himself off to bed. Not a word to me.

My colleagues gather round me, insisting that I have another drink with them, bursting to discuss what's happened.

'Well done Harold,' one of them says. 'That needed saying.'

'You think so? Well I don't. I was stupid. I put him in an impossible position. I have an awful feeling that little episode is going to cost me my job.'

I leave the room and ring Sheila, waking her up, and tell her what's happened. I also tell her that I've made an enemy and that I doubt if I can survive.

'Leave the place if things are that bad,' she says. 'Get out. You know you want to. You've been unhappy ever since Guinness arrived.'

'I'm not the only one. Guinness himself told young Tom McLachlan in London Office only last week that he knew that none of the executive directors liked him. But I can't leave until this bloody audit's over. It will look as though I'm running away.'

But there was no sign of an end to the audit. Malcolm Lees was still off work, someone told me, and the audit seemed to be going nowhere. Rumours continued to circulate about what Brian Brewer might or might not have discovered. I was told that dozens of employees were being questioned, not just me.

It was first thing in the morning and a design engineer, whom I recognised but didn't know, put his head round my office door and asked if he could speak to me. I nodded and he came in, standing at the doorway, seemingly reluctant to come right in.

'It's Malcolm Lees,' he said. 'He's dead. He's committed suicide.'

The engineer told me that Brian Brewer had been out to Malcolm Lees's home the night before. He'd told him that staying away from the office wasn't going to get him off the hook, that the audit would continue and that he was in serious trouble. I don't know how the engineer knew all this and nor do I know who found Lees's body.

My immediate reaction to the suicide was one of sorrow. Whatever Malcolm Lees had been doing it couldn't have been serious enough to justify him taking his own life, surely. My next reaction was one of anger, that something or someone had driven him to a state of mind in which he killed himself.

Then I began to turn my mind to what the death of Lees might mean for me. I felt guilty for doing so.

Would it mean that the audit would be brought to an end? Or would it simply be seen as a confession by Lees that he'd been part of a much larger financial scam than had been thought, one which I was still suspected of being part of?

An inquest took place into the death of Malcolm Lees. There it was revealed that he had left a suicide note in which he'd said something to the effect that he'd killed himself in order to protect others.

'If you knew what I know about some of the people at Risley,' it said in part, hinting at some special knowledge which, out of loyalty, he was not prepared to divulge, even unto death.

Nobody mentioned my name but I'm sure there were plenty of people in the company who thought he was talking about me. Some of my colleagues probably wanted it that way. Or was that paranoia taking hold? I felt as though I was being tried by innuendo, with no evidence placed before me and no chance to defend myself.

Malcolm Lees's suicide affected me deeply. I drank more and more and the gins got stronger. I turned to sleeping pills in order to get some sort of rest and had to force myself to get up in the morning and go to work. To make matters worse my secretary, Christine Taylor, was off ill and I had no one in whom I felt I could confide.

At night I found myself adopting the foetal position, curling up in bed, knees in Sheila's back, tossing and turning through the sleepless hours. I didn't know whether I was doing so involuntarily or because I'd heard somewhere that going back to the unborn baby state would provide me with some comfort.

Sheila was becoming more and more concerned. She urged me to go and see the doctor but I refused. It had become a matter of pride that I shouldn't seek help. I still believed that the truth would eventually emerge. It was just taking a damned long time.

I became increasingly irritable. Matthew told me later that he sensed something was going on but didn't think he should question me about it. I asked Sheila, the only person in whom I confided, not to worry Matt or the girls.

A few weeks later an escape route appeared to open up before me. Neville Chamberlain asked me if I would like to become Director General of the British Nuclear Forum, the industry's trade association, which has its offices in London.

I was already chairman of the forum, a non-executive role, and had plenty of ideas on what needed to be done to make it more effective as a political and media lobbying organisation.

I had to admit to myself that although the Director General title sounded rather grand the job would not have the status I had as company secretary and main board member of BNFL and chairman or director of several of its subsidiaries and associates.

What the hell. I wanted to get away from BNFL. If I could preserve my salary and pension conditions I would take the forum job, I told Neville, and be glad to do so – the sooner the better.

It was the night before the March 1993 board meeting at Risley, and I was working late. When we held the board at one of the sites or at head-quarters, rather than in London, the chairman hosted a dinner for local worthies, supported by his board colleagues. I was meant to be attending it. I was preparing to leave for home to change for it.

Brian Brewer came straight into my office, after a cursory knock on the door. He looked pleased with himself.

'I've something to tell you,' he said. 'I have clear evidence that you had work done on your previous property, the bungalow at Sale, not just the Culcheth house.'

'Yes. I've never made a secret of it. So?'

'You had some doors fitted. They were solid mahogany and most if not all of the cost was charged up to the company. They were worth a fortune.'

'Solid mahogany? I never asked for solid mahogany doors,' I said. 'What have those stupid bastards been up to? What have they done?' My mind was in turmoil as I absorbed this new information. I reacted – far too quickly.

'Okay. I give up. You win. I've had enough. I'm going to resign.'

'I'll go and tell Chamberlain,' Brewer said, not attempting to disguise his pleasure.

'No you won't. I'll tell him. I'd better tell John Guinness as well. We have a board dinner here tonight and he's still in the office.'

'No need. He knows everything. I've been reporting directly to him for months.'

That was the first I knew of this. I was appalled.

I walked across the corridor to Neville Chamberlain's office and told him he would receive my resignation as soon as I could write it. I explained that the reference to solid mahogany doors being fitted at my previous home had been the final straw.

Chamberlain showed little sympathy for me. His first thought didn't seem to be for me at all but the implications for that night's dinner and the following day's meeting.

'I don't suppose you'll be at the dinner tonight.'

'No.'

'Right. But you'll have to be at the board meeting tomorrow Harold. It can't go ahead unless you're there. The company secretary has to be there.'

'Okay. I'll be there. God knows what use I'll be.'

So that was it. I had just told him that I was resigning and was close to tears, and the chief executive's only thought was of the need to ensure that a board meeting took place as planned.

What had happened to all that guff about the company owing 'a duty of care' to its employees, the ritual words I'd heard from Neville on so many occasions? Who had cared about Malcolm Lees? Who gave a damn about me?

I drove home in a daze. Sheila knew something was wrong as soon as I stepped through the door. My face was ashen, she said. She was afraid I was going to have a heart attack. I told her what had happened. I began to draft my resignation letter.

That letter was written in the belief that everything I'd been told by Brian Brewer was correct. I thought that after spending over a year on the audit he must have got his facts straight, that he wouldn't dare make allegations against a director without positive proof.

In my letter – and working on that false premise – I said that I had to accept the statement from Brewer that costs which should have been met by me for work on my properties had been wrongly passed on to the company. I made it clear, however, that if this had happened it was done without my knowledge.

I handed my letter to Neville Chamberlain as soon as I arrived at the office on the day of the board meeting. It was obvious from the demeanour of the people sitting round the board table that they knew what had happened and had probably had a meeting to discuss what should now be done with me. I felt like a leper.

John Guinness didn't say much to me during the board meeting. I can only remember him making a snide remark about something in the minutes of the previous month's board meeting relating to one of my many areas of responsibility. I let it go.

I couldn't get away from that meeting quickly enough. Neville Chamberlain caught up with me and finally showed some concern for my welfare.

'Are you okay Harold? You don't look well. Do you want me to get a car to take you home?'

'I'll be all right,' I mumbled. 'I'll drive myself home.'

Alex Milroy, from personnel, was waiting to speak to me in the entrance hall of Hinton House, the headquarters building at Risley, a UKAEA policeman by his side. 'I'm sorry about this. I need your security pass,' Alex said, looking sheepish.

I handed the pass over. Without it I would not be able to enter any company building. They don't waste time, I thought. From board member to persona non grata in less than a minute.

Somehow I drove the short distance home to Culcheth, aware that I was driving badly. I broke down in tears as soon as I walked through the door, cursing the people I'd left behind, railing against my fate. Sheila rang Joan Byrne and asked to her get BNFL's Risley site doctor, Eric Barker, to call and see me as soon as possible. I didn't argue this time.

It wasn't Eric who turned up, but a doctor responsible for the health of the Atomic Energy Authority employees on a separate part of the Risley site. The UKAEA and BNFL doctors stood in for each other from time to time. I didn't know the doctor who came to the house but he turned out to be a great help to me that day.

'What's happened?' the doctor asks as he joins Sheila and me in the lounge.

'I've just resigned. I don't know where I am. Sorry. I don't know what I'm going to do I mean. Oh I don't know what I mean. I think I'm having a nervous breakdown.'

'Calm down. Take it slowly. It's the Malcolm Lees business, isn't it? It's been common knowledge for months, even on the Authority part of the site.'

'I can't take any more. Malcolm Lees's suicide on top of rumour after rumour that I've resigned or been sacked. It's been preying on my mind, going round and round, never ending. I've thought of topping myself, like Lees did.'

'That's silly. Now tell me why you feel like this.'

'Malcolm Lees left a note pointing the finger at me, blaming me for his death. At least that's how it seemed to me. Maybe he was trying to protect me. Maybe I should have done more for him. Oh I don't know.'

'It seems a funny way to try to protect someone. It must have been obvious to him that he was more likely to incriminate people by saying what he said. It seems to me that if you're really trying to protect someone you keep quiet. You don't go shouting your mouth off, all that "if you knew what I know" stuff. If he'd got something to say he should have come right out and said it.

'Anyway, who says he was talking about you? Dozens of people have been spoken to by Brian Brewer apparently. Now tell me about this nervous breakdown you think you're having.'

'I haven't been able to sleep. I've had to force myself out of bed in the

mornings. I've been having panic attacks and I've been doing a lot of crying. Lots of things.'

'Have you been drinking heavily, or taking tablets?'

'I've been hitting the gin and tonics pretty hard I suppose and I picked up some sleeping pills in the States when I was there for a BNFL Inc board meeting – you can get them over the counter there.'

'That's it then. You haven't had a breakdown Mr Bolter. You're suffering the effects of mixing drink and drugs. There's a chemical imbalance in your system. You shouldn't have been working or taking decisions in that condition. Much longer and you could have killed yourself. How long has this been going on?'

'It all started about a year ago, but it's got worse since Malcolm Lees committed suicide.'

'A year. My God. I'm amazed that you've managed to keep functioning. It's disgraceful. Someone should have put a stop to this business ages ago.'

Later that day I received a call from Neville Chamberlain. He told me that if I was prepared to allow my resignation letter to be issued to the media the board was prepared to allow me to leave the company on the early retirement terms I would have received if I'd left normally, the terms Alex Milroy had told me about earlier. I agreed.

Alvin Shuttleworth, the company's legal director who reported to me, turned up at my house with a letter containing details of my retirement package, which I signed. It was dated Thursday 4th March 1993 and I expected its contents to be implemented by the end of the month.

A press release was issued on the following day and made the front pages of every national newspaper in the country as well as the main news bulletins on radio and television. A picture of me accompanied most of the stories, the same picture, obviously made available by BNFL.

It was particularly prominently displayed in the *Daily Telegraph*. It was an old picture. In it I was smiling. It seemed out of place.

Somebody briefed the press that the work carried out for me had cost the company £2500 – a figure which bears no relationship to anything I've seen before or since. Maybe there was a mix-up over the £2500 I'd paid Lees and the contractor a year earlier. I wouldn't be surprised.

One of the press officers, Bob Philips, rang me soon after the press release had gone out and warned me that several journalists had obtained my address and were on their way round to my house, determined to speak to me. 'You might want to get out of the way Harold. Fast. It won't be pleasant.'

Sheila phoned our daughter Helen, who was off work sick. She told her what had happened. It obviously came as a shock. It was agreed that we should go to stay with Helen and her husband Philip until the dust settled. We threw a few clothes into a case and shot off, leaving Matthew at home to do what he could when the journalists arrived outside our front door in Culcheth.

I am told by neighbours that he did a splendid job, keeping his cool but making it very clear that he had no intention of telling the reporters where his mother and father were. One reporter was extremely rude to him – insisting that I had a duty to talk to him because of BNFL's open and honest public relations policy. I hadn't realised it applied to my private life.

An event like this teaches you a lot about human nature. Most of my colleagues and even some of my friends ran for cover, not wishing to be associated with the loser I'd become. But some made contact immediately to express their support and concern for me, and I will always be grateful to them.

Early callers included my old friend Colin Mears and his wife Joyce, who offered Sheila and me accommodation for as long as we needed it. More surprising, perhaps, I was even contacted by Jean Caines, who was Director of Information at the Department of Trade and Industry, and her husband Neville Gaffin, who had also worked in Whitehall as a senior press man. They offered to provide us with a bolt hole at their home in London if I needed to escape the pursuing journalists. As Jean's boss was Michael Heseltine, who ultimately was my boss, too, wouldn't that have made a story for Fleet Street if it had emerged? Sheila and I declined the offer, but the thought was much appreciated.

Some of my former colleagues dropped me a line sympathising with my position but one man, my old friend John Hayles, BNFL's former finance director, went further. He rang me up and offered lunch, beginning a regular sequence of monthly lunches over the next ten years or so which came to embrace Sheila and John's wife Glennis.

At one of the early lunches I suggested to John that because he had always been a good friend while we worked together as board members of

BNFL he would have supported me whether I was guilty of fraud or not. 'Rubbish,' he said. 'If I thought for one moment you'd done something wrong our friendship would be over.'

That meant a lot to me, more than any expression of unquestioning loyalty would have done.

Another BNFL employee who did what she could to help me was Joan Byrne, my former secretary, who kept in touch even though by then she was working for Neville Chamberlain. Joan and her husband Joe have also become great friends.

Like all news stories, the story of my departure from BNFL was soon replaced by something else and Sheila and I left England for a holiday in Menorca as soon as we could. We planned to recharge our batteries and try to decide what we were going to do with the rest of our lives. Jimmy and Rita Johnston were to join us.

When Jimmy and Rita arrived Jimmy couldn't contain himself. Before unpacking, he produced a copy of the *Whitehaven News*, his local paper, and showed me the front page. 'BNFL's Bolter To Be Investigated by Serious Fraud Squad' it said.

'It's in all the nationals as well,' Jimmy told me. 'I'm sorry Harold. You didn't need this. Perhaps I should have left it till our holiday was over.'

'No Jim. You did the right thing.'

I was furious about this latest development and tempted to cut short the holiday. I wanted to get back and confront Guinness and Chamberlain. At the very least I needed to know where this left me financially. Would I still receive my severance terms?

Sheila and the other two persuaded me that we should finish our holiday. I think they were worried what I might do or say when I met my chairman and chief executive. The holiday wasn't much fun for any of us, I'm afraid, but sitting on the rocks at the end of the promontory at Na Macaret, the village where we were staying, listening to the hiss of the waves as they broke over the shore, did help to restore my spirits a little.

When I got back to the UK I received a message to ring BNFL. I was told by Personnel that my agreed retirement terms would not be implemented in view of the serious fraud squad investigation.

Instead, I was to stay at home on full salary while inquiries took place. I could also keep my company car, a top of the range Mercedes, and continue to put petrol in it at the company's expense. Effectively, I was put on gardening leave.

I determined not to waste time sitting around waiting for the Fraud Squad's officers to get round to speaking to me. I contacted Peter Roberts and told him that if I was to be questioned by the police I must be shown any evidence he had that some of my costs had gone to the company.

I'd been trying to get that information for over five months, ever since I'd told Neville Chamberlain that the bill for £7720 which had been presented to me for work carried out on the house at Culcheth was totally unreasonable.

Peter Roberts finally sent me the so-called evidence. It consisted solely of time sheets said to have been put in to BNFL by the contractors. It took Sheila and me less than an hour to recognise that the time sheets were pure invention. We both suspected that they'd been put together long after the work was supposedly carried out. They indicated that a total of 631 working hours were spent by workmen on decorating a conventional four-bedroom house, using materials which I'd already paid for. Painters and decorators I've spoken to since found the claim risible. 'I wouldn't mind some of that,' one of them said.

Through delivery notes and invoices for the materials, which we had fortunately kept, we could show that much of this work could not have been done on the dates specified in the time sheets. The materials hadn't been bought or delivered at the time. We could also prove that the work wasn't done by the number of workers said to have been involved and that the hours they supposedly worked were also a fiction.

As an example of the sort of nonsense contained in the time sheets they indicated that floor tiles and light fittings which hadn't been bought were installed in a conservatory which hadn't been built.

I also tested the £7720 invoice passed on to me by BNFL by obtaining two alternative quotations for the work involved from other contractors in the Warrington area, chosen at random from Yellow Pages. If I'd accepted the lower of the two estimates I could have had the work done for less than £2000 – and that's without haggling. Even the higher estimate was still well below the £2500 I'd paid on account and far below the final bill of £3000 I'd been led to expect to pay by Malcolm Lees. If anything BNFL or the contractor owed me money.

Some time after I'd left BNFL I discovered that the contractor had also claimed that I'd had a new kitchen put in at the company's expense as well. If that claim had been put to me immediately I could have proved that it was a lie – we had estate agents' literature showing the kitchen in situ when we bought the bungalow – and would have challenged everything else that followed.

I learned about the kitchen allegation from Liam Sammon, the estate agent who sold me the bungalow. The man I'd bought the bungalow from had told Liam, an old friend from my amateur operatic days, that the police had been to see him. They'd asked whether there was a fitted kitchen or not when I bought the property from him. The man was furious, apparently. He thought I was preparing to sue him over a missing kitchen. 'Of course there was a bloody kitchen,' he told Liam. 'What the hell's going on?'

I also learned long after I'd departed from BNFL that any documentation relating to the bills I'd paid for work done on the bungalow, including fitting new doors, had been destroyed by the contractor concerned prior to his company being taken over and before Brewer carried out his audit.

Brewer must have known that he had no written evidence to support his claim that BNFL had paid for solid mahogany doors, just the word of people who had clearly been prepared to lie over other matters, whether he knew it or not.

Armed with the fruits of my research, incomplete as it was at that time, I went to see a local solicitor, Alastair Brown of Ridgway Greenall, and asked him to act for me. I should have approached him sooner, while I was still working for BNFL, in the same way that I should have sought the help of a doctor much earlier.

Alastair and I prepared for my meeting with the police as carefully as we could and then waited for the call.

Sheila kept me going as I waited to be interviewed, forcing me out of the house, insisting that I get out into the fresh air. One morning she threw a bathroom towel at me as I lay in bed, reluctant to stir from the bedroom. 'There you are,' she said. 'If you're going to throw in the towel there's something to do it with.'

Sheila had an unlikely accomplice as she fought to make me snap out of myself – James, my first grandchild, then a toddler. He came to look forward to grandad taking him on his daily walk round the local park in his push chair and so did I.

Eventually the call came from the police and Alastair and I went to the police station in the middle of Warrington. We were greeted by two detectives.

'I'm sorry about this,' one of them said. 'There isn't an interview room free. Would you mind the interview taking place in one of the cells?'

'What do you think, Harold?' Alastair asked. 'You don't have to do this. It's up to you.'

'Let's get on with it,' I replied. 'I've waited around long enough for this to be sorted out.'

So the four of us made our way down to one of the cells. The few sticks of furniture in it were arranged so that Alastair and I sat facing the main interrogator while the other policeman sat behind and to one side of us, presumably watching my reactions to the questions they intended to ask. I thought I was in for a good-cop bad-cop session.

I received a thorough grilling, during which I volunteered the fact that I'd done my own research into the time sheets relating to the work at Culcheth and could prove that they were a total fabrication.

The policemen didn't comment – and didn't seem to be very interested either. I sensed that their own inquiries had led them to the same conclusion.

There was just one question about the earlier work carried out at the bungalow at Sale. I was asked whether I'd paid cash for the so-called solid mahogany doors. Later I came to the conclusion that it was a trick question, asked by someone who knew there was no documentary evidence one way or another, which is more than I did.

I guess that if I'd said that I'd paid cash it could have been taken as an indication that I knew something odd was going on. I told the police officer the truth. 'I paid for all the work carried out for me at the bungalow by cheque,' I said.

I have no complaints about the way the police interview was conducted. I would categorise it as firm but polite. From it I learned that I was the last person to be questioned as part of their investigation, which they expected to complete reasonably quickly.

'What I don't understand,' my principal questioner said, 'is why you used these contractors in the first place. You could have had the work done a lot cheaper if you'd shopped around.' I knew that, of course, and said so.

'It's simple,' I said. 'I thought I knew these people and my wife felt comfortable with them. She felt happy about leaving them to get on with things while she was out of the house shopping or visiting her mother in the care home. I had to leave her to it. I was racing around here, there and everywhere on company business.'

The longer the interview went on the more relaxed I became. I began to ask a few questions myself. The answer to one of them surprised me and left me totally bewildered.

'What did Malcolm Lees get out of all this?' I asked. 'Was he having work done for nothing at his home, or taking back-handers?'

'There's no evidence that he gained a single penny or that he had any work done at his house,' was the reply.

'Then I don't get it. I just don't understand what all this has been about.'

The senior fraud squad officer then volunteered the opinion that the cost control systems in place at BNFL were a shambles, among the worst he'd ever seen. He told me that he was thinking of trying to get a consultancy with the company to sort things out when he retired. I don't believe he was joking either.

As the meeting broke up he offered me his hand. 'It's been a pleasure to meet you Mr Bolter,' he said as the four of us left the police cell and the heavy metal door clanged behind us. It seemed an odd thing to say in the circumstances.

It was several months before I heard anything more. I suppose it took time for the officers to write their report and then have it considered by the Director of Public Prosecutions, not to mention waiting for the faceless civil servants and politicians to cast their eyes over it.

Alastair Brown rang me with the news: 'It's all over Harold. No charges are going to be brought against you or anyone else,' he said. But of course it wasn't all over. That would have been far too easy.

Sheila and I were having dinner with Arthur Denny, a retired colleague, and his wife Norma the following night and it turned into a bit of a celebration, although I was still furious about what BNFL and its owners, the government, had put me through.

The phone rang at about 10 pm. It was Neville Chamberlain. The lateness of the hour should have warned me to be careful. The conversation was brief. There were no pleasantries as far as I recall. This is the nub of it.

Chamberlain: 'What do you consider your position to be Harold?'

Bolter: 'I resigned 12 months ago. I want nothing more to do with BNFL.'
Wrong answer.

What I should have said was something like: 'I have not been charged with any offence after nearly two years of investigation. You accepted my resignation, changed your mind and then suspended me. I will therefore be back in the office next week.'

If I'd done that I am sure BNFL would have been only too glad to improve my terms. They had recruited one of John Guinness's friends from the civil service to fill part of my job and distributed the rest round other people. They wouldn't want me back.

But the truth is I couldn't have gone back. There was too much anger in me, too much hurt. I didn't want to have anything to do with the sort of people who could behave in the way my board colleagues had behaved. That is why I reacted far too quickly to Neville Chamberlain's question, which he'd clearly been asked to put to me by somebody else, probably someone in Whitehall.

The next day I received a letter, hand delivered, informing me that my resignation letter of exactly 12 months earlier was now being activated, with a few improvements.

The lump sum payment of around £100,000 associated with my retirement had been enhanced to take account of the 12 months I'd been suspended and a cheque had been paid into my bank account accordingly. I was also told that my pension entitlement had been increased by two years, in line with the two for one deal I'd made with Christopher Harding when I agreed not to go to the Channel Tunnel Company.

There are those who might think that I came out of this business rather well – 12 months' salary for sitting at home doing nothing, 12 months' free use of a top of the range Mercedes, a better pension than the one I would have accepted a year earlier.

But the more I thought about the matter the more I began to think that my former employer and the company's owner, the state, had got off lightly. I still do.

I decided to see if there was any legal action I could take in search of compensation for the mental torment they'd subjected me to. Pannone and Partners, a Manchester-based law firm, was in the news at the time, having recently represented John Stalker in his fight for justice against the police, and I turned to them for advice.

I saw a senior partner and several more junior lawyers over the next few weeks and the legal bills started to mount up, to the point where they reached £10,000 and I'd still not been told what sort of case I had. The problem was that I'd resigned, not been sacked. At worst the company might be found guilty of constructive dismissal.

I began to get worried about how much of my retirement lump sum I was going to get through in legal fees, with no clear idea of what form any action might take and no apparent certainty of success. Although my children urged me to keep fighting I thought it was time to bring the matter to a head and asked my lawyers to fix a meeting with BNFL.

Alvin Shuttleworth was sent to represent BNFL. He made the company's position clear immediately.

'There's no way you're going to win you know Harold. The Treasury's not going to let you and they've got more money than you.'

He was right, of course. It is what Kafka would have expected.

I gave up and went home. And my nightmares began.

13

The New Man

My first instinct after I completed my long drawn-out and painful departure from British Nuclear Fuels was to get my revenge on those who had driven me out of the company. My second instinct was much the same. It took time for me to recognise that there was more to life than anger and even longer to discover what the alternatives were.

I floundered around, searching for a new role, something which would help to restore my confidence and self-respect, something which would return me to some semblance of emotional equilibrium.

Within a year of leaving BNFL I was offered and accepted a public relations job back in the nuclear power industry. The offer came from the chief executive of a former UKAEA company, newly privatised, which was facing pressure from environmentalists over the discharge of mildly radioactive liquid into the Thames. Later I met him and his chairman. I volunteered the story of what had happened to me at BNFL, determined that everything should be out in the open, and suggested to the company's chairman that he check with the Department of Energy that I wouldn't have any problems dealing with the civil servants responsible for nuclear power.

The job offer was withdrawn shortly afterwards. I can only think that Whitehall had no time for the old-fashioned concept of someone being innocent until proved guilty. Pure Kafka again.

I might have had a case for compensation for breach of contract, I suppose, but I simply walked away. I had no confidence in the legal process after my experience with it when I sought compensation from BNFL. I wasn't too keen to join a company which ran scared when the civil service tried to blackball me. To my surprise the company's chief executive sent me a

Christmas card that year, wishing me well. He obviously felt embarrassed about what had happened.

Then, still looking for something to do, I was persuaded by the Bangladeshi owner of the Indian restaurant which Sheila and I frequented to help him set up a textile import business. I failed to check out his credit rating and that of his partner, and lost thousands of pounds as a result. Despite everything which had happened to me I still hadn't learned to be cynical about people.

Sheila and I took up golf, but enjoyable as it was we'd taken the game up far too late. We hacked our way around the golf course together, tolerated by the more gifted golfers. We still have friends at the High Legh Park Golf and Country Club and attend a few social events there but we no longer play.

At the end of 1995 Neville Chamberlain invited me to join past and present directors of BNFL for a Christmas lunch at Risley, in an obvious attempt at reconciliation. It was a kind thought but I declined the invitation.

Instead I had lunch with Neville on my own. We discussed what had happened and he argued that Brian Brewer, whose handling of an internal audit had led to my resignation, was only doing his job. I told him that in my view there was a lot more to it than that.

If Brewer was indeed 'only doing his job' then he wasn't much good at it, I suggested. At best the man was extraordinarily credulous – as gullible as I'd been, perhaps, by accepting what he told me. At worst he had accepted false information at face value without checking it out properly.

Not long after I was cleared by the police Brian Brewer accepted voluntary early retirement terms and left BNFL.

John Guinness retired after six years or so as chairman of the company, with a knighthood for services to the nuclear power industry. There was no letter of congratulations from me. When I heard about it I couldn't help thinking of Con Allday, who'd put in nearly twice as long at the top of BNFL during a far more difficult period, even covering both the chairman and chief executive roles at the end, and who wasn't so honoured.

Neville Chamberlain has kept extremely busy over the years, with several directorships in the nuclear power industry and elsewhere.

I, meanwhile, have built a new life for myself outside the business arena. I have had plenty of time to think about the people and industries with which I was associated during my working life. All of those industries have seen enormous changes and not all of them have been for the good.

The *Birmingham Post*, the starting point for my career in journalism, has been up for sale for some time. Its daily circulation is down to around 13,000, less than a quarter of what it was when I worked for it, and there are rumours that it is in danger of being shut down. The nostalgic side of me hopes it survives.

The *Financial Times* has also had its share of problems since I left 30-odd years ago. Overall it looks healthy enough with a circulation of 450,000 a day but much of that has been achieved on the back of its international performance. Sales in the UK are down below 140,000 and this has led to concerns about its future recently – and to job losses among its journalistic staff.

As to the coal and steel industries – the two nationalised industries I wrote most about while I was industrial editor of the FT – they are both shadows of their former selves, as are most of our former heavy industries.

When the British Steel Corporation was merged with the Dutch company Koningklijke Hoogovens in 1994 to form a company called Corus, BSC had fewer than 24,000 employees – a tenth of the number it had when Tony Benn and Monty Finniston were rowing about its future size so very publicly in the late 1960s.

More recently Corus was taken over by the Indian company Tata. Because of the effects of the recession Corus made 2500 of its British workers redundant in 2009 – one in ten of the workforce – and it was its UK factories which bore the brunt of the company's redundancy programme. It is anybody's guess what will happen to future steel industry employment in the UK under its new ownership and in an increasingly competitive international climate.

The coal industry has fared even worse. The number of miners working in the mines which are still open, mainly opencast, is fewer than 10,000. At its peak the industry employed a million miners.

The National Union of Mineworkers, so powerful when Will Paynter was its General Secretary, has become a bit-part player within the Labour party and the trade union movement.

Saddest of all, perhaps, British Nuclear Fuels, which appeared to be in reasonable shape when I left it, is in the process of being killed off, just as the nuclear industry seems to be in for a revival – if, that is, our political masters have the courage of their newly expressed convictions.

Much of BNFL has either been absorbed into a new body called the Nuclear Decommissioning Authority or been broken up and sold off at a knock-down price. Unfortunately, it's BNFL's assets which have been disposed of, not radioactive waste.

To give just one example, BNFL used to own a company called Westinghouse, bought from its American owners. At the beginning of 2006 it sold this company to the Japanese-owned Toshiba group for $5.54 billion.

Within little more than a year Toshiba's profits had risen by 76 percent, due in large part to the purchase of Westinghouse. Westinghouse has also begun construction of four 1100-Megawatt reactors in China and has signed agreements for four more in the United States. By the time one is built in the UK – if one is built – Toshiba could have $60 billion of business as a result of its Westinghouse acquisition. That is business lost to BNFL and to the UK.

Why should I have my doubts about new nuclear power stations being built in the UK? Hasn't the government said this will happen? It has, sort of, but there are plenty of reasons to question its resolve.

Not so long ago the government was still forecasting that Britain's ten nuclear power stations, currently providing 18 percent of the nation's electricity, would be run down so that nuclear electricity would only be responsible for 10 percent by 2015 and 7 percent by 2020.

All that changed in 2008. John Hutton, then the Business Secretary, expressed the hope that far from nuclear's share of the energy market declining, it would expand dramatically. With some sort of guidance, presumably, the media began to talk of a nuclear contribution of 30–35 percent.

In reality that means a much bigger nuclear power station building programme than a simple doubling of capacity might imply. The current 18 percent capacity figure comes from ageing plants which will themselves have to be replaced. I doubt if that will be possible without government subsidies, despite the Business Secretary's insistence that there wouldn't be any and that any decision to build nuclear would be up to the market.

As things stand the best that potential nuclear power station builders can hope for from the government is some speeding up of the regulatory framework, but even that is uncertain. The Greens and their lawyers are likely to fight tooth and nail to prevent our laborious planning procedures being streamlined.

Those procedures have delayed important developments and added millions of pounds to our electricity bills over the years. They contrast sharply with planning practices in France, which relies on nuclear power for more than 80 percent of its electricity. Decades ago I asked a couple of French nuclear people how that country's planning system worked.

'When we want to build a new power station in a particular region we agree a package of benefits for that region,' one of them said. 'Then a book is opened in the office of the Mayor. Opponents of nuclear power can write their objections in this book.'

What happens then, I asked?

'The book is closed.'

The second man expressed himself with unconscious humour. 'It is like this. You wouldn't consult the frogs when you have decided to drain the pond. This is the same when we have decided to build nuclear power stations.'

This may seem a bit cavalier but I genuinely believe that on balance, and despite their obvious sincerity, supporters of the environmental protest movement have had a damaging rather than beneficial effect on the environment. In their eagerness to attack the nuclear power industry, which was seen as an easy target, Greenpeace and Friends of the Earth have largely ignored the adverse impact on the environment of the coal, gas and oil industries. Why?

In my view it is because the fossil fuel burning industries have traditionally employed many times more people than nuclear power. The Greens recognised long ago that they had little chance of persuading politicians to take on the trade unions and press for the adoption of the expensive clean-up procedures which had long been accepted as necessary. Some would say that was pragmatic. I would call it downright dishonest.

It is time the environmentalists told us what sort of society they are in favour of. The combination of renewables and conservation which they promote are no solution to our energy needs and they must know it. While most of us are concerned about getting out of the current painful global recession, they seem content to see the UK deprived of the secure energy supply base needed to sustain even our present, rapidly diminishing, standard of living, let alone improvements to it.

The sad thing is that my old company, British Nuclear Fuels, will not be around to take part in the renaissance of nuclear power which now seems inevitable, even if the timescale is in doubt. BNFL will soon be left with no assets and only a handful of people looking after a residual holding company, following its dismemberment. At its peak it had well over 15,000 employees and looked likely to expand further in the UK and through its growing international business.

As BNFL went into its final death throes in 2008, Con Allday wrote an 'obituary' of the company. In it he argued that the end of the company was signalled as early as 1994, a year after I had left its employment and two years after John Guinness became its chairman. The appointment of someone from Whitehall by Whitehall may have been significant as far as what happened later was concerned.

Guinness and his re-shaped board agreed to something boards led by Sir John Hill, Con Allday and Christopher Harding had fought off for more than 20 years, the inclusion of the company within the Public Sector Borrowing Requirement regime, in which the government holds the purse strings directly, agreeing expenditure on a year by year basis.

Entry into the PSBR made BNFL subject to the dead hand of the Treasury rather than its board and put control firmly in the hands of the government and the politicians. As Con pointed out, the shape of the BNFL board changed dramatically during John Guinness's time as chairman, and Con argued that this could be seen as another sign of governmental interference in the way the company operated.

For decades the board had a balance of executive and non-executive directors. When Con retired there were seven executive directors, six of whom had grown up within the nuclear industry – I was the exception – and seven non-executive directors, drawn from outside industry and the City.

This situation was changed progressively. As time went by fewer executive directors were appointed and even fewer came from within the nuclear industry. As BNFL edged its way towards oblivion in 2008 it had only four executive directors and only one of them was from within the industry. By contrast, it had seven non-executive directors, not one of whom had any previous connection with the scientific and technological business they had been made responsible for.

I date the beginning of my recovery from the trauma of my departure from British Nuclear Fuels to the point when I decided to write a book about my time in the nuclear power industry, centred on Sellafield, the industry's Achilles heel. The process of writing the book turned out to be cathartic.

My initial difficulty was deciding what sort of book I should write. I certainly had concerns about nuclear power and it was obvious that a book attacking the nuclear industry would sell better than one supporting it. But I also knew that I had to be true to what I believed in. My integrity was important to me.

The book I eventually wrote was *Inside Sellafield*, which was published by Quartet Books in April 1996. It was widely and favourably reviewed. The *Independent on Sunday* described it as 'devastating', the *Daily Telegraph*, thought it was 'explosive' and the *Guardian* agreed with them, picking up on my doubts about the viability of THORP, doubts which have been vindicated.

The *Financial Times*, my former paper, devoted the whole of the front page of its weekend review section to a piece about my 'remarkable new book', but the article which pleased me most was one by Andrew Cavenagh in *The Engineer*, a technical journal.

He described my book as 'an even handed review of one of Britain's most controversial industrial complexes, dealing with all the big issues that have arisen there, from health and safety through reprocessing to community relations'. The 'even handed' description was exactly what I'd set out to achieve.

At one stage it looked as though the BBC would devote three separate Panorama programmes to *Inside Sellafield*, shown to coincide with the publication of the book. These were heady times for a new author. I could see a new career in TV journalism beckoning.

Mike Smith, a BBC producer based in Manchester, was extremely enthusiastic and suggested three possible treatments of the book to the Panorama team in London. One option he suggested was for me to present an unusual one-off edition of Panorama or Public Eye, an 'authored film' which would contribute significantly to the debate about the whole of the nuclear industry in the run-up to privatisation. Its core question would be 'has the nuclear industry delivered on its promises?' The answer would have been no.

A second option was a more traditional edition of one or other of the two programmes, in which one of the BBC's regular reporters would ask the same core question, interviewing me and others.

The third approach suggested by Mike was that there should be a series of three half-hour programmes, shown as stand-alone specials on BBC2. Each edition would be fronted by me, as authored journalism. The programmes would break down into one devoted to 'Sellafield's secret history', another 'The world's worst PR job' and the third 'The Nuclear Black Hole', referring to spiralling decommissioning and waste treatment and disposal costs.

Mike Smith and I went up to Cumbria to film a trial piece to send down to the BBC controllers in London. It was decided that the filming should take place outside Sellafield, a nice take on the title of my book.

'You can't film here,' the policeman says.

'Rubbish. We're on a public road.'

We are filming outside one of the Sellafield site entrances, looking over the perimeter fence towards the massive plutonium pile chimneys, including the one that famously caught fire in 1957.

'You have to get permission from Mr Kelly to film here.'

'No I don't. This is public land. Anyway, I appointed Jake Kelly if that's who you mean. I recruited him from the BBC. Tell him it's Harold Bolter. He knows the form.'

The policeman looks at me quizzically.

'You really don t know me, do you?' I say. How the mighty have fallen!

'No, sir, I don't.'

'Well until a few years ago your Chief Constable reported to me. I was BNFL's Company Secretary. I was responsible for site security throughout the company.'

'I see,' the policeman says, rather more deferentially, and walks slowly back to the gate house.

Mike Smith, who's controlling the filming, asks me what's going on.

'I assume he doesn't know the law, Mike. Either that or BNFL are trying it on. They may be getting nervous. I sent them a pre-publication copy of the book to check for fact and to ensure that there were no breaches of the Official Secrets Act.

'There's been no comeback from them so I assume they accept that what I've said is accurate. But there will be parts of the book they won't like.'

'Did the Chief Constable really report to you?'

'Of course he did. I even took the salute at a passing out parade for new recruits at the UKAEA Constabulary training school at Winfrith in Dorset a couple of years ago.'

The policeman returns and walks slowly towards me.

'Mr Kelly wasn't around but someone else in the press office says it's okay for you to film outside the fence. But you'll have to get permission if you want to film inside the site.'

'I know that. Tell Jake Kelly we may well be back.'

The episode may not have meant much in itself but it meant something to me. I had faced out the armed policeman trying to bully me and shown that I was not going to be intimidated. I hoped he'd tell Jake Kelly what I'd said about filming around the factory and that he'd pass it on to my old friend Grahame Smith, the site director, and on up to Guinness and Chamberlain.

The BBC didn't maintain its interest in my book, unfortunately. I'm not sure why. Mike Smith told me it had something to do with a change of personnel within the documentary production hierarchy in London, and that may be the case.

It was also a time when the BBC was being criticised for giving too much publicity to new books and it's possible that Mike's idea of giving mine a three-programme plug was simply too much.

Border Television, which covers Cumbria, had no such inhibitions. I was interviewed by one of its reporters for several hours and the interview was then developed into three separate programmes, just as the BBC had thought of doing. The programmes led their main news bulletin on successive nights and extracts were picked up by ITN for the national network.

BNFL's reaction to *Inside Sellafield* was entirely predictable. Its initial stance was to say there was nothing new in it. Then, when the media continued to run stories gleaned from the book, the company changed its approach, accusing me of sour grapes. Two mutually contradictory statements like that would never have been allowed to get through when I was responsible for public information.

The company then persuaded Bill Wilkinson, a retired board colleague who had succeeded me as Chairman of the British Nuclear Forum, to write an article attempting to put me in my place. Bill is a good friend and a very intelligent man, but it's fair to say that he had a reputation within BNFL as being something of an optimist. It seems to be a common trait among people responsible for major engineering projects, whether they are enormously expensive nuclear reprocessing and waste treatment plants, tunnels under the sea, or aircraft such as Concorde.

In his article Bill Wilkinson insisted that Sellafield's long-awaited thermal oxide reprocessing plant (THORP), beset by construction delays, would turn out to be a huge commercial success. He couldn't have been more wrong. THORP has never managed to operate to its design capacity since it was opened in 1994, much later than Bill Wilkinson's design engineers had projected. It is years behind schedule in fulfilling international reprocessing orders, to the considerable annoyance of its overseas customers.

By 2008 it had reprocessed just 5644 tons of spent fuel since it started up 14 years earlier. Its original target, on which its costings and prices were based, was to reprocess 7000 tons of spent fuel in its first ten years.

THORP has also had far too many embarrassing incidents over the years. Most recently it was shut down for three years following a leak of a highly radioactive mix of plutonium and uranium in concentrated nitric acid within the plant's dissolver system. It seems to be a troubled plant.

THORP's several production hold-ups have also affected decommissioning costs, and ultimately they will have an impact on radioactive waste disposal charges too. It was intended that THORP-generated money would be diverted to the National Decommissioning Authority's annual clean-up budget of £2 billion for dealing with all of the UK's old nuclear facilities, more than a quarter of which was expected to come from THORP earnings. Some of that will now have to come from the taxpayer.

In all, THORP has most definitely not been a success. And my forecast in *Inside Sellafield* that there would never be another THORP must surely be correct too, given the performance of the first one and the government's very clear signal in its 2008 White Paper that spent fuel from any new nuclear power stations would not be reprocessed.

Instead this fuel – containing its cocktail of unused uranium, plutonium and waste products – will most likely be stored for at least 100 years at the nuclear power stations where it has been used before being disposed of in some unexplained way. Plans for, and the financing of, waste management are to be made on this basis, the government said. It all sounds a bit vague to me.

Bill Wilkinson also took umbrage over my insistence that his estimate of the likely cost of decommissioning old plants at Sellafield was too optimistic. Successive reports from the NDA have proved me right on that too, if its estimates are to be believed.

The situation has worsened considerably over the years as new estimates of what will be involved come in from the contractors taking an interest in this potentially huge business. It is now thought that the cost of decommissioning the country's ageing plants will be of the order of £90 billion, with over two thirds of it relating to plants at Sellafield. I expect even that estimate to turn out to be too low.

To my surprise Bill Wilkinson also had a shot at estimating the cost of burying nuclear waste, even though nobody knew where the stuff was going to go. Forecasts based on wish-think like that make astrology look like a science and discredit the industry.

We still don't know where the waste, whatever form it takes, will go. The likelihood is that it will have to stay at Sellafield, possibly buried in a repository built under the sea bed off-shore and accessed from the site, but there's no certainty about that either. As to the eventual cost – who knows?

Bill Wilkinson is one of the former directors of BNFL whom I meet once a year for lunch around Christmas time, a group centred around Con Allday who is now in his late eighties and as sharp as ever. We usually end up discussing what's happened to the nuclear power industry since we left it and its chances of enjoying a revival, with or without government financial support.

Most of us are pretty depressed about what's happened to the industry over the last decade or so and wonder whether it is now in any state to face up to the challenges which apparently lie ahead.

My interest in the nuclear power industry has latterly been confined to those once-a-year lunches with the Con Allday group and my inactive membership of an organisation called Supporters of Nuclear Energy (SONE), run until recently by my old friend Sir Bernard Ingham, whom I recruited as an adviser to BNFL, his first job after leaving Downing Street.

Sir Bernard hasn't changed much over the years. He's as vocal and pugnacious as ever and is sometimes a bit too strident in his support for the industry for my taste, but the majority of the membership love him for his irascible attacks on the Greens and their supporters in Parliament and the media. SONE has managed to keep the concept of nuclear power alive at times when it seemed that the game was up and Bernard deserves credit for that.

With the excitement of the launch of *Inside Sellafield* over, I found myself at a loose end again, but not for long. Socially, Sheila and I were persuaded by two old friends from our amateur operatic society days, Bob and Pam Lloyd, to join the International Wine and Food Society. We have thoroughly enjoyed our membership of the IWFS and I served on the committee of the society's Manchester branch until recently, with a spell as chairman. The IWFS was founded 75 years ago and is still going strong. I would recommend membership to anyone who enjoys good food, good wine and good company.

I have made lots of new friends within the IWFS, even among those who occasionally irritate me by criticising 'champagne socialists'. They appear to think that to want to see an improvement in the lot of the poor – and be prepared to help pay for it through taxation – precludes personal pleasure. That's as stupid as me suggesting that only people like me, who have made their way in the world against the odds entirely on their own merits, should be allowed to enjoy themselves gastronomically.

An important by-product of our membership of the IWFS has been the friendship which has developed between Sheila and me and Christine and Bill Redman, both former members of the teaching profession. The Redmans have encouraged us to become regular theatregoers at the Royal Exchange and Library theatres in Manchester.

I also joined the Commanderie de Bordeaux which is oriented rather more towards wine than food, Bordeaux wines, as the name suggests. I will never become a wine expert, although I've tried very hard to understand it better. There are people who can identify the different grapes and vintages with rarely a mistake but I'm not one of them. I really must put in more practice.

I nearly earned a reputation for being a wine buff though. I was at a dinner held at one of the London clubs and was sitting next to Sir Ronald Millar, chief speech writer to Margaret Thatcher and to her immediate Tory successors. Ronnie Millar is probably best known for putting the words 'The lady's not for turning' into Margaret Thatcher's mouth.

He also wrote the libretto for the musical *Robert and Elizabeth*, the story of the love affair between Robert Browning and Elizabeth Barrett, and over dinner I told him that I'd appeared as Dr Chambers in a production of it put on in Altrincham. The discussion then moved on to our antecedents – my roots in the Black Country and his in the suburbs of Reading.

'We've come a long way Harold,' he said. 'Here we are at Brooks's, enjoying fine food and excellent wines. Who'd have thought it? By the way, what is the wine? Did you notice?'

'I think it was a Bordeaux. The 1982 Chateau La Lagune Haut Medoc I think,' I responded, as though I was digging the information up from the recesses of my mind.

When the wine came round to us again Ronnie inspected the label.

'My God, Harold, you really have come a long way. You're right. It is the 82 Chateau La Lagune Haut Medoc.'

I decided to come clean, knowing that it would spoil my chances of being thought of as some sort of wine buff.

'It's not that surprising, Ronnie. I'm the host. I ordered the wine.'

At that time I was having a brief flirtation with Thatcherism, impressed by the lady's sense of purpose and total belief in what she was doing. Sheila and I were even invited to one of her receptions in Downing Street, where I spent most of my time talking to the enchanting Thora Hird, who turned out to be a fascinating conversationalist.

Margaret Thatcher supported the use of nuclear power but never made the trip to Sellafield, despite Bernard Ingham's efforts to arrange it. She did, however, get as far as Capenhurst, on the Wirral, where BNFL has its centrifuge enrichment plant. She travelled to the factory by helicopter and the director then responsible for the enrichment division, Neville Chamberlain, thought the landing area looked rather unsightly.

Whether it was his decision or somebody else's I don't know (although he was generally blamed for it) but an attempt was made to improve matters by laying turf where the helicopter was to land. The inevitable happened. Down came the helicopter and up went the loose turf.

Mrs Thatcher wasn't the only prime minister to visit one of the company's sites. Unlike Mrs Thatcher, Tony Blair did visit Sellafield – before he became leader of the Labour Party. He was persuaded to make the trip by Jack Cunningham, who warned me that our guest was thought to have a big future ahead of him.

Blair stayed at the company's guest house, the Sellapark, close to the perimeter fence of Sellafield. Over dinner the future prime minister was attentive and questioning but didn't give much away. It was impossible to decide where he stood on nuclear power at that that time but I like to think that his visit to Sellafield helped to persuade him.

He became a strong supporter as the effect of fossil fuel on the global climate became more and more apparent, and one of the last things he did before handing over the reins to Gordon Brown was to come out strongly in support of a new nuclear generation building programme.

Despite my interest in politics I felt that it was wrong to declare my political allegiance while I was a journalist or on the board of a state-owned industry. Political neutrality seemed to me to be essential in both jobs. By the time I left BNFL, however, I'd become disillusioned with what Thatcherism was doing to the social fabric of the country and, free from my self-imposed restraints, I joined the Labour Party.

I've not been particularly active since I joined, but I did act as press officer for Jane Baugh, an extremely able candidate for the Altrincham and Sale West constituency at a couple of general elections, in one of which she came within 1500 votes of success, a considerable achievement in a constituency which normally records a Tory majority of around seven or eight thousand. Jane would have made a fine MP.

My real service to the local community, however, has been in the education area. I felt that education had given me a chance in life and that it was important I did what I could to ensure that children from similarly deprived backgrounds were given at least as good a start in life as I had had.

The schools I attended – Beeches Road primary school and Holly Lodge Grammar School – are both now what has come to be known as multicultural, confirming what Enoch Powell and my father – two very different men politically – expected to happen.

Beeches Road is now known as the King George V Primary School and at the time of its last Ofsted report in 2008 it had fewer than 200 pupils, which should be a very manageable size. But it seems to be struggling. The Ofsted report is riddled with words like 'satisfactory' and 'adequate', a sign of a school which may have problems.

It would be easy to put this down to the fact that the majority of the pupils are from minority ethnic backgrounds, with around three-quarters of them speaking English as a second language. But this does not have to lead to a failing school, as my own involvement in multicultural education testifies.

Holly Lodge Grammar School has been translated into the 'Holly Lodge High School College of Science, a Community Comprehensive Secondary School', which sounds a bit of a defensive title to me. It has over 1300 pupils, which to my mind is too many. Again there is a high proportion – around three-quarters – of children who come from a minority ethnic background. Over half of them speak English as a second language and, significantly, more pupils than in most other schools in the country come from areas of economic disadvantage.

Holly Lodge's most recent Ofsted, carried out in October 2006, is a bit of a mixed bag, with descriptions of its performance at the various key stages ranging from outstanding to inadequate, by way of good and satis-factory. Maybe it's improved by now.

Trafford, the borough where I live, is a mainly affluent part of south Manchester. It still has grammar schools, resolutely defended by the local Conservative MP Graham Brady, sometimes to the annoyance of his leader, David Cameron.

The head teacher of one of these schools recently publicly congratulated Brady on his courage in fighting for the grammar school principle against the wishes of Cameron. That seems pretty naïve to me. In a place like Trafford it would have been braver – and riskier – for Brady to call for the abolition of grammar schools and their replacement by comprehensives if he wanted to be elected.

Although the grammar schools survive, the eleven plus – my route out of poverty – is on the way out. Most of the grammar schools in Trafford have introduced their own entrance exams now and I suspect that fewer young boys and girls will make their way into them from the worst of the council estates or the ghetto areas.

Despite its general air of well-being, Trafford has pockets of social depriv-ation and it was in one of these areas that I became involved in the educa-tion system and gained some understanding of what can be done in multicultural schools with hard work, enthusiasm, discipline, love and dedication on the part of the staff.

While I was still working I was persuaded by Monica Galt, an excellent teacher who'd taught two of our children, to become a governor of Kings Road Primary School, where she was head teacher. Monica had already been the head of the school for some years and had effectively doubled its size by creating a reputation for caring excellence among the immigrant community.

Kings Road is now a larger than average urban primary school serving a community with challenging social circumstances, like the two schools I attended in the West Midlands. Nearly 90 percent of Kings Road's 500 or so pupils – more than twice as many as at Beeches Road – are from minority ethnic backgrounds and for about 60 percent of them English is their second language. In fact, there are 20 or so different languages or dialects spoken by the children at the school and their parents.

Because of the lack of English, levels of attainment on entry to the school are well below national and local expectations, especially in social and language skills, as one would expect. By the end of year two, however, standards in English and mathematics are only just below average and by the end of year six standards are above average. That is a remarkable achievement.

My involvement in the governing body of the school increased after I left BNFL and had time on my hands. I became chairman of the governors, a role I thoroughly enjoyed for getting on for a decade.

Such was the quality of the teaching at the school that I didn't have to worry too much about that side of its performance. Nevertheless, I took a keen interest, because of my belief that a good education is a basic right of all children, and essential if there is to be any sort of social integration among those who form the ethnic minority communities.

The fabric of Kings Road school was a different matter. That did worry me. I made it something of a personal crusade to bring about improvements to conditions which I suspected would not be tolerated in some of the leafier parts of the borough. The school didn't have a kitchen or dining room when I became Chairman of Governors. Food had to be brought to the school in cans which looked a bit like milk churns and heated up before being served to the children through a hatch near the school entrance. Then the children had to carry the food – some of it hot food – to tables and chairs set up in the school hall. Some even had to climb steps to tables and chairs set out on a stage.

I thought it was a disgrace, worse than the conditions I'd faced when I was a primary school pupil myself over 50 years earlier. I threatened to go to the press about what I considered a dangerous, unhealthy practice. It took a long time, but the school now has a purpose-built kitchen and dining hall.

Part of the problem was that the school was built in the early 1900s and was not intended to take the 500 children which its success had attracted. As a stop-gap somewhere along the way the Local Education Authority had provided temporary, supposedly mobile, classrooms. These classrooms turned out to be neither mobile nor temporary and became more and more derelict as the years went by. In the end they were replaced. To my deep regret that happened after I had stopped being a governor of Kings Road.

I believed that Tony Blair meant it when he talked of his priority as prime minister being 'education, education, education' and when the government launched a new initiative to tackle problems of social exclusion and underachievement in 1998 I was convinced that it was doing something worthwhile and decided to get involved.

The Salford and Trafford Education Action Zone, initially with four secondary schools and 16 primary schools, was a strange and unwieldy hybrid, containing schools in Salford and Trafford which had very little in common.

The best that could be said for the arrangement was that the two sets of schools were reasonably close to each other geographically, separated only by the Manchester ship canal. Otherwise there was no logic in the union. There were certainly secondary and primary schools in Trafford which were as much in need of help as those chosen to benefit from the EAZ arrangement because they were near Salford.

The schools nominated by Trafford for inclusion in the Zone were ones with a high percentage of ethnic minority children and their religion was predominantly, but not exclusively, Muslim. In Salford the schools involved had a deprived white population and a particularly strong Church of England and Roman Catholic base.

When the Salford and Trafford EAZ (Education Action Zone) was formed it was ill prepared. It didn't even have a director or a fund raiser. The Zone was charged with the task of obtaining funding from industry to match government funding, and as there was no one else around to tackle the problem I volunteered.

I joined the small EAZ team as a full-time, unpaid worker for the first 12 months of its existence. In part this was because I believed in what it was trying to do and in part because the Zone could then claim that my previous salary level at BNFL was a benefit in kind – and get matching funding based on it from Whitehall. My 12 months as an unpaid employee of the Zone was worth £100,000 or so to it.

Later I became the Zone's chairman and came to know the effort which its director, Dr Jo Joliffe, put in to try to make a success of it. But it was always an uphill struggle, not least because of the interference from Whitehall, which seemed more interested in process than achievement.

Monica Galt had mixed feelings about the purpose of the EAZ from the start and I had some sympathy with her. Kings Road, her school, was well managed and doing very well on its own, not one in need of the sort of desperate measures which the EAZ tried to introduce.

Kings Road was so good that it became a beacon school under yet another government scheme designed to help improve standards. Under this scheme high-performing schools such as Kings Road were linked up to less-successful schools, sharing and spreading effective practice and acting as a mentor.

The EAZs only lasted five years and the Beacon programme not much longer. The two initiatives probably did some good – any injection of money should – but there were no dramatic improvements in the performance of schools in the disadvantaged areas because of either of the initiatives.

Despite the various new approaches to education dreamed up in Whitehall, poor but bright children growing up in Britain today are no better placed to climb the social ladder than their equivalents born in 1970. I'm not even sure that there's been much of an improvement since I started my first primary school and went on to grammar school in the 1940s. Much is still a matter of chance, depending more on the dedication and inspiration of head teachers such as Monica Galt and the enthusiasm and loyalty of her staff than on any of the prescriptive state initiatives tried so far.

I retired from the governing body of Kings Road a few years ago, persuaded by Bill Redman, himself a former head teacher at a difficult school in Trafford, that it would be wrong for the chairman of governors to leave at the same time as the head teacher. I took his advice and went first, but I continued to take an interest in what was happening at Kings Road.

Monica Galt retired in 2008 after 25 years as head teacher at Kings Road, a rare achievement. She also spent many years as a council member of the National Association of Head Teachers, sharing her extensive knowledge with others. In my view a record like that should have been recognised through the honours system.

I know Mrs Galt came close to receiving an award at the time of the millennium honours list because someone in the Cabinet Office rang me, seeking more information about the citation for her. He told me that she was a very strong candidate. I had prepared the citation, as I did dozens of others when I was company secretary of BNFL. In my experience 'very strong candidate' is an indication that an honour is almost certain to be awarded. So what went wrong?

I asked around and was told by 'a usually reliable source', as journalists say when protecting a contact or friend, that the explanation was that Monica had been a bit too vocal about the dress sense of someone in a position to block an award for her and the story had got back to that person. I hope something as petty as that isn't the explanation for why she wasn't honoured, but I wouldn't be too surprised.

Mrs Galt's superb record was pointed up in the 2007 Ofsted report for Kings Road, her final one before retirement. It was in stark contrast to the report produced on King George V Primary School in Beeches Road, West Bromwich, my old school, which now has a similar ethnic minority make-up and far fewer pupils.

The Kings Road report makes impressive reading by any standard, given the nature of the school. The quality of teaching and learning is given a Grade 1 on every score, the highest mark Ofsted can give. This means that it was outstanding in every respect. Tony Blair wrote to Monica Galt to congratulate her on the school's performance shortly before he stood down as prime minister, which is something I suppose.

The following is just a snapshot of what Ofsted had to say about Kings Road and its headteacher:

'The quality of teaching and learning is outstanding.'

'The outstanding curriculum meets the needs of all pupils.'

'Care, guidance and support are outstanding and a significant strength of the school.'

'The headteacher provides excellent leadership and direction for the school.'

'King's Road is an outstanding school because its pupils make excellent progress as they move through the school.'

'This is a very happy school; it is seen clearly on the smiling faces of the pupils and adults. Pupils love being at school.'

Shortly after the Ofsted report appeared I was talking to Monica about the school's excellent academic performance and the quality of enjoyment which Ofsted had recognised at Kings Road, something I had always been aware of.

We went on to discuss the reasons for this and I mentioned factors such as discipline, with children and staff understanding their place in the scheme of things, but also the love for the children shown by Mrs Galt and the teachers and support staff – and the children's love for them.

I also remarked on the efforts of the teaching staff to push the more able pupils into realising their full potential, important in a local authority area which still has secondary school selection procedures. Monica Galt's response was this telling comment:

'You're right Harold, but you also have to realise that some of the children at Kings Road, including the able ones, have difficult home lives. We have to be careful not to push them too far. For them coming to school is the best part of their day.'

When she said that, my thoughts were of a small boy in wartime West Bromwich, waking up in a cold attic bedroom, looking forward to the warmth of school, the companionship of his friends and the stimulus provided by a safe and caring learning environment.

I guess the boy must also have been wondering what the future held for him.

Index